AMERICAN
GOVERNMENT

Of the People, By the People, For the People

TBCD6-1

DARNLEY PUBLISHING GROUP

Legal deposit – Bibliothèque et Archives nationales du Québec, 2008
Legal deposit – Library and Archives Canada, 2008

ISBN 978-2-923623-40-5

Printed in Canada

First Edition: 2008

TBCD6-1

Author:
Matthew Testa

Reviewers:
Joseph Timothy Healey, Esq.
John McNeff

Editor-In-Chief:
Claude Major, Ph.D.

Project Manager:
Francine Hébert, M.Ed.

Copy Editor:
Joanne Labre

Layout and Design:
Saskia Nieuwendijk
Michael Gonzalez

SODEC
Québec ✚✚ Government of Quebec – Tax credit for book publishing – Administered by SODEC

TABLE OF CONTENTS

★

Introduction 1

Chapter 1: Government Of the People 5

   Can Any Child Really Grow Up to Become President? 5

   The Civil Service 9

   The Armed Forces 11

Chapter 2: Government By the People 17

   How Our Government Got Started 17

      Our Constitution in Action: A Case Study 21

   How Our Government Is Organized 25

      Organization of the Federal Government 25

      Organization of State and Local Governments 37

   How Our Government Is Elected 43

Chapter 3: Government For the People 53

   What the Federal Government Does for You 53

   What the State Government Does for You 71

   What the Local Government Does for You 72

Chapter 4: America in Perspective: A Quick Look at the Rest of the World . . . 75

   Other Forms and Systems of Government 75

   Alliances and International Cooperation 87

TABLE OF CONTENTS

Chapter 5: What You Can Do for Your Country 95

    Becoming Involved in Politics 95

    Becoming Involved in the Community 96

    Standing Guard 98

Appendix A: Becoming an American Citizen 105

Appendix B: The Declaration of Independence 113

Appendix C: The Constitution 119

The purpose of this text is to provide a detailed look at how America's government functions today. You will discover that our government is involved in almost every aspect of our lives. From the time you reach the age of four or five and go off to school for the first time you become answerable to American laws and a benefactor of government services. Government is more than the president and the Congress. Everyone who is on the payroll of some level of government can be considered part of our government. That ranges from the city bus driver, to police and firemen, to public school teachers, to soldiers, to the people who provide our drinking water, to those who check for foreign pests coming in with the food that we import, to those who crack down on polluters, to those help you renew your driver's license, to those who administer aid to desperate people in foreign countries, to those who are working to one day land a person on Mars.

There are big jobs and little jobs, conventional ones you might think of right away, and strange ones that might never occur to you. On a government payroll, there is someone who is responsible for getting the new guides printed that explain all this year's changes to federal income tax forms. There is someone who is responsible for checking the place settings at a White House luncheon in honor of a group of visiting dignitaries from foreign countries. There are people who spend most of their time trying to make sure that the government isn't sending Social Security checks to people who are no longer alive.

Abraham Lincoln
1809-1865

In his famous Gettysburg Address, Abraham Lincoln coined the expression "government of the people, by the people, and for the people." We will use those phrases to help organize our study of American government and society today. First, we will look at who makes up our government, from its top leaders to ordinary people like you and me. Next, we will look at how our government is organized and how its leaders are elected or appointed. After that, we will review what our government does for us, the people, at the federal, state, and local levels.

Once you have an understanding of how the U.S. government is organized and the services it provides, we will briefly shift our attention to the rest of the world. One of the most important things you need to understand about American privileges and freedoms is that they are not enjoyed by everyone in this world. There are many countries that do things very similar to the way we do, but there are also some startling and troubling differences. We will examine America's place in the rest of the world and the things America tries to do to help make that world a better place.

John F. Kennedy
1917-1963

The theme of the last part of this text will also draw from a famous speech by a great American president, John F. Kennedy. In his inaugural address, which we will look at in more detail later in the text, he posed the challenge: "Ask not what your country can do for you; ask what you can do for your country." Part of the American system and way of life is public involvement in government. As citizens, we have duties and responsibilities, as well as opportunities, not just to make our wishes and opinions heard, but to participate in the basic work of government in keeping our society strong, prosperous and free.

Finally, throughout this text you will see special boxed features called "Counterpoint." Their purpose is to encourage readers to look at both sides of a political issue by explaining or commenting on what might often be considered the "minority opinion," and by presenting the facts about various significant elements of public opinion. As to who is right or wrong on any given issue, that is the privilege and duty of each citizen to decide.

CHAPTER 1

GOVERNMENT OF THE PEOPLE

CAN ANY CHILD REALLY GROW UP TO BECOME PRESIDENT?

Throughout human history, in most parts of the world, very few people ever had any chance of becoming the leader of their nation. In many cases, this privilege was passed along from generation to generation of a royal family. In other cases, you could only emerge as leader if you were strong enough and ruthless enough to defeat your opponents on the field of battle. In those cases, you only ruled until someone stronger came along to conquer again.

For over two hundred years, American democracy has served as a model to the modern world of a government in which power is held by ordinary citizens, who all have a chance to serve and even lead the country. A traditional saying among immigrants coming to this country and learning of its history is to express awe and admiration for the fact that, here, "Every American child has a chance to one day become president."

Let's start our exploration of American government by taking a brief look at some of the interesting real-life stories of exactly how a few children have grown up to become presidents in this country. It is a process that illustrates some fundamental aspects of what it means to be an American.

American presidents have sometimes come from wealthy families — Kennedy, Theodore Roosevelt, Washington, Jefferson, to name a few. However, many have come from backgrounds so simple and obscure that it seems almost inconceivable that they could have ended up as president. A few rose to public attention on the basis of being war heroes in the military — Eisenhower, Jackson, and Washington are examples. However, some of them began their adult lives with jobs that were totally "ordinary" and had nothing whatsoever to do with politics.

Abraham Lincoln is perhaps the classic example of the American boy who made it to the top in spite of humble beginnings. His childhood could only be described as "dirt poor." He had little formal education. His early jobs included surveyor, storekeeper, postmaster, and soldier. What made the difference for Lincoln, however, was his love of learning, and his ability to give himself an education. In fact, Lincoln might be cited as perhaps the first notable American to use home study as a path toward career advancement. In Lincoln's day, it was not necessary to go to law school to become a lawyer. Rather, it was possible to get the books, study them at home, and then go and pass a licensing exam. That's exactly what Lincoln did.

Even when he developed an interest in politics, the road wasn't smooth for him. But, even Lincoln would never have imagined where it would lead him. He lost the first time he ran for the Illinois legislature. The first time he tried to run for the U.S. Senate he ended up agreeing to let another candidate take the nomination for the good of the party. Later, when he did run for Senate, he was defeated by Stephen Douglas. However, that loss turned out to be the key to his eventual success because many speeches and debates that he held during that campaign caught the eye of a national audience. Now we know them as the famous Lincoln-Douglas debates.

Let's look at some other examples. Theodore Roosevelt came from a wealthy New York family, but he was a sickly child — a fact that led him to stress fitness and the great outdoors later in life. After holding various public offices, he eventually became president when President McKinley was assassinated. Despite the roundabout way he became president, the key to the Roosevelt story is what he did to take advantage of the opportunity when it was presented to him.

Theodore Roosevelt
1858-1919

Woodrow Wilson was a minister's son who started adulthood pursuing a career in academics. He graduated from law school, earned a doctorate, and became a college professor, specializing in political science. Eventually he became interested in running for office, but that was not his original ambition in life.

Harry Truman is a classic example of a man whose early life gave no indication of what he would later go on to do. Before serving in World War I, he was a farmer in Missouri. Afterwards, he opened a clothing store. His first elected office was as an administrator in a country court house.

Truman was not the first to start out this way. Andrew Johnson grew up in poverty. He served as a tailor's apprentice until he ran away from home. Later he would open his own tailor shop. If you were to stop his life at that point and tell the people that Johnson was going to be president of the United States one day, they would have said you were crazy. It almost didn't happen.

Andrew Johnson
1808-1875

Johnson was vice president under Lincoln and was supposed to be assassinated in the same plot that killed Lincoln, but the attempt on his life failed.

More recently, Lyndon Johnson also grew up in rural poverty. He worked his way through a small teachers' college and, for a time, dedicated himself to teaching poor students of Mexican descent. Eventually, like so many others, the things he cared about and believed in prompted him to run for Congress. He succeeded, and the rest, as they say, is history.

There are many other interesting or quirky stories concerning past presidents. John F. Kennedy was commander of a patrol boat during World War II. The ship was accidentally rammed and sunk by a larger Japanese ship, but through a combination of extraordinary courage and extraordinary good luck, Kennedy survived, escaped, and became a hero by rescuing many of his crew.

Gerald Ford had a long career of public service in the House of Representatives, but never ran for

president. He became president because Richard Nixon and his vice president both resigned because of scandals.

Indeed, if you took all of the men who have ever been elected President of the United States and put them all together in a room, it might well seem that about the only thing they have in common is having held that office. However, a closer look will show at least one more element of common ground: at some point in their lives, wherever they came from and whatever they were doing, they developed a love and appreciation for their country that was strong enough to dedicate their lives to serving it.

Becoming an American president is much more than winning an election and landing a good job. It has always been a challenging and dangerous occupation, one that takes a lot out of most people who assume it. In many cases, people who get themselves elected to the higher offices in the country end up taking a pay cut. Many former presidents earned much more money as lawyers or businessmen before taking office. It is not a job someone does for the money. In many cases, it is the result of an almost religious conversion to the ideal of public service — and presidents, senators, and congresspersons are not alone in their zeal for serving their country. A great many ordinary Americans share that goal and that lifestyle, as we will see in the following sections.

THE CIVIL SERVICE

"Civil service" is the term given to government employees who are not enlisted in the military. Most Americans realize that the government employs a lot of people and that a large portion of the taxes they pay go to the salaries of these individuals. However, few people grasp the full extent of the civil service, both in size and diversity of job opportunities. In 2001, there were approximately 2,700,000 federal civilian workers — or about 1 in 100 Americans. Of those, the largest number — 2,645,000 — worked for government departments and agencies that are considered part of the executive branch. Executive branch workers can be further subdivided into three groups: civilian employees of the defense department, postal workers, and all other federal civilian workers. By comparison, the legislative and judicial branches of the federal government had much fewer employees — 30,400 and 33,800, respectively. Remember that we are only talking about the federal government here. If you were to add up employees of the state and local governments, the total would be much larger. If you consider all of these people to be, in some sense, part of the government, then the

United States has the largest and most complex government in the world.

Who are civil servants and what do they do? It might be easier to describe what they don't do. In essence, you could probably find people from almost every other walk of life on a government payroll. Some jobs are specific to the nature of government, such as courtroom stenographers. There is no precise equivalent to this job in the business world. However, the government also hires plumbers, teachers, electricians, drivers, doctors, computer programmers, secretaries, chemists, cooks, and clergymen. Among federal civilian employees who work

for the executive branch (not counting the postal workers), about 87 percent have what are called "white collar" jobs (mainly in offices and laboratories), whereas 13 percent are "blue collar."

Later in this text, in the section describing government services, you will gain a better sense of how the government manages to employ so many different people. The role of government has grown to encompass far more than our founding fathers could ever have imagined. Politicians often campaign on a promise to reduce the size of government, and some administrations do succeed in making small reductions. However, the American style of government, in all its monstrous complexity, has become a fundamental part of our lifestyle and economic system. It would be impossible to make any drastic changes to the government without changing who we are as a people and how we live.

Perhaps one day you would like to work for our government in some capacity. If so, you might want to check out a large government website called **www.usajobs.opm.gov**. This site will answer your questions and get you started toward learning what is available and what you need to qualify and apply for a government position.

We have shared this information with you close to the beginning of the text in order to make one important point about the study of American government. It is not about something "out there" that affects some people in certain ways. It is something that touches almost every aspect of your life. There are things you need to know about your government that are as fundamental to your life as learning to drive a car, use a telephone, or buy groceries at a supermarket. (And, by the way, the government is involved in some way in all three of these activities!)

THE ARMED FORCES

In discussing the civil service, the word "service" gets used somewhat casually. An electrician who works for the government is pretty much just doing a job and earning a living like an electrician working in the private sector. The idea of "serving the country" might not have been much of a factor in deciding to take that particular job. However, for many government jobs, as well as for elected officials, the concept of serving society has much more relevance — and the concept of service probably reaches its highest level when we consider the men and women who make up America's armed forces.

Back in the days of the controversial Vietnam War, there was a significant amount of public distrust and opposition toward the American military. Part of the problem at that time was that many military recruits were "drafted" into service — in other words, legally forced to join rather than enlisting voluntary. That, plus the difficult and uncertain nature of the war itself and the large number of casualties, caused the image of the military and of military service to suffer.

That has changed drastically in recent times. Today, even when groups voice opposition to a particular military campaign or operation, great care is taken to express respect and appreciation toward the soldiers and sailors themselves. This is in keeping with the reverence that has been associated with military service throughout most of American history, and especially during and after World War I and World War II. Today's American armed forces are a voluntary force, and getting people to enlist is not usually much of a problem. The military offers training, educational and health benefits, and the possibility of an attractive, lifelong career. It is not for everyone, but the men and women who do participate usually do so out of a genuine sense of pride and patriotism, and many find that the experience enriches their lives and sets them on a course for success throughout their lives.

COUNTERPOINT

To many people it seems that America's all-volunteer army has been a great success story and that it has eliminated the tensions and conflicts of past eras with regard to military service. However, the system has its critics, particularly among those who are active in supporting social change for minority rights and opportunities. Their main argument is that the military attracts a disproportionate number of racial and ethnic minorities and lower-income whites because society offers these people fewer opportunities to get ahead in any other way. As a result, when war does come, the minority groups suffer disproportionately high casualties.

Is the volunteer army really just a subtle way of getting the poor to do our fighting for us? In some parts of the world, military service is compulsory for all men, and sometimes even women, once they reach a certain age. Whether it is a time of war or peace, everyone serves in the military before going on to start an adult civilian life. In this way, if conflict arises, people from all classes of society participate equally.

Would such a system make any sense in America?

What do you think?

There are three main departments in the U.S. military, all of which answer directly to the secretary of defense, a member of the president's cabinet (you will learn more about the cabinet later in this text). The president is the commander-in-chief of the armed forces, and all senior officers answer directly to him. The three branches are the Army, Navy, and Air Force. The Marines are a separate service that comes under the branch of the Navy. The Department of Defense also includes many other agencies and groups called "unified commands." In 2002 there were about 1,370,000 active duty forces, 1,280,000 reserves, and 669,000 civilian employees. Reserves are personnel who train on a part-time basis and are ready to be called up to active duty in the event of a war or national emergency. The Defense Department's budget for 2007 was $439 billion.

If you are interested in learning more about the armed forces and possible career opportunities, there are many possible sources of information. You can call or visit a local recruitment center. You can also get a lot of information from a variety of websites. One useful starting point is the website of the Armed Forces Information Service (AFIS). Its web address is **www.defenselink.mil/afis**. On the AFIS home page, you will find a section called News Sites. By clicking there, a dropdown box will open that will take you directly to other information sites about specific forces, such as the Army or Navy.

Now that you know a little something about the size and scope of our American federal government and its employees, we will take a closer look at how our government was established, how it is organized, and the process by which we, the people, elect it and hold it accountable.

Although membership in the military has been voluntary since 1973, the government has always reserved the right to return to a conscription (draft) system if its military needs should ever prove to be greater than what the all-volunteer military can provide. For that reason, all young American men are still required to register their names and addresses at local draft boards once they reach the age of 18. This is a "just in case" policy that will allow the United States to activate the Selective Service System quickly if it is ever needed. Interestingly, while women may volunteer to serve in any branch of the services, and all branches are actively seeking female recruits, young women are not eligible to be drafted under current U.S. law, even if the country were to return to active use of the draft system.

I WANT YOU FOR U.S. ARMY
NEAREST RECRUITING STATION

CHAPTER 2

GOVERNMENT ★ BY THE PEOPLE

HOW OUR GOVERNMENT GOT STARTED

The documents that are the foundations of our government are:

• The Declaration of Independence
• The Constitution
• The Bill of Rights

In the appendix of this text, the Declaration of Independence and the Constitution are presented in their entirety.

The history of the evolution of the Constitution is a fascinating topic, but it is one that could well consume an entire text. This text will describe how the American government is structured and operates in the present day, rather than the history of how it came to be this way.

The following pages contain tables that list the contents of the seven articles of the Constitution and the ten amendments of the Bill of Rights. We are also presenting a third table that summarizes the content of the constitutional amendments that have been added since the Bill of Rights was enacted.

It is important to understand that the Constitution is the foundation of our government. It put the broad structures in place and it also established basic rights that all subsequent laws must observe in order to remain valid. Many of these structures have evolved over the last 200-plus years, but the essential framework has remained quite similar in many ways.

Unlike the Constitution, which details the basic structure of the federal government and how each branch operates, the Declaration of Independence has little to do with how America's government functions. The Declaration of Independence was written in 1776 to justify the separation of the original thirteen American colonies from Great Britain. It contains a list of reasons why the United States deserves to be independent, but it does not specify how exactly the U.S. should govern itself. However, the Declaration of Independence states a few general principles of democracy that underpin American government: that "all men are created equal" and that "it is the Right of the People" to govern themselves.

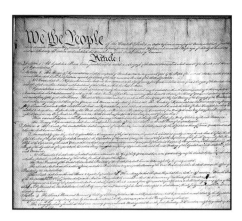

Original Copy of the Constitution of the United States

The United States Constitution is both the blueprint and the rulebook for the United States government. It was initially drafted in 1787, and Congress declared it to be in effect in the following year, after nine of the thirteen original states formally ratified it.

Almost immediately after it was passed, Congress began the work of amending it or building new provisions into it. The first ten amendments were enacted very soon after the Constitution went into effect and came to be cumulatively known as the Bill of Rights. Other amendments have been added over the years, and the Constitution itself provides a process whereby amendments can be added at any time. However, in order for this to happen, they must first pass Congress and then be ratified by at least three-quarters of the states. This provision means that amendments to the Constitution require substantial consensus across the country and cannot easily be passed.

The Main Body of the U.S. Constitution

Article I
Organization, powers, and procedures for Congress

Article II
Election, powers, and duties of the president and vice president

Article III
Powers and jurisdiction of the Supreme Court and inferior courts to be established by Congress

Article IV
Relations among states, and how new states may be admitted

Article V
How the Constitution may be amended

Article VI
Public debts and the supremacy of the Constitution

Article VII
How the Constitution must be ratified

The Bill of Rights
(Ratified Dec. 15, 1791)

First Amendment - Freedom of religion, speech, assembly, and of the press

Second Amendment - Right to keep and bear arms

Third Amendment - Protection of citizens against having to lodge soldiers

Fourth Amendment - Protection against unreasonable searches and seizures

Fifth Amendment - Rights of the accused to due process and to avoid self-incrimination

Sixth Amendment - Rights of the accused before and during trial and to a speedy trial

Seventh Amendment - Right to trial by jury in civil cases

Eight Amendment - Prohibition of excessive bail and fines, and of cruel and unusual punishment

Ninth and Tenth Amendments - Discussion of states' rights versus federal rights

Other Amendments to the Constitution

Amendment		Purpose or Effect
11th	2/7/1795	Prevented states from being sued in federal court
12th	7/27/1804	Requires electoral college to conduct separate votes for president and vice president
13th	12/6/1865	Abolished slavery
14th	7/9/1868	Prevents states from interfering with citizenship rights or failing to provide equal protection under the law to all citizens
15th	2/3/1870	Extended voting rights to African Americans
16th	2/3/1913	Authorized Congress to impose income taxes
17th	4/8/1913	Changed how U.S. senators are elected (now elected by the people)
18th	1/16/1919	Prohibition of alcohol
19th	8/18/1920	Extended voting rights to women
20th	1/23/1933	Shortened time between presidential election and inauguration
21st	12/5/1933	Repealed (cancelled) 18th Amendment on alcohol prohibition
22nd	2/27/1951	Set two-term maximum for presidents
23rd	3/29/1961	Extended voting rights to District of Columbia
24th	1/23/1964	Prohibited making voters pay a poll tax in federal elections
25th	2/10/1967	Provided rules of succession for presidents and vice presidents who die, become incapacitated, or leave office
26th	7/1/1971	Extended voting rights to persons 18 years old and older
27th	5/7/1992	Prohibited Congress from giving themselves immediate pay raises

OUR CONSTITUTION IN ACTION: A CASE STUDY

Because the Bill of Rights and the other parts of the Constitution describe principles more than procedural details, you might assume that the document tends to sit on an honored shelf in a museum of American history someplace, but that it is rarely consulted in the day-to-day operations of our modern government. Nothing could be further from the truth. All laws that have been passed by any level of government in this country are answerable to the Constitution, and constitutional rights are cited in court cases every day across this land. On several occasions, the U.S. Supreme Court has overturned laws passed by Congress or by a state legislature because they violated some principle established by the Constitution. This has happened many times in our history and it is by no means a rare event. No matter how many new laws are passed, they have to conform to the Constitution, or else they won't endure. In fact, when a law is first passed, it is often challenged by opponents who ask the courts to rule on whether or not it is constitutional.

Interpretation of how the principles of the Constitution apply to specific cases and situations is one of the fundamental activities of our courts, and one of the bases upon which judicial decisions are made. It is one thing to say that people have a right to free speech, to due process, or to protection from unreasonable searches. However, deciding exactly what actions taken by police or government officials do or do not violate those rights is complicated, and the process is ongoing.

The following court case, and related cases, gives you a glimpse of how the Constitution affects the outcomes of many important court cases. It shows how one court decision becomes a precedent that has a direct effect on how later court cases are settled.

Terry v. Ohio

In October 1963, a Cleveland police detective stopped three men who were repeatedly walking past a store. He identified himself, asked their names, and then searched them by patting down the outside of their clothes. In doing so, he found that two of the men were carrying handguns. He arrested them and they were charged with carrying concealed weapons.

One of the main arguments advanced by defense attorneys was that the search that resulted in these charges violated the Fourth Amendment's protection against unreasonable searches and seizures. Despite the fact that the men were not doing anything obviously illegal at the time, they were stopped and searched. The reason the detective stopped them was that he believed, in his judgment, that their actions suggested they were "casing the store," looking it over in preparation for a robbery attempt.

This case ended up going to the U.S. Supreme Court because it finally brought to a head an issue that had long been controversial in law enforcement procedures: what makes a search or a detention "reasonable?" Can the police stop anyone they like at any time for any reason, just because they claim to have a hunch or a suspicion about that person? If that were to be the policy, some would fear that police could use detentions and searches to harass people they simply didn't like, or to unfairly target people simply because they belong to minority groups.

In deciding this case, the Supreme Court decided to set guidelines that would apply not only to this case but to all similar cases. They created six specific guidelines that must now be observed in a "stop and frisk" procedure:

1. There has to be some specific and reasonable grounds for police to suspect that there is criminal activity underway.

2. There has to be some specific and reasonable reason to think that the subject might be armed and dangerous.

3. The police must identify themselves before conducting the stop and search.

4. Before conducting the search the police must make a reasonable

attempt to ask the subject to explain his or her behavior.

5. After conducting this verbal inquiry, the police may then proceed with the search only if they did not hear any explanation that would cause a reasonable person to no longer have reasonable fears about points one and two.

6. If all the preceding conditions still allow, the police may then conduct a search only of the subject's outer clothing to discover weapons.

You will notice that the decision was supposed to address a definition of what is reasonable, and yet at several points in these guidelines the word "reasonable" is still used. However, the guidelines do get more specific about what police should do in this set of circumstances. For example, they should ask some questions before conducting the search. Suppose the detective had spotted the men pacing outside the store, then asked them what they were doing, and one of them had explained that his son was inside the store using the public washroom and they were waiting for him to come out. Then subsequently a child appeared. It would then no longer be reasonable to suspect that the purpose of pacing back and forth in front of the store was a preparation for a robbery, and the detective should not proceed with the search unless there was some other specific reason for suspicion.

The next thing we want to show you is how this case became a precedent for some other cases. It is important to understand that rarely are two court cases identical. One of the challenges facing judges is applying a previous court decision to a new set of circumstances. In doing so, the judge has to consider not only the detailed pronouncements of the previous decision, but also its clear spirit and intent.

In 1979, the U.S. Supreme Court considered a case in which an officer stopped a vehicle, apparently at random, smelled marijuana, saw it on the floor, and made an arrest. This is a different set of circumstances from the previous case, but it has the same central problem: can police stop cars

anytime they want, without receiving any complaint, spotting a traffic violation or illegal activity, or having any specific reason to be suspicious of the occupants of that vehicle? This time, based on the principles of *Terry v. Ohio*, the court said no. It disallowed the marijuana taken from the vehicle search to be used as evidence at the time of trial.

The principles of *Terry v. Ohio* came up again in the case of *U.S. v. Place*. This time the issue was detaining luggage in a public place to allow time for a drug-sniffing dog to be brought in to examine it. One of the main issues was how long can you reasonably hold up luggage for this type of search. The Court got very specific and established a guideline of 90 minutes.

Again, in the 1994 case of *U.S. v. Bautista* the Court had to rule on some specific aspect of what was permissible during a "stop and frisk." This time the issue was whether or not police could handcuff the subject during the search, or if handcuffing was only permissible once the officers decided to make an arrest. The Court ruled that sometimes the use of handcuffs was justified, depending on the attitude and behavior of the suspect. The whole purpose of a frisk is to look for weapons — in other words, to ensure that police officers are not at risk if they continue to question this individual. Handcuffs are designed to make sure that officers are not at risk while they conduct the frisk. However, the Court set limits on the use of handcuffs. The application of force must be no more than necessary, and the purpose must clearly be to protect police and/or to prevent escape. Under these guidelines, the Court could decide that handcuffing a suspect who was not being arrested was not reasonable in cases where the suspect remained calm and cooperative.

Finally, let us quickly look at the case of *Sibron v. New York*. In this case, while frisking for weapons, a police officer put his hand into the suspect's pocket and pulled out a bag of marijuana. An arrest was made and charges levied. This time the Court said the evidence was not legally seized. Why? If a person is being arrested a more thorough search is permissible, including a search of pockets. However, if someone is simply being stopped for questioning, the search is only supposed to be a pat for weapons. Whatever was in the bag in the suspect's pocket was clearly not a weapon. Therefore, the officer did not have a right to remove it.

There have been hundreds of other court cases where the judgment in the *Terry v. Ohio* case has been considered. In fact, it has become such an important part of how cases are handled that many law enforcement officials and lawyers now refer to a "stop and frisk" as a "Terry stop."

The preceding discussion is simplified, and *Terry v. Ohio* is only one of several famous court decisions that deal with the Fourth Amendment. However, hopefully it gives you a general idea of how we have gone from a single sentence in the Fourth Amendment to a series of more detailed

guidelines on police conduct. It also shows you something we will talk about more in the next section: how the courts have a role that is just as important as the Congress in deciding precisely how law enforcement officials must deal with the public.

HOW OUR GOVERNMENT IS ORGANIZED

ORGANIZATION OF THE FEDERAL GOVERNMENT

The Broad Strokes

Now that we are clear on the documents and processes that set our

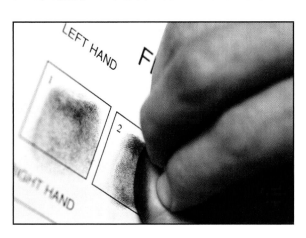

government in motion, it is time to take a closer look at how that government is structured in the twenty-first century. We will begin with a review of the main elements that you may remember from your history courses. Then we will look at those elements in more detail.

The "broad strokes" of the government's organization structure and interaction can be summarized quickly in the following list of points:

- The federal government is divided into three branches: the executive, which is headed by the president; the legislative, which is the Congress; and the judicial, which is headed by the U.S. Supreme Court.

- The capital of the U.S. is Washington, D.C. This city is home to Congress, the White House, the Supreme Court, and many other institutions that make up the federal government.

- The president is the chief executive officer. He is also commander-in-chief of the armed forces. Presidential elections are held every four years, and the longest any president may serve is two terms. Elections are held in November and a new president takes office in January.

- The vice president is the second in charge. He is elected with the president, and would become president should the president die, resign, or be impeached and convicted (a legal process to remove a president from office). The vice president also presides over the Senate and may cast a vote there in the event of a tie.

- The Senate and the House of Representatives make up the two bodies of Congress. To become law, a bill must be passed by both bodies. There are two senators for each state. Since there are fifty states, this means that there are 100 senators. The number of representatives from each state depends on that state's population, with more populous states like New York and California having more representatives than small or medium-sized states. There

TIP

If you ever want to try to calculate how much time is remaining until the next presidential election, remember that these elections are always held in even-numbered years that can be evenly divided by four with no remainder: 1988, 1992, 1996, 2000, 2004, 2008, etc.

and publish a "minority opinion." This does not affect the outcome of the case, but could have an influence upon legislators and the public. Supreme Court justices are appointed by the president and must be confirmed by the Senate.

are a total of 435 representatives in the House. Senators are elected to a six-year term, representatives to a two-year term. This means that a federal election is held every two years, at which time all of the representatives and one-third of the senators are elected. There are no term limits on how long a person may serve in Congress, and several distinguished members have been re-elected over and over for lifelong careers that span decades.

- The Supreme Court has authority over all other courts in the country, both state and federal. Cases from lower courts may be appealed to the Supreme Court and any cases involving the Constitution may be brought to the Supreme Court. There are nine Supreme Court justices, including the chief justice, who presides over proceedings. Cases are settled by a majority (at least five of the justices agreeing). However, sometimes judges who vote against the majority will get together

- The Constitution establishes a system of checks and balances to prevent any one branch of government from having absolute power. Laws are passed by Congress, but they must be signed by the president before becoming law. A president may veto (overrule) a law passed by Congress. However, Congress may then pass the law over the president's veto if on a second vote they can get a two-thirds majority in both the House and the Senate. The president prepares a budget for the federal government and sends it to Congress for approval. The president may not spend money without Congress's approval. Nor can the president declare war without such approval, even though, once war is declared, the president may wage the war as he sees fit. The Supreme Court provides a check on the power of both other branches, because it is able to strike down any laws that it considers to be in violation of the principles of the U.S. Constitution. However, even the Supreme Court does not have the last word. The Constitution itself can be amended (changed) with the approval of Congress plus ratification by three-quarters of the states. As you have seen this has happened twenty-seven times in our history.

• The Constitution establishes a distinction between federal and state areas of power and jurisdiction. The federal government has the power to raise an army, go to war, and enact trade agreements with other nations. It also looks after matters that extend beyond state lines, such as interstate transportation. The states look after social services, public works like state highways and bridges, and the regulation of city and county governments. They have their own courts and can pass a broad range of laws affecting both civil and criminal matters. Both levels of government can enact and

collect taxes. In practice, there are some areas where both levels of government are active. For example, public education is primarily a state responsibility, but the federal government is also active, in limited ways, in this area.

The Finer Points

In a previous section, we gave you a sense of the scope of our modern federal government by providing some recent statistics on numbers of federal employees. You might suspect from that discussion that there is more to

the federal government than simply the president, Congress and the Supreme Court.

In a later section of this text, we will look more specifically at what the government does by identifying specific departments and agencies. However, before leaving the topic of government structure, we want to give a better understanding of the overall organization.

As you learned earlier, the executive branch of the federal government is the largest and the most complex. Although answerable to the president, it is too vast an organization for one person to manage. The president relies on the help of his cabinet to manage the various departments of the executive branch. Cabinet members are appointed by the president and ratified by the Senate. Fourteen cabinet positions were established gradually between 1789 and 1989. Recently, a new cabinet position, Department of Homeland Security, was established, restructuring parts of other departments under a new cabinet post. We will look at this new development later in the text, where we also survey the responsibilities of the other traditional departments. For the moment, we will simply list the departments as follows:

- Defense Department

- State Department

- Treasury Department

- Interior Department

- Justice Department

- Commerce Department

- Agriculture Department

- Labor Department

- Housing and Urban Development Department

- Transportation Department

- Energy Department

- Health and Human Services Department

- Education Department

- Veterans Affairs Department

- Department of Homeland Security

Each senior cabinet official is called a secretary (Secretary of Defense,

Secretary of Transportation, etc.). There is a second-in-command called a deputy secretary or undersecretary, then there are assistant secretaries — all appointed by the president.

Each secretary works somewhat independently on matters under his or her jurisdiction. However, each is directly answerable to the president, and, on a regular basis, the entire cabinet conducts formal meetings with the president. Sometimes key issues or crises are discussed at such meetings. In this way, cabinet members can serve as general advisers to the president on matters both inside and outside of their specific fields.

The executive branch also includes several other offices, councils, or agencies. For example, the National Security Council includes some cabinet members and senior members of the military who advise the president on military and foreign policy matters. The Office of Management and Budget prepares the federal budget and watches over spending. There is also a Domestic Policy Council that is subdivided into specific offices, such as the Office of National Drug Control Policy and the Office of Science and Technology Policy. There are also about 100 agencies. The names you are most likely to recognize are NASA,

which operates our space program, the Environmental Protection Agency, which is a pollution watchdog, and the Central Intelligence Agency (CIA), which conducts "intelligence operations" to help protect U.S. interests and security around the world.

By comparison, the other two branches of the federal government are much simpler than the executive branch. However, each has its own complexities, especially the Congress.

We told you earlier that Congress has two main bodies, the Senate and the House of Representatives. However, each of these has various officers and various subdivisions, which we will briefly summarize.

Addressed earlier was that the vice president is the president of the Senate. However, the vice president has many other duties and rarely attends the Senate on a day-to-day basis. When the vice president is away, sessions of the full Senate are led or moderated by a chairperson called the President Pro Tem, who is selected by the party with the most senators. The House of Representatives also has a chairperson called the speaker of the House. This is a much more powerful and important position than the Senate president pro tem. The Speaker of the House directs the path of legislation through the House and can strongly influence what matters are discussed in the House.

The Senate and House both have a system of leadership within the group of members that belong to each of the political parties. The group chooses a "floor leader," who is assisted by others called "whips." Their main role is a political one. They keep the members of their own party organized and "on the same page" and ensure that legislation is as favorable as possible to the principles or interests of their own party.

The most important formal structure within the House and Senate is the committee structure. Each legislature has approximately twenty committees that deal with a variety of specific topics. The permanent committees are called "standing committees." There are also special and select committees that may only meet occasionally or that are organized for a specific, temporary purpose. Finally, there are joint committees that include members from both the House and the Senate. Examples of the titles of committees are: Agriculture, Budget, Judiciary, Rules and Administration, Armed Services, Science, Governmental Affairs, and Foreign Relations. In some cases, both the House and Senate have separate committees with the same name and purpose (example: the Budget Committee). However, the Senate has some committees that the House does not, and vice versa. Either body can and does create special committees from time to time. Furthermore, most of the committees also have smaller subcommittees that deal only with very specific issues.

Senators and representatives are assigned to specific committees by party leaders depending upon their background and personal expertise, as well as their seniority (number of terms they have served). There are members of both parties on all committees. The party with the most seats (most elected members) ends up controlling most or all of the committees.

Committees are important because members actually spend more time working at the committee level than they do meeting as a complete body. When a law is proposed by a senator or a representative, it is directed to the committee that is most directly concerned with the topic of the proposed law. The draft of a proposed law is often called a bill. The committee has a lot of power in deciding the fate of the bill. Not all bills end up coming before the full House or Senate for a vote — in fact, a great many do not. The committee chooses what bills will come to a general vote and which ones will not. The committee may choose to modify the bill before proposing it for a general vote.

Bills that have to do with the spending of money always start in the House before ending up in the Senate. Authorization bills create new federal projects and define how much money can be spent on them. Appropriation bills provide the specific money for each program or project.

Besides passing bills, Congress has certain other duties. For example, the Senate must approve all important appointments made by the president, including cabinet secretaries, Supreme Court justices, other federal judges, and ambassadors (ambassadors represent the U.S. government in foreign countries). In addition, the House has the authority to impeach (formally accuse) public officials, including the president. If a person is impeached in the House, he or she will be tried in the Senate, which has the authority to remove the person from office if it receives the two-thirds majority needed for a conviction. The action in the House that starts the process requires only a simple majority. Two presidents have been impeached in the House, Andrew Johnson and Bill Clinton. Neither was convicted by a two-thirds majority in the Senate, so neither was removed from office.

The preceding discussion of how bills start at committees before coming up for a general vote may give you the

impression that the House and Senate are closed groups that deliberate entirely among themselves. This is not true. Committees often convene public hearings about a proposed bill that is significant and perhaps controversial. People who are for or against the bill may also submit written statements to committees. Congress also sometimes conducts special investigations if there is an important problem, crisis, or scandal affecting the government.

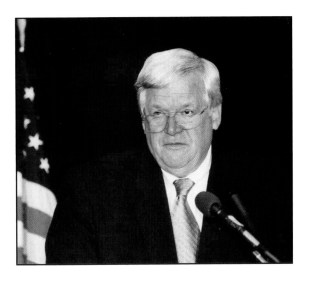

These investigations can call public officials to testify and often allow members of the public to express their concerns publicly.

Beyond the structure of the elected members themselves, Congress also has a large structure of support staff. Each senator or representative has a large staff that maintain offices in Washington and in the member's home district. This staff handles the large volume of calls, letters, e-mails, and personal appointments that result from ordinary citizens contacting their elected members. Sometimes a member will handle a minor complaint about a specific problem a citizen is having with some government benefit or service directly by contacting the officials or bureaucrats involved. At other times, people are contacting the member to express an opinion about some legislation, or to complain about a situation that they feel warrants new legislation. Congressional offices handle and respond to all contacts. If you write to your senator or representative you are almost guaranteed to get a response, although that response may come from a staff member rather than the elected member directly. Staff also handle reporters and lobbyists. Lobbyists are hired by private groups to contact and persuade legislators to vote in their favor.

COUNTERPOINT

Lobbyists are an important part of the American law-making process. They represent large and powerful groups within society, such as the tobacco industry, the petroleum industry, labor unions, and professional or trade associations. Special-interest groups, such as the National Rifle Association, also hire lobbyists to help represent their interests.

Some people argue that the activities of lobbyists tend to "drown out" the smaller or weaker voices of individual citizens or the general public. Officially, lobbyists have no power and are not entitled to specific privileges.

Defenders of the lobby system point out that the right of free speech should apply to companies and organizations as much as it does to individual citizens. They also argue that lobbyists are in a position to contribute useful information to the debate. They are simply there to exercise the right of all citizens to participate in the democratic process and have their voices heard.

What do you think?

In addition to the personal staff of each member, Congress has a staff that serves its needs as a whole. Each committee has an administrative staff that conducts most of the day-to-day chores involved in the processing of bills and other congressional activities. Congress also has a staff that maintains the Library of Congress and the Congressional Research Service. There is also a General Accounting Office and a Congressional Budget Office that work full-time investigating financial matters and providing information that is helpful in analyzing and approving budgets.

Last, but not least, we turn our attention to the structure of the third branch of our federal government, the Supreme Court. The structure of the Supreme Court is relatively simple. The eight associate justices and the chief justice tend to work together as a group rather than split up into committees or deal directly with the public as individuals. However, the court has a sizeable administrative staff to help in the work of the court with scheduling and conducting oral arguments, publishing decisions, and other tasks. One of the important tasks of the Supreme Court is deciding which cases it is willing to review. Far more cases are appealed to the Supreme Court than it has time and resources to hear. Since its main responsibility is reviewing significant constitutional issues in cases already judged by lower courts, the Court looks over proposed cases and either agrees or refuses to hear them based on whether or not it feels such issues are at play.

It is important to understand, however, that the Supreme Court is not the only federal court. Below the Supreme Court, and directly accountable to it, is a network of Federal District Courts and Appeals Courts spread across the country. These courts have separate areas of responsibility or jurisdiction from state courts. For example, they try cases involving federal laws, disputes between states, foreign governments and treaties, disputes between parties from different states, or cases involving U.S. diplomats, as well as anything involving an alleged violation of constitutional rights. For each type of case, there is a hierarchy or flow of the case from the trial court that hears the original case, to an appeals court that may be asked to review the judgment of the lower court and possibly overturn it, to the Supreme Court, which may agree to review a case that has been judged by any of the lower courts. In a few rare circumstances, a case may originate at the U.S. Supreme Court, but its main role is to examine cases that have already been judged by at least one, and usually two, lower courts.

ORGANIZATION OF STATE AND LOCAL GOVERNMENTS

In a nutshell, most state governments mirror the federal government in many significant ways. They too have clearly defined executive, legislative, and judicial branches. As outlined above, the structure of the judicial branch is very much like that of the federal court system. State legislatures are also a lot like Congress in that most are divided into two chambers. Finally, the roles of governor and lieutenant governor mirror that of the president and vice president. The terms, procedural details, and areas of

NOTE

The term "Supreme Court" can sometimes be confusing, because the same term is also used for the highest state court in each state. To be fully clear, the high court of the land should be referred to as the U.S. Supreme Court. As with the federal court system, the state courts are divided into a hierarchy, starting with the lower courts and general trial courts, then to the state appellate (appeals) courts, then to the state Supreme Court.

STATE JUDICIAL BRANCH

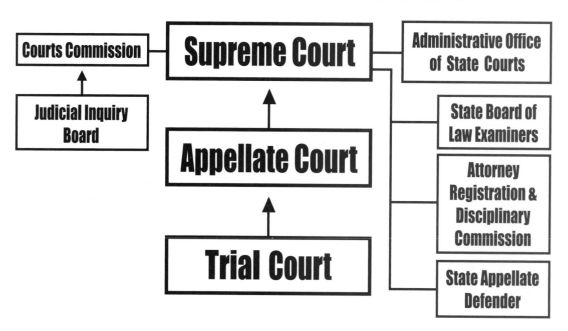

jurisdiction are where the differences occur. We will describe what state governments do for citizens in a later section of this text.

When it comes to local governments, there is considerable variety from one part of the country to another, and from urban to rural areas. This is partly because local governments are not specifically mentioned in the U.S. Constitution. They exist at the discretion of the states, which maintain authority over them and the right to change their structure if they wish to do so.

There is usually a distinction between the local governments in cities versus more rural areas. To become a city, an area with sufficient population must apply to the state legislature for a charter and thereby become incorporated. The charter will specify the style of municipal government the city will adopt. City governments are generally responsible for fire and police protection, maintaining city streets, public works such as sewers and water, trash collection, public libraries, and recreation. They also take on some of the state's responsibilities with regard to health and welfare. Cities may also levy their own taxes with the consent of the state. A major form of municipal tax is the property tax, which is based on the assessed value of all residential

and commercial properties in the municipality.

One form of government found in many large cities is the mayor-and-council. The city is divided into districts or wards, each of which votes for mayor and elects a local council person. The council meets to prepare and administer the municipal budget and to pass local laws called ordinances. The main variation in this style of local government concerns how much power is given to the mayor by the charter. In some cities, the mayor has a great deal of power. He or she appoints municipal department heads and may veto ordinances passed by the council. In other cities, the council has more power and the mayor may be little more than the moderator at council meetings.

Medium-sized and small cities have often modified this design to what is termed a council-manager format. There is no elected mayor. The only elected officials are the council persons, who may be elected to specific wards or may be chosen by all the voters in the city as a whole. The council hires a manager to supervise the city staff. The manager is directly answerable to the council, which holds all the power. There are a few variations on this municipal structure.

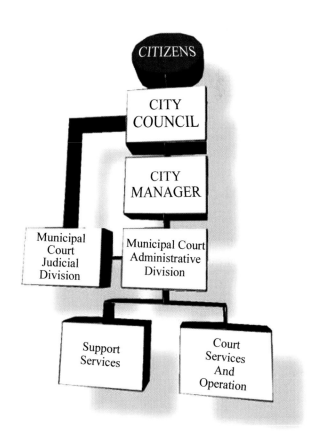

In Louisiana, counties are called parishes, and in Alaska they are called boroughs. Counties are geographically larger than cities — in fact, cities fall within one county or another. Some counties may be sparsely populated. The style and level of importance of county governments varies from place to place. Many counties have three to five elected commissioners or supervisors. There is often also a county sheriff, who is the senior law enforcement officer. Many counties also elect a district attorney who is the chief prosecutor for the county. In counties that include one or more significant cities, there is considerable variation as to what is handled by the municipal government and what is left to the county.

Many counties are subdivided into small units that represent a single distinct community. In some places, these units are called towns. In other places, they are referred to as townships or villages. The specific type of local government varies from state to state. In some states, the people of the town meet once a year and may actually enact important local ordinances at these meetings, as well as decide on property taxes and the town budget. However, day-to-day managing of the town is turned over to elected officials that may be called selectmen, trustees, or supervisors. These representatives tend to function much like a smaller version of a city council. In some towns, local elections also include voting for town officials such as the tax assessor, town clerk, and town treasurer. Depending upon the locality and style of organization, there may also be an elected executive to serve much like a mayor, whether or not that is the actual title of the position. Some larger towns or villages also follow the council-manager model and hire a professional manager.

The final form of local government involves the managing of public schools. The costs of running schools are shared by state and local governments. The state is subdivided into school districts that may or may not follow city or town boundaries, depending on the concentration of the population. Each district is managed by an elected body called a school board. In some places, school board elections are held in "off years" when there is no other office that is up for re-election. Unfortunately, these elections tend to draw poor voter turnout, perhaps because citizens don't feel they get a chance to know the candidates or the issues very well. However, school boards do have an important influence over the quality of local schools. In some states, this has led to an uneven quality of education from one district to another, and some states are taking steps to correct this situation. Remember that the state government has ultimate authority over the public school system and can intervene when school boards don't seem to be managing things properly.

When you put it all together, from the president and Congress, through the governor and state legislatures, to the county and local governments with their boards, elected officials, and school board members, the American voter has a lot of decisions to make when going to the polls. It takes some time and effort to keep informed on the candidates and the issues so that wise choices can be made and the people elected will come as close as possible to representing the real concerns, values and issues on the community. Unfortunately, not all Americans take this privilege and duty seriously. In some elections in some parts of the country, less than half of the eligible voters actually turn up to cast a ballot. The people who don't show up are often significant enough that they could have changed the outcome one way or another had they made the effort. There is currently nothing forcing citizens to vote. However, it's often been said that if you don't vote, don't complain about the government or what it ends up doing.

Voter apathy — people who are eligible to vote but don't — is a serious problem in our democratic system. It means that sometimes people with very enthusiastic and active supporters, but who don't reflect the values and beliefs of the general public, can get themselves elected. People who are discontented and want to make radical changes are more likely to be sure to show up to vote, whereas people who feel that things are more or less okay may not bother, assuming that the present government will probably be re-elected. That assumption can prove to be very wrong.

There are various reasons or excuses people give for not voting. They often say that they don't feel that their one vote will make any difference in the thousands or millions that are being cast. It is true that very few elections are ever decided by a single vote. However, some important elections have been decided by only a few dozen or a few hundred. What the apathetic voter doesn't realize is that other people are coming up with the same excuse, enough other people that together their absence does make a difference to the outcome.

Another reason some people offer is that "They're all the same." They have grown cynical about politics and politicians, and think nothing will change regardless of which party wins. This viewpoint is not supported by facts. There are often important differences between parties and candidates on issues that seriously affect all of our lives: how much taxes we pay, the approach taken to law enforcement and fighting crime, the level of social services provided to the poor and disadvantaged, even whether or not the nation goes to war.

What do you think?

HOW OUR GOVERNMENT IS ELECTED

Elections are the most significant way in which American citizens participate in their government. Rather than voting on all the individual issues that a government must face, voters elect a representative who will vote on their behalf. In theory, candidates are supposed to make their feelings known about important issues during the campaign that precedes an election. Then, presumably, each voter chooses the candidate whose views are the closest match to his or her own views. Of

course, it is not possible to predict how an elected official will vote on every item that comes before Congress or a state legislature. Sometimes a candidate you vote for may take a position with which you do not agree. When that happens, there are two things you can do to continue to exercise your participation. You can contact your elected member by phone, mail, or email to express your dissatisfaction with a policy he or she has taken. If enough people do this, sometimes an elected official will change his or her position. However, the final and decisive way you exert power over elected officials is when they come up for re-election. Their terms are limited and they know it. If they fail to follow the wishes of the people who elected them, they will not be re-elected the next time.

The first thing you need to do to be able to participate in the election process is register as a voter. To do so you must be at least 18 years old, a resident of the state in which you plan to vote, and a U.S. citizen. In most states, you must register ahead of time if you want to vote in an election. When registering to vote you will need to show proof of your identity and citizenship (which is usually done by presenting a birth certificate). You will be asked to provide your name and address. You will also be asked if you wish to register as a member of any political party. The main political

parties in the United States are the Republicans and the Democrats, although there are other smaller parties. You do not need to belong to a political party in order to become a registered voter. On the registration form, you can indicate that you are "unaffiliated" or "independent." However, if you want to become a Republican or Democrat, it will be necessary for you to register as such at the county office in order to vote in that party's process of choosing candidates prior to the election. If you register as an independent, you are only allowed to vote in the general election and choose one of the candidates already selected by the parties. However, if you are registered

with a party, then, in most states, you get to vote two times, first at the preliminary election or "primary" in which only members of that party vote to select candidates, and then again in the general election where you try to get those candidates elected. Note: some states do not conduct primaries. Rather, candidates are selected by caucuses. In this system, party members choose delegates to represent them, then the delegates actually vote for the candidates.

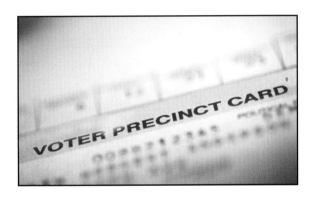

The election process is controlled by the states — meaning it is a little different from one place to another. The main difference is in the system or equipment actually used to cast the ballot. However, the main parts of the process are approximately the same everywhere. When you register, you will be told which polling place (voting location) you should go to. When you get there, you will be asked to write your name and address and signature on an application form. The clerk will take your form and read your name aloud so that a second person, called a

challenger, can hear it. The challenger's job is to double-check that you are actually a registered voter and the person you say you are. The challenger will often look up your registration form and compare the signature there with the signature on the application. If there is any doubt that you are the right person, you may be asked additional questions. If the challenger is satisfied you will be allowed to cast your vote. The challenger may initial your application indicating that he or she is satisfied as to your identity. In most places, there are at least two challengers, one representing each major political party. They are present because over the years various attempts have been made to "fix" elections by sending people to vote in areas where they don't belong or sending them to vote more than once.

The actual voting area is supervised by judges who make sure that every person has privacy when making the vote and to help with any problems. This is the point where the process becomes different in different places. In some places, voters use paper or cardboard cards. In other places, they pull a lever of a machine. Some ballots require you to mark an X in a circle beside the name (paper ballots). Others require you to punch out a perforated hole next to the name of the candidate (punch card ballots).

Still others require you to use a pencil to fill in a circle next to a name (scanned ballots). In some places, votes are made using electronic monitors with touch screens or buttons similar to those you would find at an automatic banking machine. It is critically important that you ensure that you understand how to use the ballot or machine in your area or you could end up voting for someone you do not intend. This allegedly happened to large numbers of voters in Florida during the 2000 presidential election and may have made the difference between George W. Bush or Al Gore being elected.

Ballots can be complicated for two reasons. First, it is common to have five or six candidates running for the same office, because in addition to the Democrats and Republicans some smaller parties may be running candidates. Secondly, you are often voting for several different positions at the same time. If you don't have a clear understanding of the ballot, you should ask for help. Many voters accidentally "spoil" their ballots by not marking or punching them correctly. On punch ballots, if you don't punch the hole all the way through, the card may not be read by the machine that tabulates the votes. If you accidentally vote for two candidates for the same office, your vote will be rejected.

Presidential elections are held every four years. Members of the House of Representative are up for election every two years. Senators are elected to six-year terms, but one third of them face re-election every two years. In addition, some states hold elections for governor, state legislature and local offices at the same time as the presidential or congressional elections. Other states wait and hold these elections during odd-numbered years when there are no federal offices at stake.

A further cause of complicated ballots is the fact that many states will also ask citizens to vote on specific questions during the general election. These questions may be put on the ballot by government officials, but often they result from action taken by a citizens' group. If such a group gets enough signatures and follows the applicable administrative rules, they can have their issue placed on the ballot. There are two general ways in which this happens. An initiative is when the citizens' group wishes to propose a new law of its own. A referendum is when a citizens' group wishes to challenge a law that has already been passed by the state or local government. Referendums sometimes happen when there is a controversial issue at hand. For example, there may be a plan to build an expensive new sports arena that could cause an increase in state or local taxes and there may be a local citizens' group that is against the plan.

COUNTERPOINT

Some people believe that allowing different systems for voting from state to state, and sometimes from county to county within a state, gives rise to a subtle form of discrimination against some voters. For example, in the 2000 Presidential election there was a bitter dispute about the different methods of voting within the state of Florida - and exactly where in the state those methods were used. It is generally true in many states that poorer people in cities vote Democratic and people in more affluent areas tend to vote Republican. Some journalists who reviewed the situation in Florida concluded that some of the more affluent counties in Florida had updated their voting equipment, whereas poorer ones had not. The newer equipment was easier and less confusing to use. Many voters in the traditionally Democratic areas realized after they voted, and began to hear about the problem in the news, that they had become confused by the layout of the ballot and had accidentally voted for the wrong candidate. Of course, it was too late to change their votes. Many historians believe that if Florida had been required to have a modern voting procedure everywhere, Al Gore might have received enough additional votes, votes intended for him in the first place, to win the state and thereby the presidency.

What do you think?

The one thing that is standard across the nation is that general elections are held the first Tuesday in November after the first Monday. However, sometimes special elections for a specific purpose may happen at some other time. For example, it may be necessary to replace an official who has died in office, or it may be necessary to have a second election, called a run-off election, if no candidate receives a clear majority in the first election (usually because there are more than two candidates). Some elections require a candidate to win a majority of the votes cast. There is an important difference between majority and plurality. Majority means 50% plus one vote. Plurality simply means more than anyone else. Suppose there are three candidates. One gets 40% of the vote, another gets 35%, and the third gets 25%. In this case, the first candidate has a plurality, but does not have a majority.

When it comes to the process of choosing candidates within a particular political party, each state has its voice within the party by choosing its preferred candidate by means of primaries or caucuses, as previously mentioned. Republican and Democratic candidates for president are then actually selected at a large national convention. The party in each state sends delegates to this convention. The number of delegates is in proportion to the size of the state's population. In states that conduct primaries or other formal selection systems, the delegates are expected to vote for their chosen candidate on the first ballot. However, when there are more than two candidates, sometimes one candidate doesn't receive a clear majority (50% plus one) on the first ballot. When this happens, other

ballots are held until there is a winner. After the first ballot, the delegates are free to change their votes. Candidates that finish further back in the first round may drop out before the second ballot. However, in doing so, they may encourage their supporters to vote for another particular candidate. In this way, even candidates that have little chance of winning can exert considerable influence at a convention.

In addition to selecting presidential and vice presidential candidates (the vice presidential candidate is almost always chosen by the winning presidential candidate in consultation with party advisers, then approved by the convention), the delegates at the

convention prepare a "platform." This is a statement of where the party stands on the key issues of the election, and reading the platform is one good way to help voters choose candidates.

The procedure outlined in the Constitution for electing a president is much more complex than for other elections. The actual election of the president takes place at a meeting of a group called the electoral college, several weeks after the general election. The electoral college works a bit like a virtual convention. Each state "sends" a set of electors to the college, the number depending on the state's population (states with larger populations send more electors). If a presidential candidate wins the popular vote in a particular state, then that state sends electors to the college who support that candidate. If you win a state by even just a single vote, then all of the electors from that state vote for you. Thus, it is very important for presidential candidates to get more votes than opponents in several key states that have a large number of electors. You can win several small states that have only a few electors, but still lose the election if your opponent wins some of the larger states.

Many people dislike the electoral college system, and there is often talk of doing away with it. The 2000 presidential election renewed this debate. Because of where his votes were positioned in key states, George W. Bush won the election (got more votes at the electoral college), even though when you counted up the popular vote of the nation as a whole, Al Gore got slightly more votes than Bush. However, amending the Constitution is a long and complicated process, and it seems unlikely that the electoral college system will be changed any time soon.

COUNTERPOINT

To many people it seems that the electoral college is a pointless and unfair complication to the election process. Why shouldn't the winner of the popular vote automatically become president? If a candidate can win the election while having fewer votes than an opponent (which has happened four times in U.S. history) then obviously some votes count for more than others.

There is an opposing point of view on this issue. Some analysts believe that the electoral college system is actually fairer and helps to make all votes across the nation more important. Here is why: If the only thing that mattered were the popular vote, presidential candidates would spend almost all their time campaigning in high population-density areas, where they could reach more people with their message in a shorter amount of time. You could see and be seen by half a million people at a time at a major rally in New York City, Chicago, or Los Angeles. It would take days of traveling around the countryside to contact that many people in states like Wyoming, Montana, North Dakota or Utah. Even under the present system, voters in small states don't get as much attention as voters in larger ones. However, that sometimes changes as we draw close to election day. The various campaigns conduct surveys called polls to try to find out how people in each state plan to vote. Candidates then decide to spend as much time as possible in states, even small ones, where the poll shows that they are in a close race. If the poll shows they will take the state by a large margin, or lose it by a large margin, there is no point in going there. However, if the poll shows a close result, then the thinking is that a couple of last-minute campaign visits to the state might be enough to push the balance in the candidate's favor. A candidate will try to win as many states as possible, even small states, especially if the overall race appears to be close and the electoral college outcome is uncertain.

There is another aspect of the electoral college system that helps smaller states get more attention. The number of electors from each state is determined by adding together the state's number of senators and representatives. As you will recall, the number of representatives is in proportion to each state's population, but each state gets two senators no matter what. So, if a state has twenty-two representatives, it gets 24 electors (22+2). If it is very small and has only two representatives, it gets 4 electors (2+2). Thus, by adding the fixed number of senators, a small state may double its representation at the college, whereas a large state only adds to its total by a slight amount. In a majority-of-popular-vote system, each state would only have votes in proportion to its population, without getting the "bonus two" that end up being more significant to smaller states than to larger ones.

What do you think?

CHAPTER 3

GOVERNMENT ★ FOR THE PEOPLE

WHAT THE FEDERAL GOVERNMENT DOES FOR YOU

Earlier in the text, we presented statistics about the large number of people who work for the American government. Now it is time to give you a better idea of what some of these people do. At least in theory, every one of them is there because our government leaders felt that there was something specific that government needed to do to make your life safer and better.

If we were to try to list every government department and agency at every level and then explain all the things it does, this text would need to be the size of a city telephone directory. We can only give you an overview that focuses upon the main departments and their main contributions. However, just so you get some glimpse of the complexity of government organizations, we will start by looking in some detail at the federal government's newest body, the Department of Homeland Security. Then we will summarize the activities of each of the other departments, but in somewhat less detail.

Department of Homeland Security

The creation of this department in 2003 was the most significant structural change to our federal government since World War II. The main impetus for the change were the events of September 11, 2001, when two of our major cities were attacked by terrorists and more than 3,000 Americans lost their lives. Prior to that

1) Border and Transportation Security

2) Emergency Preparedness and Response

3) Science and Technology

4) Infrastructure Protection

(Note: the term "infrastructure" refers to physical assets managed by the government: roads, bridges, buildings, monuments, etc.)

Without going into detail about what each agency does, the following listing of DHS agencies will give you a quick view of the range of activities that are involved. Remember, each of these is a separate entity with its own staff, facilities, and mission.

date, most of the agencies that now come under Homeland Security already existed. However, they were scattered amongst various other federal departments. Bringing them all together under one Secretary and management structure was an attempt to better coordinate their activities so the country would be better prepared for a similar event in the future and, more importantly, could do everything possible to prevent it from happening.

The Department of Homeland Security (DHS) combines 22 separate agencies under four major directorates:

Border and Transportation Security

Immigration and Naturalization Service

Transportation Security Administration

Federal Law Enforcement Training Center

Animal and Plant Health Inspection Service

Office of Domestic Preparedness

Emergency Preparedness and Response

Federal Emergency Management Agency

Strategic National Stockpile and the National Disaster Medical System

Nuclear Incident Response Team

Domestic Emergency Support Team

National Domestic Preparedness Office

Science and Technology

CBRN Countermeasures Program

Environmental Measurements Laboratory

National BW Defense Analysis Center

Plum Island Animal Diseases Center

Infrastructure Protection

Critical Infrastructure Assurance Office

Federal Computer Incident Response Center

National Communications System

National Infrastructure Protection Center

Energy Security and Assurance Program

The Secret Service

The Coast Guard

Together, these agencies exist to worry about every conceivable thing that could ever go wrong — either accidentally or through a deliberate act of an enemy — that might harm large numbers of Americans in any way. This means anything from terrorist bombings, to immunizations against diseases that could be used as weapons, to protecting livestock and wildlife from foreign diseases, to protecting the internet and communications systems from hackers or saboteurs; to ensuring emergency supplies of oil and other energy in the event of war or some other world crisis, to dealing with tragedies that could be the result of major storms, natural events, or industrial accidents. Other government departments would participate in various ways in many of these tasks, but the job of planning and coordinating the major first responses falls to the Department of Homeland Security.

Department of Defense

In recent times, the Department of Defense has once again become an extremely important and high profile part of the executive branch of our government. The Secretary of Defense is one of the most critical and powerful of presidential advisers. The American military that he supervises is also the single largest and most expensive group of government-paid workers.

The general purpose of the Defense Department is fairly self-evident. It manages our military in both war and peace. However, sometimes the boundaries of its authority or jurisdiction can become difficult to assess, as it is not always clear what the separation is between acts of war and acts of international diplomacy during or after a war. For example, after the U.S.-led invasion of Iraq in 2003 there was some disagreement between Defense Secretary Donald Rumsfeld and Secretary of State Colin Powell, not only over policy for postwar Iraq, but over which department should have primary responsibility for implementing it.

Department of State

The State Department is another powerful and influential wing of the executive branch. The State Department directs all dealings with foreign countries except those regarding acts of war. This means that formal talks between world leaders, American participation in international meetings and conventions, visits from foreign dignitaries, and the participation of the U.S. at the United Nations are all handled through the State Department. Primary attempts to solve problems and avoid war through diplomatic pressure or international agreements and compromises are handled at the State Department.

When all these measures fail and war becomes the only resort, the Defense Department takes over.

The main justification for the State Department is the safeguarding of American citizens and American interests around the world. However, in the twenty-first century, with America widely regarded as the only remaining superpower, there is a strong view in America that problems in other parts of the world are also our problems — in part because they end up affecting us, and in part because we often feel a duty to use our power to help those who are powerless and oppressed. For this reason, you will see State Department officials doing things like intervening to help resolve the conflict between the Israelis and the Palestinians.

Apart from handling the large issues, the State Department also carries out day-to-day chores that assist and protect Americans, especially when they are traveling to foreign countries. It establishes embassies and consulates in almost all countries throughout the world. These serve as a home base for our ambassadors, who are the official representatives of our government to foreign governments. However, they also serve as places of information and assistance to American travelers who encounter dangers or difficulties. If an American is arrested in a foreign country, whether justly or unjustly, the embassy is often active in ensuring fair treatment and providing some communication link with family or colleagues back home.

A final important service of the State Department is issuing passports. A passport is a document that is formatted like a small booklet. It serves as proof of identity and proof of U.S. citizenship. Only citizens can receive passports. These documents are necessary for most international travel. Canada will often allow Americans to enter without showing a passport, but it is an exception to the rule. Much of the rest of the world requires not only passports but visas. A visa is a document giving a foreign person permission to enter a country. Most countries in Western Europe, and a few in other geographical areas, allow Americans to enter with only a passport. Most others require visas. The United States requires visas of people from

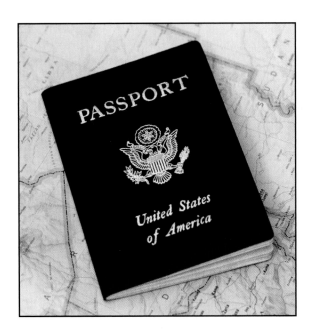

many countries who wish to enter the United States. A foreign person who wishes to visit the United States from any of these countries must first apply for a visa at the local American embassy. The main purpose of visa requirements is security. Before a visa is issued, a background check will be conducted to ensure that the person is not on any list of known criminals or undesirables.

Treasury Department

The Treasury Department is literally the only money-making agency of the federal government. It operates mints (factories that make coins) and special engraving and print shops that produce paper currency. It is also responsible for managing the monetary resources of the federal government. This is no small task when you consider that the federal government's annual spending is in the ballpark of three trillion dollars.

The two main agencies or systems that manage money are the Internal Revenue Service and the Federal Reserve System. We all know what the IRS does: it collects taxes. The action of the Federal Reserve System is more complex and it is not as well understood by Americans because it tends to operate somewhat behind the scenes. It is a separate government agency from the Treasury Department, and we will discuss its role later in the text.

Department of Justice

Although some agencies within the Justice Department have recently been moved to the Department of Homeland Security, the Justice Department remains the key agency of

law enforcement in our country. It operates the Federal Bureau of Investigation (FBI), the largest and most important federal police force. The Office of the Attorney General, which is the head of this department, also directs federal prosecutions. Special divisions within the Justice Department enforce specific aspects of federal laws, such as drug enforcement, antitrust (preventing illegal business monopolies), and civil rights.

Department of the Interior

The Department of the Interior looks after public lands, relations with Native Americans, national parks, monuments, and historic sites. It also has some responsibility for overseeing the mining of natural resources.

Department of Agriculture

The Department of Agriculture carries out programs of research, education, conservation, forestry,

marketing, credit, export expansion, food distribution, grading and inspection, and development of rural areas.

Among the major units are The Cooperative State Research Service and The Agricultural Research Service, who work with state agencies to improve the effectiveness of research in areas such as human nutrition, soil and water conservation, processing and distribution of farm products, and climatic environmental conditions. Another major unit, The Food and Nutrition Service administers food assistance programs, including food stamp, school breakfast and lunch, and summer food service programs.

Department of Commerce

The Commerce Department looks after a handful of somewhat unrelated matters that affect the health of the American economy. In our free market system there are limited areas in which businesses are regulated and enforcement of those regulations is distributed among several different departments. What the Commerce Department specifically looks after are the census, trademarks and patents, and standards for weights and measurements. These are fairly indirect services to business, but they are important. The census (a head

count of the American public held every ten years) provides useful data to business and government planners, and has an effect upon the reshaping of the boundaries of Congressional districts. Patents allow inventors to have exclusive right to sell their ideas for a period of time before others can copy their designs. Trademarks allow companies to own their product names or slogans and prevent other companies from causing confusion by trying to use these protected names themselves.

While we've made it sound like the Commerce Department is relatively simple, a look at a detailed organizational chart for this department would show about thirty different offices or agencies dealing with everything from Minority Business Development, to the National Oceanic and Atmospheric Administration, to export administration and enforcement.

Department of Labor

The Labor Department does several specific things that are intended to help protect the American worker. They act to enforce safe working conditions, minimum wages, and pension rights. They also collect and publish data about the work force, and encourage cooperation between labor unions and management. Again, however, in a free market system the federal government's ability to regulate workers, other than federal employees, is somewhat limited.

Department of Health and Human Services

The Department of Health and Human Services touches virtually every American at one time or another. Health and Human Services has an important role in administering Social Security, Medicare, and Medicaid. It also runs the Public Health Service and the Food and Drug Administration — and a host of other departments and agencies related to these topics. Anything that has to do with health issues, epidemics, or the safety of food or drugs comes under its jurisdiction.

Department of Housing and Urban Development

The Department of Housing and Urban Development is the federal agency responsible for national policy and programs that address America's housing needs, that improve and develop the nation's communities, and enforce fair housing laws.

HUD's business is helping create a decent home and suitable living environment for all Americans, and it

has given America's communities a strong national voice at the cabinet level. HUD plays a major role in supporting homeownership by underwriting homeownership for lower- and moderate-income families through its mortgage insurance programs.

Department of Education

Public education is largely the responsibility of the states. The main way the federal government has become involved is by funding various special programs, such as for persons with limited English skills or for physically challenged students, among others. Once the federal government is offering money to the states, it gets to have some input into the standards that the states must fulfill in order to qualify for the federal money. One of the more significant policies in recent years was the No Child Left Behind Act of 2002, which established standardized testing requirements for schoolchildren and gave parents more flexibility to transfer their children to another school. The Department of Education also provides grants and loans for America's college students. In principle, every American who wants to go to college can, if necessary, borrow money from the government to finance their education.

Department of Transportation

The responsibility for transportation is another gray area of federal/state jurisdiction. The federal department becomes involved in areas like interstate highways, railroads, mass transit — and perhaps most importantly, air travel. The federal government sets detailed standards for the construction and operation of aircraft, and has primary responsibility for investigating crashes and accidents. Before 2003, DOT also managed the Coast Guard, but as you have already learned, that service has been shifted to the Department of Homeland Security.

Department of Energy

The Department of Energy emerged after the great oil shortage of the late 1970s. Its role is to develop a national energy policy and to encourage research and development of new technology. It tries to ensure that the country has enough reserves of oil on hand to make it through any short-term crisis that could develop and it plays a role in regulating the interstate piping or transmission of gas and electricity. In a free market system, however, the ability of the government to control the energy industries is limited and there has been a trend in recent years to decrease the amount of regulatory control over energy producers. Differing views exist as to whether the government is getting too involved in helping the major oil companies, or not doing enough to ensure security of supply. The one thing of which there is little doubt is that the dependence of the American economy on foreign oil is a source of vulnerability.

Department of Veteran Affairs

There has always been a department that looked after programs for veterans of military service, but, in 1989, in part because of many complaints about how veterans were being treated, this department was elevated to a cabinet-level position. The department operates some hospitals specifically for veterans and offers many different assistance programs for veterans and their families.

Independent Agencies and Corporations

There are several important bodies in the federal government that are not directly attached to cabinet departments. Some of these are considered to be part of the executive branch, while others are truly

Serving Those
Who
Served

independent. The organizational structure and chain of command gets complicated and it is not the main thing we want to cover here. It is more important that you understand what these agencies do for the public.

Perhaps most important is the Federal Reserve System (often called the Fed). This is essentially a national government-owned bank with branches across the country. This system is managed by a board of directors and a chairperson selected by the president and approved by the Senate for a four-year term. However, once in office, the board acts independently of the president or Congress and can even criticize government policies, tax measures, or spending if it feels they are harmful to the health of the economy.

The Fed has various roles with regard to banking regulation, consumer credit, and controlling the circulation of the nation's currency. It uses various tools at its disposal to influence the commercial banks and to shape the monetary policy of the nation. It does this in various ways. It manipulates the interest rate that it charges to commercial banks that borrow money from it, thereby directly affecting their lending rates to businesses and consumers. It also sets requirements for reserves that commercial banks must deposit with it in order to ensure that they will be able to honor requests for withdrawals, even if there is a sudden increase in them. It also buys and sells government securities and bonds that affect the investment climate in the country and impact the stock market and the value of the U.S. dollar.

A detailed explanation of how our economic system works is beyond the scope of this text. However, a simplified view can be offered as follows. There are two economic problems that the Federal Reserve System seeks to head off. Solving one

of these problems often leads directly to the other, so it is a constant balancing act. First, when the economy is slow and not growing or creating new jobs fast enough, the Fed acts to lower interest rates. This makes it easier for businesses and consumers to borrow money, much of which will end up being spent on products and business expansion to get the economy revved up again. However, revving up the economy too much leads to a different but equally serious problem: high inflation. The term inflation refers to a process in which wages and prices keep steadily creeping up, so that in a short period of time everything costs more and people are constantly fighting for higher wages to keep pace with the increases. When this happens, the Fed will raise interest rates to try to slow down the economy just enough to keep inflation at a reasonable rate. Interest rates also have some effect on the value of the dollar. The term "value of the dollar" refers to how much the U.S. dollar is worth as compared with other world currencies. Again, the value of the dollar can be a double-edged sword. If the value of the dollar falls, it costs Americans more of our money to buy goods from foreign countries — and imported goods are an important part of our economy. On the other hand, if the value of the dollar gets too high, then some American products suddenly become too expensive for people in other countries to afford, and this hurts industries that rely on exports (sales to other countries) for their livelihood.

COUNTERPOINT

The ups and downs of the American economy can truly complicate the government's plans, programs and budgets.

A budget is an estimate of revenues (mainly from taxes) and of expenses. The expenses can only be justified and achieved if the revenue forecasts are accurate. However, most of the main ways in which governments collect taxes are directly proportional to the health of the economy. For example, a large source of government revenue is income tax. However, income tax is based on a percentage of earnings by American corporations and citizens. When the economy drops, businesses show less profit, and citizens are earning less in wages, and the government's take can fall off significantly. If the spending proceeds as originally planned but the revenues fall short, the government ends up running a deficit.

Over the years, either deliberately or accidentally, the federal government has run so many deficits that the nation has accumulated a huge national debt. As of April 2008, this debt was a whopping $9.4 trillion.

How does the government get into debt? By borrowing money when it doesn't have enough revenue to meet its commitments. However, borrowing money is not free, even for the government. The interest payments on the debt (just interest, not repaying any of the principal) can be almost as high as the entire defense budget, which is the government's largest area of expense.

The United States is not the only country that has faced this problem. During the Clinton administration, deficits were steadily lowered, and eventually, annual budgets showed a surplus. However, this was made possible mainly by a very strong economy during much of that period. The Bush administration chose to return to intentional deficits so that it could fight the war on terrorism while at the same time trying to stimulate a lagging economy by cutting taxes, so more money was left in the hands of taxpayers and businesses.

This has become a significant economic and moral issue. Should today's government be allowed to create problems for tomorrow's government by intentionally adding to the public debt?

What do you think?

We will complete our survey of federal government activities and services by examining a few more independent agencies whose general activities are significant and of which you should be aware. On the topic of money, one of these is the Federal Deposit Insurance Corporation (FDIC), which insures bank accounts of certain types up to a certain amount. This provides protection to citizens if the bank goes out of business.

In mentioning the important government services, we should not forget the post office. The United States Post Office (USPS) operates as a government corporation. The

distinction between that and a government department is often a subtle one. Essentially, it means that it is managed much in the style of a private corporation, but it receives money from Congress whenever it needs it.

In the category of "independent agencies" rather than "government corporations" there are two (of about 100) to which we wish to call your attention. The first is the Environmental Protection Agency. Since 1970, this agency has set goals and standards for controlling atmospheric pollution and helping enforce federal laws. It is designed to be a public watchdog over our environment. However, there are also several private groups such as Greenpeace and the Sierra Club that also serve as environmental watchdogs and most of them tend to feel that the EPA does not do enough and that it gives in easily to government pressure to look the other way in cases of projects or industries which have the administration's support.

Before the Bush Administration's War on Terrorism largely distracted the nation from many issues on the homefront, environmental protection was one of the hot — and controversial — political topics. It was a favorite cause of former vice president and presidential candidate Al Gore. In general, it can be said that consistently over the past 30 years, Democrats have stressed environmental protection far more than have Republicans. During Democratic presidencies, environmental laws tend to be passed or strengthened; during Republican administrations they tend to be revoked or weakened.

Why wouldn't everyone be in favor of cleaner air and water, and controlling harmful chemicals in the environment? The problem is that protection and cleanup of the environment costs money — both government money, and money that private industries must spend meeting tougher standards, or that they lose because those standards place limits on their activities. If industries were to suffer high enough losses in this area, it could lead to a slowdown in the American economy and loss of jobs for American workers. Of course, the great debate is whether or not that would actually happen, or if it is simply being used as an excuse to allow big business to do what it pleases and maximize profits.

During the Clinton administration, the countries of the world got together in Japan and signed the Kyoto Protocol on global warming. Scientists have shown that certain gases produced as part of air pollution are causing a steady and permanent warming of the Earth's atmosphere, leading to more severe weather patterns, and droughts in many parts of the world. The United States originally signed the agreement, but when George W. Bush took office he pulled the United States out of it, for economic reasons. Since America is the single largest producer of the gases that are causing global warming, there is fear that the Kyoto Protocol has little chance of succeeding without us. President Bush has also angered environmentalists by some of his other decisions, such as to open sensitive wilderness in Alaska to oil exploration.

Opponents of environmentalism say that it goes too far in its definitions of what environmental protection should entail. They point to examples of situations where a major construction project was halted because a little-known species of rare frog lived in the area and might be driven to extinction by the project. They say that American jobs are more important than American frogs. However, environmentalists point out that there are thousands of species of plants and animals around the world that have become extinct or are threatened with extinction because of human development and industry. They also point out that 75% of our medicines are derived from plants or animals, some of which are rare and only found in environments such as rainforests, which are rapidly being destroyed in many parts of the world.

What do you think?

The last federal agency we will look at in this section is perhaps the most famous one: the National Aeronautic and Space Administration, commonly known as NASA. NASA has operated the American space program, which got a strong boost of support during the administration of John F. Kennedy and has been active ever since. The crowning achievement of the program was landing a man on the moon in 1969 and returning him to Earth safely, a feat they eventually repeated so many times that the public almost seemed to take it for granted. However, in recent years, the agency has suffered problems that have damaged its reputation. Two space shuttles, the Challenger and Columbia, malfunctioned and exploded, killing all crewmembers. A couple of consecutive unmanned missions to Mars failed due to engineering miscalculations or other technical problems. Part of the underlying problem has been a

cutback in NASA's funding in recent years. However, they also appear to have had internal management and quality control issues that cannot entirely be blamed on the budget.

The agency's future is uncertain. The United States is presently committed to participating, with other nations, in the International Space Station project, which will conduct important scientific research in space. Many within NASA still hope to land an astronaut on Mars within the foreseeable future; however, as NASA continues to have serious problems with missions much closer to home, that is becoming increasingly unlikely. Most of NASA's success stories in recent years have involved unmanned

scientific missions sent to photograph and explore the solar system, or to launch important satellites and space telescopes. Few people predict that NASA will ever disappear, but many see the future of the agency as one of launching unmanned scientific probes, as well as helping the military and the telecommunications industry launch satellites that serve a practical purpose.

COUNTERPOINT

Even during the high profile success stories of the 1960s and 1970s there was considerable opposition in America to the space program. The main complaint was the huge expense of space research and exploration. Many people felt that with so many problems here on Earth, such as poverty in American cities and Third World countries, the money could be better spent. Some characterize the space program as largely an extravagant ego-enhancing sport for engineers and military pilots. Much of the original impetus for landing a man on the moon was to get there before the Russians did, during the Cold War period of tension between the U.S. and Russia.

Proponents of the space program can point to ways in which space research has had practical benefits in civilian society. Many products that we use in our homes were first developed for use in space, such as Velcro fasteners. They also argue that above and beyond any practical contributions to society, the space program enriches mankind's understanding of the universe, advances human technology and achievement, and can serve as a vehicle for international cooperation.

What do you think?

WHAT THE STATE GOVERNMENT DOES FOR YOU

After seeing how complex the federal government is, it might come as a surprise to learn that most of the things government does that touch citizens most directly are all handled by the states. State governments create and maintain the civic structure of our lives. Their areas of responsibility include the following:

- public schools, including state colleges
- public health
- many types of social services and welfare
- state criminal law
- state prosecutors, courts and prisons
- state highways and bridges

- state parks
- state police
- state licensing and supervision of trades and labor laws
- regulation of business practices, utilities, and consumer protection
- pollution control (responsibility shared with federal government)

Any one of these broad categories can be opened into a detailed listing of individual services and responsibilities. For example, in the category of public health, the states do the following:

- licensing doctors and dentists
- regulating the sale of drugs
- providing financial assistance to hospitals and other health institutions
- running public treatment clinics
- regulating vaccinations for children
- maintaining medical testing laboratories
- inspecting and licensing of restaurants
- maintaining air and water quality
- managing hazardous waste
- administering Medicaid, which provides medical services to the disadvantaged

WHAT THE LOCAL GOVERNMENT DOES FOR YOU

Remember that the local government is really just an extension of the state government. Therefore, it provides many of the programs and services listed in the preceding section, under state supervision. While we mentioned that the states have responsibilities for schools, in practice, it is the local governments that operate many public schools at the elementary and high school levels. Also, many social services programs, such as welfare, are run at city level, even though state and federal governments pay some of the costs. If someone needs low cost public housing, they would often work with a social worker employed by the city.

Local governments also run many important basic day-to-day services, such as collecting the trash and operating police and fire departments. The town or city may provide drinking water directly, or may contract to a private company for this service. Larger towns and cities also operate mass transit systems of public buses and subways.

Finally, local governments make decisions on a street-by-street and building-by-building basis. They give out building permits and condemn unsafe structures. They set up zoning ordinances that limit what types of buildings and businesses may be built or operated in specific neighborhoods. They set standards for how properties must be maintained, and they regulate issues that pertain to public order or nuisance type complaints. They also regulate parking and traffic patterns on local streets.

Both state and the local governments share in the responsibility for various types of record keeping, such as birth certificates, academic records and recording property deeds.

COUNTERPOINT

Civil libertarians are people who believe that the government spends too much time and money telling people what to do. They believe that government should regulate as few aspects of our lives as are absolutely necessary for public safety and order and nothing more. They stress individual rights and freedoms.

Sometimes civil libertarians and local government officials end up clashing because of local attempts to regulate or prohibit something. Often a local government will decide to take a stand on how residents take care of their lawns, where and how children can ride bicycles and what pets people may or may not own.

Many people see these types of laws as overstepping the reasonable boundaries of what local government should be doing. If government is going to get involved at all, they would prefer to see the state government study the problem closely and then come to a reasonable decision that will apply everywhere.

Even though states have the authority to overturn unreasonable local bylaws, they rarely do so. They view the actions of local governments as reflecting local community concerns and values.

What do you think?

CHAPTER 4

AMERICA IN PERSPECTIVE:
A QUICK LOOK AT THE REST OF THE WORLD

OTHER FORMS AND SYSTEMS OF GOVERNMENT

It is difficult to fully appreciate our freedoms and lifestyle here in America without taking a look at the rest of the world - particularly in places where freedom, prosperity and even basic human rights, are lacking. There are many countries in the world today that enjoy a political system and social structure much like ours. However, at the time our country was established in 1776, democracy was a radical new idea not being practiced to any significant degree anywhere else in the world. It had been tried in some earlier eras, notably ancient Greece, and to some degree ancient Rome, but at the time our country was founded the rest of the world was ruled by kings, dictators, or warlords. The success of the American experiment was an important factor in influencing many other nations to adopt a democratic system - although that system was often different in important ways from ours.

There are no two countries in the world that operate in exactly the same way. For that reason, it is hard to classify political and economic systems without resorting to oversimplifications. For example, countries like Canada and England have governments and social systems that are very much like ours. When we visit those countries things are familiar and we feel safe. We feel that our security and basic rights will be respected and protected. We get this same feeling in many other European countries, even some whose governments function in a very

different way from ours. They share the same values and regard for human rights as we do. There are also democracies in Asia, South America and a few in Africa. We feel at home there to varying but often lesser degrees, not only because of differences in languages and customs, but also because the rights of citizens and the actions of governments, police and military are sometimes noticeably different from us in ways that do not put us completely at ease.

Governments around the world can be classified in two different ways. The first classification is based on the political system, including not just the political leaders, but the courts, laws, and basic human rights. The second classification is based on the economic system, which involves public or private ownership of land and business and the powers of government to control employment, wealth, and the economy. The fact that there are two different ways of looking at other countries means

that we cannot easily divide them up into two simple camps based on only one factor. A country may have a political system that is much like ours, but an economic system that is very different.

Our economic system is sometimes referred to as capitalism. The main principle of capitalism is private ownership and economic freedom of individuals with some government restrictions, but as few as possible. In a capitalist country, you can own land, start your own business, take or quit jobs without government permission, and accumulate as much wealth as you are able. (Of course, you will be taxed to some degree on your earnings, however.)

At the opposite end of the spectrum is a system called communism. It was founded as a kind of protest movement because it believed that capitalism was allowing some people to get very rich while other people stayed poor no matter how hard they worked. It tried to change this by declaring that the basic tools of the economy — land, factories and natural resources — would all belong to the state. The state would decide how best to use them on behalf of all the people. In theory, this meant that there were few, if any, wealthy people in society and all of the working classes were looked after by the government, provided with jobs, medical care, education, and all the other necessities of life.

In practice, communism didn't work out nearly that well, and almost all of the countries in the world that once adopted it have since abandoned it. The three notable exceptions are North Korea and Cuba, which still practice a strict, old-fashioned style of communism, and China, which is still a communist country, but one that is gradually modernizing and allowing more and more capitalist economic influences.

In theory, communism was an economic system. In and of itself, the philosophy did not necessarily mean that people living under communism would be deprived of basic rights and freedoms. However, that is what started to happen in every country where communism was adopted. The government had too much power, and it failed to use it solely for the good of the citizens.

There is an attempted middle ground between capitalism and communism. It is a system called socialism. Socialism adopts some of the economic philosophies of communism without the manipulation and suppression of human rights and freedoms. Socialist governments do not usually try to have the government own and control absolutely every aspect of the economy. They may take control of certain industries or occupations they consider essential to

THUMBNAIL REFERENCE CHART

Concepts	Capitalism	Socialism	Communism
Private Ownership	Yes	No	No
Individual Enterprise and Profits	Yes	No	No
Government Control of Industry	No	Yes	Yes
Automatic Right of Each Citizen to Share in the Wealth of Society	No	Yes	Yes
Right of Each Citizen to Gain as Much of the World's Wealth as His Abilities Can Earn Him	Yes	No	No
Employment Guaranteed	No	Yes	Yes
Unemployment Compensation	Yes	No	No
Right to be Unemployed	Yes	No	No
Old Age Provisions	Yes	Yes	No
Right to Vote for Public Officials	Yes	Yes	(?)Yes
Right to Criticize the Government	Yes	Yes	No
Right to Voice Opinions on Laws to be Made	Yes	Yes	(?)Yes
Right to Civil Trial	Yes	Yes	(?)Yes
Spiritual Concepts as well as Economic Included in Philosophy	No	No	Yes
Freedom of Worship	Yes	Yes	No
Recognition of Established Moral Codes	Yes	Yes	No
Recognition of a God	Yes	Yes	No
Acceptance of the Duty of Revolutionizing World Society	No	No	Yes
Recognition of a Need for a Government	Yes	Yes	No
Freedom of Speech and Press	Yes	Yes	No
Freedom of Thought	Yes	Yes	No
Freedom of Choice of Radio Programs and Reading Material	Yes	Yes	No
Freedom of Entertainment	Yes	Yes	No
Freedom of Movement and of Choice of Living Quarters	Yes	(?)Yes	No
Freedom of Choice in General	Yes	Yes	No
Freedom from Religion	Optional	Optional	Yes
Freedom from an Employer	Optional	Yes	Yes
Free Educational Facilities (Limited)	Yes	Yes	Yes
Censored Books for Use in Schools	No	Yes	Yes
Recognition of Privileged Classes of Society	No	Yes	Yes
Desire for Peace	Yes	Yes	No
Right to Form Unions and to Collective Bargaining	Yes	Yes	(?)Yes
Free Medical Services	No	Yes	Yes

public well-being and leave the rest of them to operate in a capitalist style system of free enterprise and private ownership.

The Scandinavian countries have experimented with socialism, and to a lesser extent, so have countries like Canada and Great Britain. For example, these two countries have "socialized," or taken government control over, the medical and health care system. If you need to see a doctor in Canada, the government pays for the visit. The government also regulates doctors' salaries and drug costs and owns most hospitals and medical clinics. The Canadian government also regulates and participates in agriculture, transportation and natural resources in a somewhat different way than we do. However, almost every other aspect of Canadian business operates in the same way as ours.

COUNTERPOINT

The United Sates has always been staunchly opposed to government control over any business, even the medical profession. While close allies and friends of ours like Great Britain and Canada have taken some drastic steps to take control of medical care to ensure that all citizens have access to good health care, we have more or less maintained the traditional system that has been in place for the past hundred years or more. If people need or want to see a doctor or stay in a hospital, they must pay for it. If they can afford it, they can buy insurance from private companies that will at least partially protect them from high medical bills. The government regulates medical issues only to a minor degree, and only steps in to provide direct care or government-sponsored insurance in a few special circumstances, such as for veterans, seniors, or people on social assistance. Most Americans who are employed purchase medical insurance through their employers. However, many small employers do not offer insurance plans and if a person is laid off or fired from a job he or she often loses medical insurance coverage. As a result, many Americans do not have any medical insurance, or do not have enough of it. If they experience a serious medical problem, bills can total tens or even hundreds of thousands of dollars and can cost a family their savings or even their home.

These tragic outcomes rarely occur in countries like Great Britain and Canada. The government offers insurance to all citizens and permanent residents. People do not pay directly for this insurance; it comes out of tax revenues. There are no limits to the amount of coverage a person can receive and usually no co-payment or percentage that the patient has to pay. While there are a few optional services that are not covered, most services and procedures are covered 100%.

At first glance, if we were to ask you which system you would prefer based only on what we have just told you, most people would prefer the British or Canadian system. However, there are problems, especially in Canada. While good quality medical care is available to everyone, there are so many people trying to take advantage of that care that there are long waiting lists for many important services. While most Canadians report that they still prefer their system to what they know of the U.S. system, they are clearly increasingly frustrated with it. During the 1990s, when governments tried to eliminate their deficits, spending on health care was reduced, causing shortages and tensions within the system.

The Canadian system is affordable in part because the government pays the bills, but also because it regulates the industry itself. The government controls doctors' income, hospital fees, drug costs and many other aspects of the system. Critics of socialized medicine argue that this builds both bureaucracy and mediocrity into the system. Doctors in the United States can earn considerably more money than Canadian doctors - and this has led directly to a doctor shortage in parts of Canada, because many Canadian doctors have moved to the U.S. so they can enjoy the greater freedom and higher incomes. Also, while Canada performs some medical and pharmaceutical research, they are not as active in these fields. Most medical breakthroughs come from the U.S. and the profit motive is certainly a factor that keeps the big U.S. drug companies and medical technology labs on the quest for cures and better treatments.

Early in his administration, President Clinton vowed that he would introduce a new medical care system in the U.S. that would be somewhat like the Canadian model. He named his wife Hillary to head up the group that would implement the plan. It never got off the ground. It was found that converting to a public system would be too expensive and there was too much opposition from the medical industry and from Congress. However, some would argue that declaring it would be too expensive to give all Americans public health care amounts to admitting that many Americans are not getting proper health care at the present time. Is the present American system better than the Canadian or British systems, or is it only better for the middle and upper classes, while largely under-serving the needs of the poor and working classes? Should free enterprise be the overriding value here, or is medical care essential enough to the public well being that our government should step in and run it in the best interests of society?

What do you think?

When it comes to political systems, the countries in the world can be roughly divided into democracies and others. The "others" may be monarchies, where the country is ruled by a royal family, or dictatorships, where one individual, often a general in the army, has taken control of the government by force and uses the military to stay in power.

It is important to understand that the measure of a true democracy is whether or not the people have the power to elect (or vote out) a government, and whether there are reasonable alternatives to choose from.

This means more than just having "elections." Some countries that are actually dictatorships pretend to be "democratic" by holding elections in which the people don't have any real

regimes that do not let their people have any say in how the country is run. However, not all dictators are tyrants like Saddam Hussein. Historically, a few of them have ruled their countries much more fairly and reasonably, and have been important allies of America. They are the exceptions, however. Most dictators have one overriding concern in how they govern their countries: keeping themselves in power and suppressing any attempt by anyone else to share or take that power. This can lead to a level of government-sponsored violence that is so foreign to us in the United States that it can be hard for us to imagine. After Saddam Hussein was overthrown in Iraq, we got a glimpse of some of the methods he used to oppress opposition to his regime.

choices. For example, in Iraq, shortly before Saddam Hussein was driven from power by the U.S.-led coalition, he held "elections" in which he supposedly received 100% of the vote. The fact was that there were no other candidates. Anyone who tried to form an opposition party to Saddam was either killed or driven from the country. Likewise, in the days when Russia was a communist country they held elections to pick leaders of the Communist Party. This was not a true democracy, however, because the candidates were all chosen by the party and all supported the communist dictator of the day. There was no real choice.

In general, the United States has generally frowned upon dictators or

When a government has no accountability to its own people or to the rest of the world, some truly horrible things can happen. Iraq is by no means an isolated case in today's world.

Earlier, we mentioned monarchies as another alternative to democracy. True monarchies, where the royal family has supreme power, are very rare in the world today. Other than the notable exception of Saudi Arabia, most of them are small islands in the Pacific. However, a few countries, such as Japan, Great Britain, Sweden and the Netherlands have blended the old style monarchies with modern style democracy. These are called constitutional monarchies. The royal family are mainly figureheads. Their role is ceremonial. The real political and decision-making power is held by democratically elected officials.

The United States would never accept living under a monarchy or dictatorship. However, our democratic system is not a static thing frozen in time. It evolves and changes over time, as we consider new and better ways of doing certain things. One way that we can examine ourselves and decide whether any possible changes might be necessary or beneficial is to look at the somewhat different ways that other democratic governments around the world have chosen to structure themselves and handle their affairs. The comparisons are interesting and sometimes we can see both advantages and disadvantages to the way things are done in other places.

For example, it is useful to make a quick comparison between the systems of government in the United States and in Canada. On the surface, the two countries are about as similar as any two countries on earth. Canadian provinces function very much like American states, with only relatively minor differences concerning their areas of responsibility and jurisdiction. The elected leader of the province is called the premier, not the governor, but the roles are very similar. Likewise, on the federal level Canada has a prime minister, not a president.

There are some differences, however, that go a little deeper than names and titles. Earlier, you learned about the clear and distinct division the U.S. Constitution makes between the executive, legislative and judicial branches of government. In Canada, these distinctions are not so precise. In a sense, Canada's "executive branch" of government is drawn directly from its "legislative branch." The prime minister and all of the various heads of the Cabinet departments are elected members of parliament, much like the members of our House of Representatives. In fact, Canadians do not vote directly for their prime minister. Each electoral district of the country elects a member of parliament. The party that wins the most seats in parliament gets to "form a government." This means that the designated leader of that party automatically becomes prime minister.

Canada has a similar system at the provincial level. Voters elect only the members of their provincial legislatures; they do not vote directly for provincial premiers. The leader of the party that has the most seats in the legislature automatically becomes premier.

A further distinction is that Canada does not have an elected Senate. The members of the Senate are appointed by the prime minister and usually serve for life, much like our Supreme Court justices. The end result of all these differences is that while Canada is clearly a democracy, the Canadian people get to do a lot less voting than we do. We vote separately for a senator, and representative and a candidate for President, Canadians only vote for a member of parliament and the rest of the government comes together based on the outcome of that one type of voting.

It would be easy to find fault with the Canadian system, but in practice it does have some advantages. Because the Canadian prime minister always has more seats in Parliament than any other party, he or she is usually able to run the country effectively and efficiently. The government can organize a program and be fairly sure of getting its most important elements passed by Parliament. Here, in the United States, we often find ourselves in a situation where we have a president who is a member of one party (Democrats or Republicans) but one or both houses of Congress are controlled by the other party. When this happens the country often sinks into something called a gridlock. The Democratic Congress thinks it was elected to push through one set of policies and programs, whereas the Republican President (or vice versa) feels he was elected to do something quite different. In a sense, the voters have sent a mixed message to Washington as to which party and which programs it wants to support. We end up with the President and Congress quarreling about most important legislation and trying to block one another's programs and laws from being enacted.

Another feature of the Canadian system is that there is no fixed interval between federal elections. There is a maximum amount of time after which a new election must be held. However, an election can be "called" sooner under various circumstances. If the government is unable to get any of its more significant bills passed by Parliament, this can automatically set the stage for a new election. Thus, if the ruling party has a very small majority and it does something to annoy or disappoint the public, it can find that some disgruntled members of Parliament fail to support the government, and can thereby lead to its downfall in a new election. One thing that makes this a fairly common occurrence in Canadian political history is that Canada has more than two major political parties. There are presently three major national parties in Canada and a fourth that is active

The Canadian Hierarchy

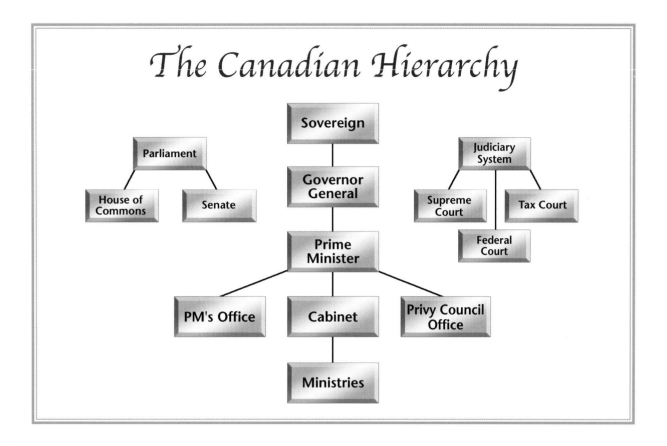

only in the French-speaking province of Quebec. Because of this fact, it is possible for an election to end up with no single party having won a majority of seats in Parliament. When this happens the party that gets the most seats usually has to make a deal with one of the other parties to join forces to form a government. This situation is called a "minority government." It is particularly fragile, because if the party with the most seats doesn't keep its partner happy, the partner may abandon the coalition and force a new election.

Minority governments are not unique to Canada. In fact, most democratic countries in the world have more than two political parties and frequently face a situation where two or more parties must get together and form a coalition in order to end up with a government that has a majority. This is often the situation in countries like Israel, Italy and several other European nations.

In theory, there is no reason why the United States might not one day face a similar problem. If this were to happen, it is unclear how we will deal with it. There is no American law that says the Republicans and the Democrats are the only two national political parties we are allowed to have, or will ever have. In fact, there are "minor" third parties that are active all the time and at several times in our history, there has been a significant attempt to organize a major third party. The most recent politician to come close to significance on a national scale was Ross Perot, who ran for President in 1992.

This is not to say we do not have small parties that attempt to become contenders in the electoral process. In the 2000 presidential election, Pat Buchanan ran as an independent, and there was also a field of candidates from the Green Party. Because the election results between Al Gore and George Bush were so very close, these small "fringe parties" actually had an indirect effect on the outcome. Because of the way the ballots were designed, a significant number of people in one part of the State of Florida who intended to vote for Democrat Al Gore ended up accidentally voting for Pat Buchanan. It is likely that these errors, like various other factors we have already mentioned, were enough

in themselves to allow Republican George W. Bush to win the state.

Nonetheless, America's political system makes it very hard for a new party to get started and gain enough momentum ever to become an important factor at the national level. It would have to organize offices and candidates across the country all at the same time in order to win more than an insignificant handful of seats in Congress to have any realistic shot at electing a President. Also, Americans tend to like to support a winner. As a result, many of us are reluctant to vote for a candidate we feel has little realistic chance of winning, even if we like what he or she stands for.

of America's involvement in the Vietnam War. Voters who would like to see any significant changes in American government or policy often feel frustrated going to the polls, because the only two candidates that have any chance of winning are unlikely to make any significant changes to the system.

In other parts of the world, there is often a significant difference in philosophy between the four or five major political parties competing for votes. However, some voters complain that in the United States the differences between the Democrats and Republicans have become relatively minor. At one time you could have said that the Democrats tended to support more spending on social programs and were therefore more likely to increase taxes or run up high deficits. However, in recent years, it was the Democrats under Bill Clinton who eliminated federal deficits and George W. Bush's Republicans who decided to run them up again when the economy fell into a deep slump. Some people think of Republicans as being more "hawkish" or likely to go to war. Certainly there was a lot of military activity during George W. Bush's administration. However, it was Democrat Bill Clinton who waged the war over Kosovo, and Democrat Lyndon Johnson who supervised much

ALLIANCES AND INTERNATIONAL COOPERATION

A popular phrase today is "globalization." The world is trying to become a more open place where people and goods flow freely from country to country and social, political and economic inequalities that lead to tension and conflict are slowly dissolved. Whether the countries leading that struggle are succeeding is open to debate. Another significant impetus for international cooperation has been the War on Terrorism, and the perceived need to correct trouble spots around the world where war or conflict are not only causing great suffering for the local people, but threaten world peace and stability.

The largest and most prestigious internal organization to which the United States belongs is the United Nations. It was formed in 1945 at the end of the Second World War with the ambitious aim of preventing future wars and helping nations work together to solve disputes and problems. The U.N. has three main bodies: the General Assembly, to which all 165 member nations send representatives; the International Court of Justice, which resolves some types of disputes between member nations when they voluntarily choose to employ this service; and, arguably the most important part of the U.N., the Security Council. The General Assembly and Security Council meet in New York City. The International Court, which also now includes the International Criminal Court and International War Crimes Tribunal, meets in the Hague, Netherlands.

The United Nations also operates a large number of commissions and relief agencies that look at medical, social and environmental issues and problems in the world, including the United Nations Children's Fund (UNICEF).

The U.N. Security Council has five permanent members and another ten that are elected to two-year terms by the General Assembly. The permanent members are the U.S., Russia, China, France and Great Britain. The Security Council passes resolutions that may authorize military or peacekeeping actions, condemn actions taken by other nations, or impose punishments such as trade sanctions and embargos (blockages). This would seem to make the Security Council a very powerful body. However, getting a resolution passed requires approval of at least 9 of the 15 members and any one of the five permanent members can block the resolution and effectively kill it, even if they are the only ones to oppose it.

Also, since the United Nations doesn't have a significant permanent military force, it cannot enforce its resolutions unless member nations decide to form a coalition of their own troops to act on the U.N.'s behalf.

Some people see the United Nations as the best ultimate hope for world peace - despite the fact that over its first sixty years of existence the world has experienced dozens of significant wars and continues to do so into the new millennium. Others see the U.N. as a fundamentally flawed organization that is weak when it comes to resolving major international conflicts. Because it only takes one key vote to stop a major Security Council initiative, the council only seems to be effective in situations where one country is so clearly in the wrong that there can be no argument, and where no council member has a political or economic stake in one of the countries involved in the dispute.

In many ways, the United Nations is still a figurehead organization. While it plays an important role in distribution of relief to the needy, it is not the place where the world's most important political, economic and military decisions are being made. The reality is that there are various other levels of formal and informal alliances between countries that are much more influential.

One of the most influential alliances in the world today is called NATO: The North Atlantic Treaty Organization. This is another group formed shortly after World War II. NATO has a more limited membership and a more specific purpose than the U.N. At the end of World War II, Europe was divided between allies of the U.S. and countries that had been taken over by Communist Russia. Russia was the main perceived threat to future peace in Europe and most of Europe's democratic countries formed a military pact with the United States and Canada that basically declared, "An attack on any one of us will be seen as an attack on us all."

While NATO has continued to conduct joint military training exercises and has had a few real life military engagements over the years, today most of the countries NATO originally feared have become members of the organization. All the countries Russia once controlled are now free nations, most of whom have joined NATO. Likewise, Russia itself, while not yet offered a full membership, has been given a seat on the NATO joint council. It was primarily NATO that conducted the war in Kosovo in 1999 that led indirectly to the overthrow and imprisonment of Serbian President Slobodan Milosevic.

Other organizations in which the United States participates are the Rio Pact and the Organization of American States (OAS), which are alliances between the United States and the countries of Latin America, and the ANZUS Pact, a security arrangement with Australia and New Zealand. The United States also has treaties of alliance with some countries individually, notably Japan, the Philippines and South Korea.

Another important, though less formal association of powerful countries, is the G-8. It is like a country club of the world's richest countries, the ones with the most powerful economies - not to mention militaries. Its main purpose is to resolve economic problems in the world rather than military ones. The countries in the G-8 are the United States, Great Britain, France, Canada, Italy, Germany, Japan, and the most recent addition, Russia. The leaders of these countries get together about once a year to discuss elimination of trade barriers, Third World development and debt relief, and sometimes various environmental and health issues affecting the world community. These meetings are always heavily targeted by protesters who believe that G-8 policies are unfair to other nations and causing the world more harm than good.

Trade Agreements

The major new area of international alliances and cooperation is trade. Free trade agreements essentially mean that nations agree to do business with one another with a minimal amount of government interference in the process of open competition. The United States originally signed a free trade agreement with Canada, our largest trading partner. In 1994, the agreement was expanded to include Mexico and came to be known as NAFTA. In that same year an older agreement called GATT (General Agreement on Trade and Tariffs) was revitalized and signed by 23 countries. It sets some rules for limiting government interference in international trade and is designed to keep markets as fair and open as possible. In practice, members of both these conventions frequently get into disputes about one another's trade practices. GATT set up a regulatory body called the World Trade Organization (WTO) to help resolve some of these disputes.

A typical dispute starts with an allegation that the government of some member nation is giving some sort of subsidy or special economic assistance to a particular industry in a way that gives it an unfair competitive advantage over similar industries in other member countries. The WTO must decide whether or not the allegation is justified - which is not an easy task because there are often fundamental differences in the way governments of the various member nations handle their own social welfare programs and forms of assistance to business and industry. One of the drawbacks to entering into trade agreements is that they tend to limit a government's ability to take action to boost its own economy and employment situation, or to protect key industries that may experience hard times.

Free trade is one of the most controversial political and economic issues of our day. To fully understand why, you would need a fuller explanation of economic principles than we have room to provide to you here. In a nutshell, the opposite of free trade is restricted or protected trade. Governments restrict trade to protect their own workers and businesses from foreign competition - usually when they fear that competition will win out and will place their own workers at a disadvantage. Historically, the main ways governments have restricted trade is by placing special taxes called tariffs and duties on goods coming from foreign countries. This inflates the cost of those goods and gives consumers in the protected country more reason to buy from their own local industries and producers. This makes tariffs popular with some local business owners and with workers and unions. However, since countries that are affected by tariffs usually retaliate by placing tariffs on goods coming from the restricted country into their own country, these trade barriers pile up in a retaliatory fashion and make it hard for businesses in either country to export goods. Therefore, larger businesses that are well positioned to compete successfully in a freer market oppose such trade restrictions. Consumers also tend to oppose them. They would rather be able to buy cheap foreign goods if they want to. In a way, trade restrictions punish consumers for not "shopping at home." It is ultimately the consumers, not the foreign producers, who end up paying the extra taxes.

The United States is an expensive place in which to manufacture goods. Our workers earn higher wages than workers in almost any other part of the world. We also pay our workers a higher level of benefits and we have a variety of environmental and consumer protection laws that force industries to spend more money on American-based operations. Opponents of free trade argue that since other parts of the world don't face these extra costs, opening our doors to an unrestricted supply of foreign goods places American jobs and the American way of life in danger. How can an American shirt manufacturer who pays its workers an average of $15.00 per hour compete with a clothing manufacturer in Asia that pays workers something closer to 50 cents an hour?

Large American companies actually do often compete fairly successfully in a less-restrictive trade environment. A fast food chain like McDonald's has probably opened about as many outlets in the U.S. as it can. If it wants to continue to grow, it needs to find new markets in other parts of the world. As for having to pay those high American wages, corporations get around that by setting up plants in foreign countries and paying local workers what they expect to earn in their local currency. The "American" sneaker can easily compete with the Asian sneaker when they're both made in Asia.

Some American companies don't have to set up shop in Third World Countries to compete well under free trade. They rely instead on high technology and efficiency. Automation and computerization reduce the labor component of many manufacturing processes. It doesn't matter so much if your workers make five times as much money as foreign workers if your superior equipment allows them to be ten times as productive.

Many would argue that consumers are the big winners under free trade. The selection of both foreign and domestic goods becomes a shopper's dream, and the fierce competition keeps prices as low as possible. Your dollar will definitely go a lot farther in a globalized free trade marketplace - unless you're one of the unfortunate ones who loses his or her job because your particular employer or industry ends up being one of the free-trade losers, rather than a free-trade winner.

Apart from the economic and labor issues, there are social issues. Free trade, over time, causes world nations to become increasingly similar in the way they do things, their economic systems, their labor and environmental laws, their social programs, even their tastes and habits. Some believe this will make the world a happier, friendlier and safer place. Others believe that globalization makes the rich get richer and leads many people to resistance that is sometimes violent.

What do you think?

CHAPTER 5

WHAT YOU CAN DO FOR YOUR COUNTRY

BECOMING INVOLVED IN POLITICS

No doubt as you have read this text you have formed your own opinions on some of the issues we are discussing. That is a healthy and important process for everyone. Perhaps you will discover that you hold some of these opinions strongly, strongly enough that you may want to get involved in helping either to preserve or to change some aspect of our society that means a lot to you.

In the United States of America, politics is not only for politicians. It is for everyone. Our elected leaders are at the top of huge pyramids that include at their bases, millions of "ordinary Americans" who join our major political parties and work to help get their candidates elected.

For some, voting on election day is enough participation in the democratic process. However, many find they want to do more. It is very easy to register as a member of a political party when you register to vote. Becoming a member of a party means that you get to attend local party meetings. You can vote on matters of policy and help choose candidates to run in elections. If you wish, you can even go out and help in a campaign, either as a fundraiser or by going door to door in support of a candidate. Many people who start out volunteering to help a party in these ways later go on to become candidates themselves.

Besides the major political parties and the smaller ones, there are other organizations that take an interest in specific issues and work to persuade politicians to adopt their policies. These groups often get permits to stage political rallies to demonstrate their concern about an issue, and to help persuade the public about the validity and importance of their cause and position. Attendance at these rallies - when they are legal and conducted peacefully - is another important way to have a voice in the political affairs of our country.

The simplest and most direct thing you can do to participate politically doesn't require you to join any organization at all. You simply need to make your views known to your elected officials by phone, by letter or by email. If you care strongly about something, let your state and federal representatives and senators hear

about it. All mail and messages are read, and in most cases responded to, and trends in these communications are an important factor politicians use in deciding how to vote in the legislature or at Congress. Politicians know that if they ignore you and others like you too many times, chances are that when the next election comes around you will be voting for some other candidate.

BECOMING INVOLVED IN THE COMMUNITY

After everything you have now learned about the American government and all the things that it does for us, it might surprise you to hear that America is largely a nation of volunteers. In many key areas of our lives the work that is done in the public sector is overshadowed by that done in the private sector - by corporations, and by large and important nonprofit organizations. These organizations rely heavily on volunteers to carry out much of their work.

President George W. Bush called upon all young Americans to volunteer to help fulfill a need in their communities. Volunteering is an excellent way to foster core American values about caring for one another and building a safe, healthy and just society. Volunteer work can also bring substantial benefits to those who

The Peace Corps was founded in 1961 to give young Americans a chance to see and help the world at the same time. Peace Corps volunteers have been assigned to 135 countries around the world. The specific nature of the work varies depending on the local needs and on the background and skills of individual volunteers. There are many situations for which no previous experience is necessary.

participate. Sometimes it is difficult for young people - or older ones who have been away from the work force for a while - to get that first job that can become the foundation for a satisfying working life. Without skills or experience it can be very hard to get started. Volunteering is an excellent way to pick up meaningful work experience that will later impress prospective employers. Often volunteer work resembles work done by paid employees - in some cases it can lead directly to such employment. In others the skills learned while volunteering will look good on your resume - as will what volunteering says about your personal character.

There are large and small opportunities to serve your community as a volunteer. The large opportunities include some programs managed by the federal government. The most notable of these are the Peace Corps and the Corporation for National and Community Service.

The Corporation for National and Community Service is like a Peace Corps that helps out here at home. This government agency runs three major programs:

1) Senior Corps

2) Learn and Serve

3) AmeriCorps

Senior Corps and Learn and Serve are for seniors and students respectively. AmeriCorps recruits volunteers from various age groups and backgrounds and makes them available to some of our country's important nonprofit organizations such as Habitat for Humanity, The American Red Cross, and Boys and Girls Clubs of America. Volunteers work between 20 and 40 hours a week, and generally receive some pay for their time to offset their living expenses.

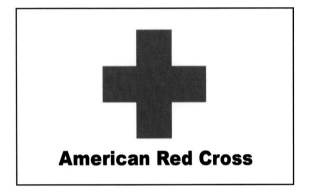

American Red Cross

There are also many privately managed nonprofit organizations. Some provide meals or companions for seniors or shut-ins. Others help find homes for stray pets, build playgrounds, or champion a cause such as local environmental protection or saving endangered species. Many parks and historical sites have citizens' groups that help protect the sites and keep them clean. There are also national and local charities associated with all major diseases and infirmities. Much of the money required for research and helping patients is collected by volunteers who go door to door or handle the phone lines.

There are many smaller but no less significant opportunities to serve in every city and town across the country. Most churches need volunteers to help out with their charitable activities. Schools and hospitals also need volunteer help to run many of their programs. Some people also find opportunities to help out in their own neighborhoods. Perhaps there is an elderly couple living on your street that could use a hand with snow shoveling or cutting the grass. If you look for ways to offer your services, you will not fail to find them.

STANDING GUARD - YOUR ROLE IN AMERICA'S FUTURE

America has been blessed to have been created and guided by some of the truly great leaders in human history - not only at its founding, but at critical points in its history. Each new

generation of Americans needs to find new leaders who are willing and able to renew the greatness of the nation in the face of new problems and situations. However, placing the care and maintenance of this country in the hands of a few elected officials is not good enough to preserve the high ideals upon which America was founded. As President Lincoln said, this is a nation "of the people, by the people, and for the people." It will be ordinary Americans who will determine what it will be like to be an American and what America's place in the world will be, ten, twenty or fifty years from now.

Some of America's greatest presidents have understood the importance of keeping the American people interested and involved in preserving the dream. Some of their most famous and significant speeches have been moments not of making promises to the public, but of issuing challenges to us. We will close this text by taking a look at two of those memorable speeches in American history, both of which placed the burden of guarding and preserving our freedoms squarely on the shoulders of "average Americans."

The first is one of the earliest preserved speeches of Abraham Lincoln, delivered when he was only 28

years old. It was titled "The Perpetuation of our Political Institutions," but it is commonly known as the Lyceum Address. The speech is too long to be reproduced completely here, but the following is one of its more relevant passages:

I know the American people are much attached to their government; — I know they will suffer much for its sake; — I know they would endure evils long and patiently, before they would ever think of exchanging it for another. Yet, not withstanding all this if the laws be continually despised and disregarded, if their rights to be secure in their persons and property are held by no better tenure than the caprice of the mob, the alienation of their affections from the Government is the natural consequence; and to that sooner or later, it must come.

The question recurs, "how shall we fortify against it?" The answer is simple, Let every American, every lover of liberty, every well wisher to his posterity, swear by the blood of the Revolution, never to violate in the least particular the laws of the country; and never to tolerate their violation by others. Let reverence for the laws.... become the political religion of the nation; and let the old and the young, the rich and the poor, ... of all sexes and tongues, and colors and conditions, sacrifice unceasingly upon its altars..."

In this speech, Lincoln compares dedication to country to a religion, to something sacred. He points out that people will not feel pride in their country or support for its government unless they can live in a just society where rights are respected and laws are obeyed. Lincoln is describing our civic duty as being much more than showing up to vote each election day. We need to stand up for what is right in our day-to-day lives. Without respect for the law and for personal and public property, we risk descending into the chaos that still exists in many parts of the world.

The second speech we will examine is the famous Inaugural Address of John F. Kennedy. The speech was delivered at a time in history when tensions between the free world and the communist nations were very high and international crises were the main

things on the minds of Americans. Much of the speech dealt with world problems and threats. However, the words from the speech that are still most quoted and remembered are about the civic duty of ordinary Americans in keeping the country strong, brave and focused on its values.

John F. Kennedy
Inaugural Address
Friday, January 20, 1961

Fellow citizens, we observe today not a victory of party, but a celebration of freedom — symbolizing an end, as well as a beginning — signifying renewal, as well as change. For I have sworn before you and Almighty God the same solemn oath our forebears prescribed nearly a century and three quarters ago.

The world is very different now. For man holds in his mortal hands the power to abolish all forms of human poverty and all forms of human life. And yet the same revolutionary beliefs for which our forebears fought are still at issue around the globe — the belief that the rights of man come not from the generosity of the state, but from the hand of God.

We dare not forget today that we are the heirs of that first revolution. Let the word go forth from this time and place, to friend and foe alike, that the torch has been passed to a new generation of Americans — born in this century, tempered by war, disciplined by a hard and bitter peace, proud of our ancient heritage — and unwilling to witness or permit the slow undoing of those human rights to which this Nation has always been committed, and to which we are committed today at home and around the world.

Let every nation know, whether it wishes us well or ill, that we shall pay any price, bear any burden, meet any hardship, support any friend, oppose any foe, in order to assure the survival and the success of liberty.

This much we pledge—and more.

To those old allies whose cultural and spiritual origins we share, we pledge the loyalty of faithful friends. United,

there is little we cannot do in a host of cooperative ventures. Divided, there is little we can do — for we dare not meet a powerful challenge at odds and split asunder.

To those new States whom we welcome to the ranks of the free, we pledge our word that one form of colonial control shall not have passed away merely to be replaced by a far more iron tyranny. We shall not always expect to find them supporting our view. But we shall always hope to find them strongly supporting their own freedom — and to remember that, in the past, those who foolishly sought power by riding the back of the tiger ended up inside.

To those peoples in the huts and villages across the globe struggling to break the bonds of mass misery, we pledge our best efforts to help them help themselves, for whatever period is required —not because the Communists may be doing it, not because we seek their votes, but because it is right. If a free society cannot help the many who are poor, it cannot save the few who are rich.

To our sister republics south of our border, we offer a special pledge — to convert our good words into good deeds — in a new alliance for progress — to assist free men and free governments in casting off the chains of poverty. But this peaceful revolution of hope cannot become the prey of hostile powers. Let all our neighbors know that we shall join with them to oppose aggression or subversion anywhere in the Americas. And let every other power know that this Hemisphere intends to remain the master of its own house.

To that world assembly of sovereign states, the United Nations, our last best hope in an age where the instruments of war have far outpaced the instruments of peace, we renew our pledge of support — to prevent it from becoming merely a forum for invective — to strengthen its shield of the new and the weak — and to enlarge the area in which its writ may run.

Finally, to those nations who would make themselves our adversary, we offer not a pledge but a request: that both sides begin anew the quest for peace, before the dark powers of destruction unleashed by science engulf all humanity in planned or accidental self-destruction.

We dare not tempt them with weakness. For only when our arms are sufficient beyond doubt can we be certain beyond doubt that they will never be employed.

But neither can two great and powerful groups of nations take comfort from our present course — both sides overburdened by the cost of modern weapons, both rightly alarmed by the steady spread of the deadly atom, yet

both racing to alter that uncertain balance of terror that stays the hand of mankind's final war.

So let us begin anew — remembering on both sides that civility is not a sign of weakness, and sincerity is always subject to proof. Let us never negotiate out of fear. But let us never fear to negotiate.

Let both sides explore what problems unite us instead of belaboring those problems which divide us.

Let both sides, for the first time, formulate serious and precise proposals for the inspection and control of arms — and bring the absolute power to destroy other nations under the absolute control of all nations.

Let both sides seek to invoke the wonders of science instead of its terrors. Together let us explore the stars, conquer the deserts, eradicate disease, tap the ocean depths, and encourage the arts and commerce.

Let both sides unite to heed in all corners of the earth the command of Isaiah — to "undo the heavy burdens ... and to let the oppressed go free."

And if a beachhead of cooperation may push back the jungle of suspicion, let both sides join in creating a new endeavor, not a new balance of power, but a new world of law, where the strong are just and the weak secure and the peace preserved.

All this will not be finished in the first 100 days. Nor will it be finished in the first 1,000 days, nor in the life of this Administration, nor even perhaps in our lifetime on this planet. But let us begin.

In your hands, my fellow citizens, more than in mine, will rest the final success or failure of our course. Since this country was founded, each generation of Americans has been summoned to give testimony to its national loyalty. The graves of young Americans who answered the call to service surround the globe.

Now the trumpet summons us again — not as a call to bear arms, though arms we need; not as a call to battle, though embattled we are — but a call to bear the burden of a long twilight struggle, year in and year out, "rejoicing in hope, patient in tribulation" — a struggle against the common enemies of man: tyranny, poverty, disease, and war itself.

Can we forge against these enemies a grand and global alliance, North and South, East and West, that can assure a more fruitful life for all mankind? Will you join in that historic effort?

In the long history of the world, only a few generations have been granted the role of defending freedom in its hour of maximum danger. I do not shrink from this responsibility — I welcome it. I do not believe that any of us would exchange places with any other people or any other generation. The energy, the faith, the devotion which we bring to this endeavor will light our country and all who serve it — and the glow from that fire can truly light the world.

And so, my fellow Americans: ask not what your country can do for you — ask what you can do for your country.

My fellow citizens of the world: ask not what America will do for you, but what together we can do for the freedom of man.

Finally, whether you are citizens of America or citizens of the world, ask of us the same high standards of strength and sacrifice which we ask of you. With a good conscience our only sure reward, with history the final judge of our deeds, let us go forth to lead the land we love, asking His blessing and His help, but knowing that here on earth God's work must truly be our own.

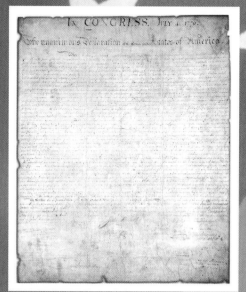

APPENDIX A

BECOMING AN AMERICAN CITIZEN

Citizenship law is a complicated field. There are lawyers and non-profit organizations who specialize in helping individuals comprehend and work with the finer points of regulations that apply to them. For every general rule, there are many exceptions. The information we will provide here is a general guideline, but it will not answer all questions in complex or unusual cases. The best

way to get more information is to visit the federal government website at **www.usais.org.** The site has general information, answers to common questions, various tests of eligibility, sample questions that are asked at interviews and information on obtaining and filing the necessary paperwork. You can also start an application directly online.

There are three ways of becoming a U.S. citizen. The first is to be born on U.S. soil. The vast majority of people born on U.S. soil automatically become U.S. citizens, whether or not their parents are citizens. However, there are exceptions. For example, children of foreign diplomats do not automatically become citizens even if they are born here. The second way to become a citizen is to have at least one parent who is an American citizen. However, if that person is living in some other part of the world at the time the child is born, the regulations become somewhat complicated as to eligibility.

The third way to become a citizen is by a process called naturalization. This is how immigrants may become citizens after they have resided in the United States for a period of time, provided they meet some basic qualifications. Naturalization is handled by the Immigration and Naturalization Service (INS), an agency of the federal government.

The first qualification is that you must have entered the United States legally. If this is not true, you need to straighten out this problem before you have any chance of becoming a citizen. It is not sufficient for you simply to state that you have been here for a period of time. You need to be able to prove it by showing that you entered the United States legally and that before coming and/or while here you obtained any necessary cards or visas to permit you to remain in the United States legally. For example, visitor's visas or student visas have an expiration date, and a person who remains in the United States after such a document has expired is no

longer in legal residence here. Again, this is a complicated matter, and if your situation has any aspect of this problem you would be well advised to contact an immigration lawyer before making an application.

Assuming you arrived and remained here legally, the next basic requirement concerns the length of time you have been here. The general rule is that you must have been here 5 years. However, for spouses of citizens, the waiting time is reduced to 3 years. Again, there are some complicated rules concerning people who may have become a legal resident three to five years ago but have left the U.S. for periods of time during that interval. You should also note that you are allowed to start the application process 3 months before the required 5 year time frame, because the process takes longer than three months so you will have fulfilled the requirement by the time it is concluded. There is also a requirement that you must have resided in the state where you are making the application for at least three months.

The next requirement is that you must be able to demonstrate that you can read, write and speak English. This is necessary because the government feels that people who lack these language skills may not be able to fulfill their duties as citizens adequately. Once again, there are exceptions. The main exception is for people over the age of 50 who have resided in the U.S. for at least 20 years. However, there are various other circumstances where the INS can modify or waive both the length of residency and the language requirements.

Finally, there are some basic requirements that apply to everyone and cannot be waived. You must be able to demonstrate that you have a good moral character, that you have loyalty to the principles of the U.S. Constitution and that you have a favorable disposition toward the United States. Anything in your background that contradicts these

requirements (such as a criminal record in your country of origin, or previous membership in a terrorist organization) may cause your application to be rejected. It is important to be honest about these matters. Failing to disclose a conviction, even for a minor offense, could cause you to be rejected. Again, if you feel you may have a problem in this area, talk to an immigration lawyer.

The naturalization process generally takes 6 to 9 months, though sometimes longer. There are a variety of forms that need to be submitted depending on whether you are applying by yourself or being sponsored by a spouse or adoptive parent. There is a fee required for having your application processed and there may be an extra fee for fingerprinting.

After your paperwork has been filed, your claim will be investigated. If the investigation turns up no obstacles to your application, you will be called in for a interview. During the interview you will be asked questions that concern your moral character and integrity. You will also be expected to demonstrate the necessary English language skills and you will be asked some basic questions about American history and government. These questions are usually simple and straightforward and do not pose a problem for anyone who has completed a course in U.S. history and government. The INS website offers sample test questions, and, for a small fee, will even provide an online course for those who need it. As part of the verification of your character, you may be asked to provide two witnesses who know you personally and will vouch for your character and integrity.

If your application is refused for any reason, you have the right to appeal that decision. However, assuming you make it successfully through all these stages and requirements, you will be called to what is called a "final hearing" in a federal district court. This "hearing" is really just a formality. You know ahead of time that you will become a citizen at this hearing. However, in order to become a citizen, you must take an Oath of Allegiance to the United States. In this oath you promise to:

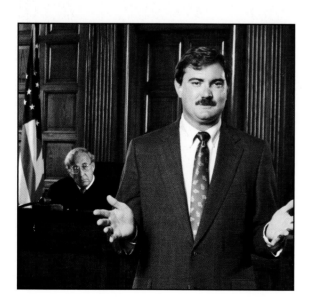

- Renounce loyalty to former governments in places where you previously lived.

- Defend the Constitution and laws of the United States.

- Bear arms on behalf of the United States when required by law.

These sound like very serious commitments. However, you should note that after becoming a U.S. citizen, your status in your country of birth or origin is mainly determined by their laws. Some countries allow you to become a citizen of a second country without losing your citizenship in your first country (called dual citizenship). For example, if you immigrate to the United States from Canada, when you become an American citizen you do not lose your Canadian citizenship. You end up having both.

Concerning the duty to bear arms, as you learned previously in the text, at the present time America's armed forces are all volunteers. Therefore, you will not be forced into the military unless the government reinstates the draft for all eligible Americans.

U.S. citizens have a general duty to know about their rights and the laws of the country and to participate in the democratic process of the

nation. The main way to do this is to register to vote and vote on each election day. Soon after becoming a citizen you should register as a voter in the town or city where you live. As a citizen you may also be called to serve on a jury in a court case. However, if you fail to vote or to appear for jury duty you do not invalidate your citizenship. In fact, it is very hard to lose U.S. citizenship, other than by taking on citizenship of another country. There are a small number of serious crimes such as treason, which could cause your citizenship to be taken away. Your citizenship can also be revoked by a process called denaturalization. This happens if it is later learned that you

committed fraud or deception in your application for citizenship.

The citizenship ceremony is a happy occasion for new Americans. You receive a Certificate of Nationality, a letter from the President of the United States and various other documents as keepsakes. The atmosphere is friendly. Photographs are permitted and encouraged. The presiding judge does everything he or she can to make you feel proud and welcome.

Federal Judge Congratulates a New U.S. Citizen

As a new U.S. citizen, you have certain rights and protections. You can obtain a U.S. passport, which is necessary for travel to other countries. You will receive protection and assistance from the U.S. government if you have certain types of problems while traveling abroad. You may also petition for "green cards" (residency and work permits) for children or close relatives.

If you commit a crime (except for a high offense like treason) you will not be deported to your country of origin. If convicted you will go to prison in the United States. While there, you will still be a U.S. citizen. However, certain privileges, such as the right to vote, may be denied to you during incarceration.

The investigative phase of a citizenship application can be a frustrating process for many applicants; the background check is thorough and takes time. You need to follow all of the minor rules, such as making sure you show up at the right INS Service Center for where you live. You will be asked to furnish photos and various documents proving who you are and your background. Missing or incorrect items can cause delays.

You should not take these requirements personally. They are done for reasons of national security, and everyone goes through them. The United States does not want to give citizenship to fugitives from foreign justice, terrorists, convicted felons, or illegal immigrants. The only way to maintain fairness and avoid discriminating against certain groups or types is to put everyone through the same process. However, you will find that the process is fair and that most immigration officials will make it as pleasant for you as they can. You won't be asked any trick questions. The exam questions about history are not unduly complex or difficult. Any person who meets the basic requirements and makes a reasonable effort to prepare for the interview should have little difficulty. However, unless he or she falls under some exception, a person who does not have good English skills would be well advised to improve that situation before starting the naturalization process.

DECLARATION OF INDEPENDENCE

Complete Text – Transcription

IN CONGRESS, JULY 4, 1776.

THE UNANIMOUS DECLARATION OF THE THIRTEEN UNITED STATES OF AMERICA,

When in the Course of human events, it becomes necessary for one people to dissolve the political bands which have connected them with another, and to assume among the powers of the earth, the separate and equal station to which the Laws of Nature and of Nature's God entitle them, a decent respect to the opinions of mankind requires that they should declare the causes which impel them to the separation.

We hold these truths to be self-evident, that all men are created equal, that they are endowed by their Creator with certain unalienable Rights, that among these are Life, Liberty and the pursuit of Happiness. — That to secure these rights, Governments are instituted among Men, deriving their just powers from the consent of the governed, — That whenever any Form of Government becomes destructive of these ends, it is the Right of the People to alter or to abolish it, and to institute new Government, laying its foundation on such principles and organizing its powers in such form, as to them shall seem most likely to effect their Safety and Happiness. Prudence, indeed, will dictate that Governments long established should not be changed for light and transient causes; and accordingly all experience hath shewn, that mankind are more disposed to suffer, while evils are sufferable, than to right themselves by abolishing the forms to which they are accustomed. But when a long train of abuses and usurpations, pursuing invariably the same Object evinces a design to reduce them under absolute Despotism, it is their right, it is their duty, to throw off such Government, and to provide new Guards for their future security. — Such has been the patient sufferance of these Colonies; and such is now the necessity which constrains them to alter their former Systems of Government. The history of the present King of Great Britain is a history of repeated injuries and usurpations, all having in direct object the establishment of an absolute Tyranny over these States. To prove this, let Facts be submitted to a candid world.

He has refused his Assent to Laws, the most wholesome and necessary for the public good.

He has forbidden his Governors to pass Laws of immediate and pressing importance, unless suspended in their operation till his Assent should be obtained; and when so suspended, he has utterly neglected to attend to them.

He has refused to pass other Laws for the accommodation of large districts of people, unless those people would relinquish the right of Representation in the Legislature, a right inestimable to them and formidable to tyrants only.

He has called together legislative bodies at places unusual, uncomfortable, and distant from the depository of their public Records, for the sole purpose of fatiguing them into compliance with his measures.

He has dissolved Representative Houses repeatedly, for opposing with manly firmness his invasions on the rights of the people.

He has refused for a long time, after such dissolutions, to cause others to be elected; whereby the Legislative powers, incapable of Annihilation, have returned to the People at large for their exercise; the State remaining in the mean time exposed to all the dangers of invasion from without, and convulsions within.

He has endeavoured to prevent the population of these States; for that purpose obstructing the Laws for Naturalization of Foreigners; refusing to pass others to encourage their migrations hither, and raising the conditions of new Appropriations of Lands.

He has obstructed the Administration of Justice, by refusing his Assent to Laws for establishing Judiciary powers.

He has made Judges dependent on his Will alone, for the tenure of their offices, and the amount and payment of their salaries.

He has erected a multitude of New Offices, and sent hither swarms of Officers to harrass our people, and eat out their substance.

He has kept among us, in times of peace, Standing Armies without the Consent of our legislatures.

He has affected to render the Military independent of and superior to the Civil power.

He has combined with others to subject us to a jurisdiction foreign to our constitution, and unacknowledged by our laws; giving his Assent to their Acts of pretended Legislation:

For Quartering large bodies of armed troops among us:

For protecting them, by a mock Trial, from punishment for any Murders which they should commit on the Inhabitants of these States:

For cutting off our Trade with all parts of the world:

For imposing Taxes on us without our Consent:

For depriving us, in many cases, of the benefits of Trial by Jury:

For transporting us beyond Seas to be tried for pretended offences:

For abolishing the free System of English Laws in a neighbouring Province, establishing therein an Arbitrary government, and enlarging its Boundaries so as to render it at once an example and fit instrument for introducing the same absolute rule into these Colonies:

For taking away our Charters, abolishing our most valuable Laws, and altering fundamentally the Forms of our Governments:

For suspending our own Legislatures, and declaring themselves invested with power to legislate for us in all cases whatsoever.

He has abdicated Government here, by declaring us out of his Protection and waging War against us.

He has plundered our seas, ravaged our Coasts, burnt our towns, and destroyed the lives of our people.

He is at this time transporting large Armies of foreign Mercenaries to compleat the works of death, desolation and tyranny, already begun with circumstances of Cruelty & perfidy scarcely paralleled in the most barbarous ages, and totally unworthy the Head of a civilized nation.

He has constrained our fellow Citizens taken Captive on the high Seas to bear Arms against their Country, to become the executioners of their friends and Brethren, or to fall themselves by their Hands.

He has excited domestic insurrections amongst us, and has endeavoured to bring on the inhabitants of our frontiers, the merciless Indian Savages, whose known rule of warfare, is an undistinguished destruction of all ages, sexes and conditions.

In every stage of these Oppressions We have Petitioned for Redress in the most humble terms: Our repeated Petitions have been answered only by repeated injury. A Prince whose character is thus marked by every act which may define a Tyrant, is unfit to be the ruler of a free people.

Nor have We been wanting in attentions to our Brittish brethren. We have warned them from time to time of attempts by their legislature to extend an unwarrantable jurisdiction over us. We have reminded them of the circumstances of our emigration and settlement here. We have appealed to their native justice and magnanimity, and we have conjured them by the ties of our common kindred to disavow these usurpations, which, would inevitably interrupt our connections and correspondence. They too have been deaf to the voice of justice and of consanguinity. We must, therefore, acquiesce in the necessity, which denounces our Separation, and hold them, as we hold the rest of mankind, Enemies in War, in Peace Friends.

We, therefore, the Representatives of the united States of America, in General Congress, Assembled, appealing to the Supreme Judge of the world for the rectitude of our intentions, do, in the Name, and by Authority of the good People of these Colonies, solemnly publish and declare, That these United Colonies are, and of Right ought to be Free and Independent States; that they are Absolved from all Allegiance to the British Crown, and that all political connection between them and the State of Great Britain, is and ought to be totally dissolved; and that as Free and Independent States, they have full Power to levy War, conclude Peace, contract Alliances, establish Commerce, and to do all other Acts and Things which Independent States may of right do. And for the support of this Declaration, with a firm reliance on the protection of divine Providence, we mutually pledge to each other our Lives, our Fortunes and our sacred Honor.

THE CONSTITUTION

Complete Text – Transcription

CONSTITUTION OF THE UNITED STATES OF AMERICA

WE THE PEOPLE of the United States, in Order to form a more perfect Union, establish Justice, insure domestic Tranquility, provide for the common defense, promote the general Welfare, and secure the Blessings of Liberty to ourselves and our Posterity, do ordain and establish this Constitution for the United States of America.

Section. 1.
All legislative Powers herein granted shall be vested in a Congress of the United States, which shall consist of a Senate and House of Representatives.

Section. 2.
The House of Representatives shall be composed of Members chosen every second Year by the People of the several States, and the Electors in each State shall have the Qualifications requisite for Electors of the most numerous Branch of the State Legislature.

No Person shall be a Representative who shall not have attained to the Age of twenty five Years, and been seven Years a Citizen of the United States, and who shall not, when elected, be an Inhabitant of that State in which he shall be chosen.

Representatives and direct Taxes shall be apportioned among the several States which may be included within this Union, according to their respective Numbers, which shall be determined by adding to the whole Number of free Persons, including those bound to Service for a Term of Years, and excluding Indians not taxed, three fifths of all other Persons. The actual Enumeration shall be made within three Years after the first Meeting of the Congress of the United States, and within every subsequent Term of ten Years, in such Manner as they shall by Law direct. The Number of Representatives shall not exceed one for every thirty Thousand, but each State shall have at Least one Representative; and until such enumeration shall be made, the State of New Hampshire shall be entitled to chuse three, Massachusetts eight, Rhode-Island and Providence Plantations one, Connecticut five, New-York six, New Jersey four, Pennsylvania eight, Delaware one, Maryland six, Virginia ten, North Carolina five, South Carolina five, and Georgia three.

When vacancies happen in the Representation from any State, the Executive Authority thereof shall issue Writs of Election to fill such Vacancies.

The House of Representatives shall chuse their Speaker and other Officers; and shall have the sole Power of Impeachment.

Section. 3.

The Senate of the United States shall be composed of two Senators from each State, chosen by the Legislature thereof for six Years; and each Senator shall have one Vote.

Immediately after they shall be assembled in Consequence of the first Election, they shall be divided as equally as may be into three Classes. The Seats of the Senators of the first Class shall be vacated at the Expiration of the second Year, of the second Class at the Expiration of the fourth Year, and of the third Class at the Expiration of the sixth Year, so that one third may be chosen every second Year; and if Vacancies happen by Resignation, or otherwise, during the Recess of the Legislature of any State, the Executive thereof may make temporary Appointments until the next Meeting of the Legislature, which shall then fill such Vacancies.

No Person shall be a Senator who shall not have attained to the Age of thirty Years, and been nine Years a Citizen of the United States, and who shall not, when elected, be an Inhabitant of that State for which he shall be chosen.

The Vice President of the United States shall be President of the Senate, but shall have no Vote, unless they be equally divided.

The Senate shall chuse their other Officers, and also a President pro tempore, in the Absence of the Vice President, or when he shall exercise the Office of President of the United States.

The Senate shall have the sole Power to try all Impeachments. When sitting for that Purpose, they shall be on Oath or Affirmation. When the President of the United States is tried, the Chief Justice shall preside: And no Person shall be convicted without the Concurrence of two thirds of the Members present.

Judgment in Cases of Impeachment shall not extend further than to removal from Office, and disqualification to hold and enjoy any Office of honor, Trust or Profit under the United States: but the Party convicted shall nevertheless be liable and subject to Indictment, Trial, Judgment and Punishment, according to Law.

Section. 4.

The Times, Places and Manner of holding Elections for Senators and Representatives, shall be prescribed in each State by the Legislature thereof; but the Congress may at any time by Law make or alter such Regulations, except as to the Places of chusing Senators.

The Congress shall assemble at least once in every Year, and such Meeting shall be on the first Monday in December, unless they shall by Law appoint a different Day.

Section. 5.

Each House shall be the Judge of the Elections, Returns and Qualifications of its own Members, and a Majority of each shall constitute a Quorum to do Business; but a smaller Number may adjourn from day to day, and may be authorized to compel the Attendance of absent Members, in such Manner, and under such Penalties as each House may provide.

Each House may determine the Rules of its Proceedings, punish its Members for disorderly Behaviour, and, with the Concurrence of two thirds, expel a Member.

Each House shall keep a Journal of its Proceedings, and from time to time publish the same, excepting such Parts as may in their Judgment require Secrecy; and the Yeas and Nays of the Members of either House on any question shall, at the Desire of one fifth of those Present, be entered on the Journal.

Neither House, during the Session of Congress, shall, without the Consent of the other, adjourn for more than three days, nor to any other Place than that in which the two Houses shall be sitting.

Section. 6.

The Senators and Representatives shall receive a Compensation for their Services, to be ascertained by Law, and paid out of the Treasury of the United States. They shall in all Cases, except Treason, Felony and Breach of the Peace, be privileged from Arrest during their Attendance at the Session of their respective Houses, and in going to and returning from the same; and for any Speech or Debate in either House, they shall not be questioned in any other Place.

No Senator or Representative shall, during the Time for which he was elected, be appointed to any civil Office under the Authority of the United States, which shall have been created, or the Emoluments whereof shall have been encreased during such time; and no Person holding any Office under the United States, shall be a Member of either House during his Continuance in Office.

Section. 7.

All Bills for raising Revenue shall originate in the House of Representatives; but the Senate may propose or concur with Amendments as on other Bills.

Every Bill which shall have passed the House of Representatives and the Senate, shall, before it become a Law, be presented to the President of the United States: If he approve he shall sign it, but if not he shall return it, with his Objections to that House in which it shall have originated, who shall enter the Objections at large on their Journal, and proceed to reconsider it. If after such Reconsideration two thirds of that House shall agree to pass the Bill, it shall be sent, together with the Objections, to the other House, by which it shall likewise be reconsidered, and if approved by two thirds of that House, it shall become a Law. But in all such Cases the Votes of both Houses shall be determined by yeas and Nays, and the Names of the Persons voting for and against the Bill shall be entered on the Journal of each House respectively. If any Bill shall not be returned by the President within ten Days (Sundays excepted) after it shall have been presented to him, the Same shall be a Law, in like Manner as if he had signed it, unless the Congress by their Adjournment prevent its Return, in which Case it shall not be a Law.

Every Order, Resolution, or Vote to which the Concurrence of the Senate and House of Representatives may be necessary (except on a question of Adjournment) shall be presented to the President of the United States; and before the Same shall take Effect, shall be approved by him, or being disapproved by him, shall be repassed by two thirds of the Senate and House of Representatives, according to the Rules and Limitations prescribed in the Case of a Bill.

Section. 8.

The Congress shall have Power To lay and collect Taxes, Duties, Imposts and Excises, to pay the Debts and provide for the common Defence and general Welfare of the United States; but all Duties, Imposts and Excises shall be uniform throughout the United States;

To borrow Money on the credit of the United States;

To regulate Commerce with foreign Nations, and among the several States, and with the Indian Tribes;

To establish an uniform Rule of Naturalization, and uniform Laws on the subject of Bankruptcies throughout the United States;

To coin Money, regulate the Value thereof, and of foreign Coin, and fix the Standard of Weights and Measures;

To provide for the Punishment of counterfeiting the Securities and current Coin of the United States;

To establish Post Offices and post Roads;

To promote the Progress of Science and useful Arts, by securing for limited Times to Authors and Inventors the exclusive Right to their respective Writings and Discoveries;

To constitute Tribunals inferior to the supreme Court;

To define and punish Piracies and Felonies committed on the high Seas, and Offences against the Law of Nations;

To declare War, grant Letters of Marque and Reprisal, and make Rules concerning Captures on Land and Water;

To raise and support Armies, but no Appropriation of Money to that Use shall be for a longer Term than two Years;

To provide and maintain a Navy;

To make Rules for the Government and Regulation of the land and naval Forces;

To provide for calling forth the Militia to execute the Laws of the Union, suppress Insurrections and repel Invasions;

To provide for organizing, arming, and disciplining, the Militia, and for governing such Part of them as may be employed in the Service of the United States, reserving to the States respectively, the Appointment of the Officers, and the Authority of training the Militia according to the discipline prescribed by Congress;

To exercise exclusive Legislation in all Cases whatsoever, over such District (not exceeding ten Miles square) as may, by Cession of particular States, and the Acceptance of Congress, become the Seat of the Government of the United States, and to exercise like Authority over all Places purchased by the Consent of the Legislature of the State in which the Same shall be, for the Erection of Forts, Magazines, Arsenals, dock-Yards, and other needful Buildings;—And

To make all Laws which shall be necessary and proper for carrying into Execution the foregoing Powers, and all other Powers vested by this Constitution in the Government of the United States, or in any Department or Officer thereof.

Section. 9.

The Migration or Importation of such Persons as any of the States now existing shall think proper to admit, shall not be prohibited by the Congress prior to the Year one thousand eight hundred and eight, but a Tax or duty may be imposed on such Importation, not exceeding ten dollars for each Person.

The Privilege of the Writ of Habeas Corpus shall not be suspended, unless when in Cases of Rebellion or Invasion the public Safety may require it.

No Bill of Attainder or ex post facto Law shall be passed.

No Capitation, or other direct, Tax shall be laid, unless in Proportion to the Census or enumeration herein before directed to be taken.

No Tax or Duty shall be laid on Articles exported from any State.

No Preference shall be given by any Regulation of Commerce or Revenue to the Ports of one State over those of another; nor shall Vessels bound to, or from, one State, be obliged to enter, clear, or pay Duties in another.

No Money shall be drawn from the Treasury, but in Consequence of Appropriations made by Law; and a regular Statement and Account of the Receipts and Expenditures of all public Money shall be published from time to time.

No Title of Nobility shall be granted by the United States: And no Person holding any Office of Profit or Trust under them, shall, without the Consent of the Congress, accept of any present, Emolument, Office, or Title, of any kind whatever, from any King, Prince, or foreign State.

Section. 10.

No State shall enter into any Treaty, Alliance, or Confederation; grant Letters of Marque and Reprisal; coin Money; emit Bills of Credit; make any Thing but gold and silver Coin a Tender in Payment of Debts; pass any Bill of Attainder, ex post facto Law, or Law impairing the Obligation of Contracts, or grant any Title of Nobility.

No State shall, without the Consent of the Congress, lay any Imposts or Duties on Imports or Exports, except what may be absolutely necessary for executing it's inspection Laws: and the net Produce of all Duties and Imposts, laid by any State on Imports or Exports, shall be for the Use of the Treasury of the United States; and all such Laws shall be subject to the Revision and Controul of the Congress.

No State shall, without the Consent of Congress, lay any Duty of Tonnage, keep Troops, or Ships of War in time of Peace, enter into any Agreement or Compact with another State, or with a foreign Power, or engage in War, unless actually invaded, or in such imminent Danger as will not admit of delay.

ARTICLE. II.

Section. 1.

The executive Power shall be vested in a President of the United States of America. He shall hold his Office during the Term of four Years, and, together with the Vice President, chosen for the same Term, be elected, as follows:

Each State shall appoint, in such Manner as the Legislature thereof may direct, a Number of Electors, equal to the whole Number of Senators and Representatives to which the State may be entitled in the Congress: but no Senator or Representative, or Person holding an Office of Trust or Profit under the United States, shall be appointed an Elector.

The Electors shall meet in their respective States, and vote by Ballot for two Persons, of whom one at least shall not be an Inhabitant of the same State with themselves. And they shall make a List of all the Persons voted for, and of the Number of Votes for each; which List they shall sign and certify, and transmit sealed to the Seat of the Government of the United States, directed to the President of the Senate. The President of the Senate shall, in the Presence of the Senate and House of Representatives, open all the Certificates, and the Votes shall then be counted. The Person having the greatest Number of Votes shall be the President, if such Number be a Majority of the whole Number of Electors appointed; and if there be more than one who have such Majority, and have an equal Number of Votes, then the House of Representatives shall immediately chuse by Ballot one of them for President; and if no Person have a Majority, then from the five highest on the List the said House shall in like Manner chuse the President. But in chusing the President, the Votes shall be taken by States, the Representation from each State having one Vote; A quorum for this purpose shall consist of a Member or Members from two thirds of the States, and a Majority of all the States shall be necessary to a Choice. In every Case, after the Choice of the President, the Person having the greatest Number of Votes of the Electors shall be the Vice President. But if there should remain two or more who have equal Votes, the Senate shall chuse from them by Ballot the Vice President.

The Congress may determine the Time of chusing the Electors, and the Day on which they shall give their Votes; which Day shall be the same throughout the United States.

No Person except a natural born Citizen, or a Citizen of the United States, at the time of the Adoption of this Constitution, shall be eligible to the Office of President; neither shall any Person be eligible to that Office who shall not have attained to the Age of thirty five Years, and been fourteen Years a Resident within the United States.

In Case of the Removal of the President from Office, or of his Death, Resignation, or Inability to discharge the Powers and Duties of the said Office, the Same shall devolve on the Vice President, and the Congress may by Law provide for the Case of Removal, Death, Resignation or Inability, both of the President and Vice President, declaring what Officer shall then act as President, and such Officer shall act accordingly, until the Disability be removed, or a President shall be elected.

The President shall, at stated Times, receive for his Services, a Compensation, which shall neither be increased nor diminished during the Period for which he shall have been elected, and he shall not receive within that Period any other Emolument from the United States, or any of them.

Before he enter on the Execution of his Office, he shall take the following Oath or Affirmation:—"I do solemnly swear (or affirm) that I will faithfully execute the Office of President of the United States, and will to the best of my Ability, preserve, protect and defend the Constitution of the United States."

Section. 2.

The President shall be Commander in Chief of the Army and Navy of the United States, and of the Militia of the several States, when called into the actual Service of the United States; he may require the Opinion, in writing, of the principal Officer in each of the executive Departments, upon any Subject relating to the Duties of their respective Offices, and he shall have Power to grant Reprieves and Pardons for Offences against the United States, except in Cases of Impeachment.

He shall have Power, by and with the Advice and Consent of the Senate, to make Treaties, provided two thirds of the Senators present concur; and he shall nominate, and by and with the Advice and Consent of the Senate, shall appoint Ambassadors, other public Ministers and Consuls, Judges of the supreme Court, and all other Officers of the United States, whose Appointments are not herein otherwise provided for, and which shall be established by Law: but the Congress may by Law vest the Appointment of such inferior Officers, as they think proper, in the President alone, in the Courts of Law, or in the Heads of Departments.

The President shall have Power to fill up all Vacancies that may happen during the Recess of the Senate, by granting Commissions which shall expire at the End of their next Session.

Section. 3.

He shall from time to time give to the Congress Information of the State of the Union, and recommend to their Consideration such Measures as he shall judge necessary and expedient; he may, on extraordinary Occasions, convene both Houses, or either of them, and in Case of Disagreement between them, with Respect to the Time of Adjournment, he may adjourn them to such Time as he shall think proper; he shall receive Ambassadors and other public Ministers; he shall take Care that the Laws be faithfully executed, and shall Commission all the Officers of the United States.

Section. 4.

The President, Vice President and all civil Officers of the United States, shall be removed from Office on Impeachment for, and Conviction of, Treason, Bribery, or other high Crimes and Misdemeanors.

ARTICLE III.

Section. 1.

The judicial Power of the United States shall be vested in one supreme Court, and in such inferior Courts as the Congress may from time to time ordain and establish. The Judges, both of the supreme and inferior Courts, shall hold their Offices during good Behaviour, and shall, at stated Times, receive for their Services a Compensation, which shall not be diminished during their Continuance in Office.

Section. 2.

The judicial Power shall extend to all Cases, in Law and Equity, arising under this Constitution, the Laws of the United States, and Treaties made, or which shall be made, under their Authority;—to all Cases affecting Ambassadors, other public Ministers and Consuls;—to all Cases of admiralty and maritime Jurisdiction;—to Controversies to which the United States shall be a Party;—to Controversies between two or more States;— between a State and Citizens of another State;— between Citizens of different States;—between Citizens of the same State claiming Lands under Grants of different States, and between a State, or the Citizens thereof, and foreign States, Citizens or Subjects.

In all Cases affecting Ambassadors, other public Ministers and Consuls, and those in which a State shall be Party, the supreme Court shall have original Jurisdiction. In all the other Cases before mentioned, the supreme Court shall have appellate Jurisdiction, both as to Law and Fact, with such Exceptions, and under such Regulations as the Congress shall make.

The Trial of all Crimes, except in Cases of Impeachment, shall be by Jury; and such Trial shall be held in the State where the said Crimes shall have been committed; but when not committed within any State, the Trial shall be at such Place or Places as the Congress may by Law have directed.

Section. 3.

Treason against the United States, shall consist only in levying War against them, or in adhering to their Enemies, giving them Aid and Comfort. No Person shall be convicted of Treason unless on the Testimony of two Witnesses to the same overt Act, or on Confession in open Court.

The Congress shall have Power to declare the Punishment of Treason, but no Attainder of Treason shall work Corruption of Blood, or Forfeiture except during the Life of the Person attainted.

ARTICLE. IV.

Section. 1.

Full Faith and Credit shall be given in each State to the public Acts, Records, and judicial Proceedings of every other State. And the Congress may by general Laws prescribe the Manner in which such Acts, Records and Proceedings shall be proved, and the Effect thereof.

Section. 2.

The Citizens of each State shall be entitled to all Privileges and Immunities of Citizens in the several States.

A Person charged in any State with Treason, Felony, or other Crime, who shall flee from Justice, and be found in another State, shall on Demand of the executive Authority of the State from which he fled, be delivered up, to be removed to the State having Jurisdiction of the Crime.

No Person held to Service or Labour in one State, under the Laws thereof, escaping into another, shall, in Consequence of any Law or Regulation therein, be discharged from such Service or Labour, but shall be delivered up on Claim of the Party to whom such Service or Labour may be due.

Section. 3.

New States may be admitted by the Congress into this Union; but no new State shall be formed or erected within the Jurisdiction of any other State; nor any State be formed by the Junction of two or more States, or Parts of States, without the Consent of the Legislatures of the States concerned as well as of the Congress.

The Congress shall have Power to dispose of and make all needful Rules and Regulations respecting the Territory or other Property belonging to the United States; and nothing in this Constitution shall be so construed as to Prejudice any Claims of the United States, or of any particular State.

Section. 4.

The United States shall guarantee to every State in this Union a Republican Form of Government, and shall protect each of them against Invasion; and on Application of the Legislature, or of the Executive (when the Legislature cannot be convened), against domestic Violence.

ARTICLE. V.

The Congress, whenever two thirds of both Houses shall deem it necessary, shall propose Amendments to this Constitution, or, on the Application of the Legislatures of two thirds of the several States, shall call a Convention for proposing Amendments, which, in either Case, shall be valid to all Intents and Purposes, as Part of this Constitution, when ratified by the Legislatures of three fourths of the several States, or by Conventions in three fourths thereof, as the one or the other Mode of Ratification may be proposed by the Congress; Provided that no Amendment which may be made prior to the Year One thousand eight hundred and eight shall in any Manner affect the first and fourth Clauses in the Ninth Section of the first Article; and that no State, without its Consent, shall be deprived of its equal Suffrage in the Senate.

ARTICLE. VI.

All Debts contracted and Engagements entered into, before the Adoption of this Constitution, shall be as valid against the United States under this Constitution, as under the Confederation.

This Constitution, and the Laws of the United States which shall be made in Pursuance thereof; and all Treaties made, or which shall be made, under the Authority of the United States, shall be the supreme Law of the Land; and the Judges in every State shall be bound thereby, any Thing in the Constitution or Laws of any State to the Contrary notwithstanding.

The Senators and Representatives before mentioned, and the Members of the several State Legislatures, and all executive and judicial Officers, both of the United States and of the several States, shall be bound by Oath or Affirmation, to support this Constitution; but no religious Test shall ever be required as a Qualification to any Office or public Trust under the United States.

ARTICLE. VII.

The Ratification of the Conventions of nine States, shall be sufficient for the Establishment of this Constitution between the States so ratifying the Same.

The Word, "the," being interlined between the seventh and eighth Lines of the first Page, the Word "Thirty" being partly written on an Erazure in the fifteenth Line of the first Page, The Words "is tried" being interlined between the thirty second and thirty third Lines of the first Page and the Word "the" being interlined between the forty third and forty fourth Lines of the second Page.

Attest William Jackson Secretary

Done in Convention by the Unanimous Consent of the States present the Seventeenth Day of September in the Year of our Lord one thousand seven hundred and Eighty seven and of the Independence of the United States of America the Twelfth In witness whereof We have hereunto subscribed our Names.

Exterior Repairs & Projects

Complete Handyman's Library™
Handyman Club of America
Minneapolis, Minnesota

Published in 1996 by
Handyman Club of America
12301 Whitewater Drive
Minnetonka, Minnesota 55343

Published by arrangement with Cy DeCosse Incorporated
ISBN 0-86573-684-7

Printed on American paper by
R. R. Donnelley & Sons Co.
99 98 97 96 / 5 4 3 2

CREDITS:
Created by: The Editors of Cy DeCosse Incorporated
and the staff of the Handyman Club of America
in cooperation with Black & Decker. **BLACK&DECKER®**
is a trademark of Black & Decker (US), Incorporated
and is used under license.

Handyman Club of America:
  Book Marketing Manager: Cal Franklin
  Book Marketing Coordinator: Jay McNaughton

Contents

Introduction 5
    Inspecting Your House 6
    Exterior House Maintenance Checklist 9
    Working Safely 10
    Using Caulk & Wood Filler 14
Replacing & Repairing Roof Systems 17
    Evaluating Roof Systems 18
    Planning a Roofing Project 20
    Roofing Materials & Tools 22
    Removing Roof Coverings & Replacing Sheathing 24
    Installing Drip Edge & Building Paper 26
    Installing Flashing 28
    Shingling a Roof 32
    Repairing Shingles & Flashing 38
    Repairing Fascia & Soffits 42
    Repairing Gutters 46
    Installing a Vinyl Snap-together Gutter System...............50
    Installing Soffit & Roof Vents 52
Repairing Siding & Trim 57
    Evaluating Siding & Trim 58
    Repairing Siding 60
    Repairing Trim 68
Repairing Concrete 70
    Identifying Concrete Problems 72
    Safety & Tools 74
    Filling Cracks 76
    Patching Holes 78
    Resurfacing Concrete 80
    Repairing Steps 82
    Miscellaneous Concrete Repairs 84
    Sealing & Maintaining Concrete 86
Repairing Brick & Block Structures 88
    Identifying Brick & Block Problems................................90
    Repairing Brick & Block Walls 92
    Repairing & Replacing Chimney Caps 98
    Cleaning & Painting Brick & Block.................................100
Insulating & Weatherizing 103
    Detecting Energy Loss 104
    Insulating & Weatherizing Products 106
    Improving Insulation 108
    Weatherizing Your House 112
    Maintaining Storm Doors & Windows.............................120
    Replacing Storm Windows 127
Painting Your House...129
    Evaluating Painted Surfaces 130
    Tools & Materials..132
    Preparing Surfaces for Paint 134
    Applying Primer & Paint 140
Protecting & Maintaining Your Home 149
    Quick Fixes for Asphalt 150
    Pestproofing Your Home 152
    Improving Home Security 154
Index..158

Introduction

The roof, windows, doors, and exterior walls of your house work together to create a shield that keeps your home healthy and protects your family from the elements. By adhering to a program of scheduled maintenance and inspection and making timely repairs and improvements, you can ensure that your home provides maximum enjoyment for you and your family, with a minimum of work and expense.

Exterior Repairs & Projects shows you how to maintain the outside of your house by developing the ability to spot trouble and make repairs that improve the appearance and keep minor problems from becoming major headaches. Once you have determined a course of action to correct problems or make improvements, we give you clear instructions on how to accomplish the most common exterior home repairs and improvements.

This book begins with some helpful information on how to inspect the exterior of your home— what to look for, how to investigate beyond the surface, and where to look for solutions to any problems you detect. Then, we cover the basics of working safely outdoors and at heights. From there, the book is divided into seven sections that give you further information on identifying and solving specific problems.

Replacing & Repairing Roof Systems contains information on repairing roofs and flashing; reshingling a roof; repairing and replacing gutters, soffits and fascia; and adding roof and soffit vents.

Repairing Siding & Trim covers repairs for all the most common siding types: wood lap, vinyl, metal, stucco, shakes, and board-and-batten. It also contains instructions for repairing exterior trim.

Repairing Concrete provides instruction for filling cracks and holes; resurfacing areas such as sidewalks and patios; repairing steps; and other miscellaneous repairs. You will also see how to seal and maintain concrete to help prevent future repairs.

Repairing Brick & Block Structures has everything you need to know about repairing brick and block walls, repairing and replacing chimney caps and cleaning and painting brick and block.

You also learn how to identify brick and block problems and recognize those that need professional evaluation.

Insulating & Weatherizing shows you how to analyze the energy efficiency of your home, and how to upgrade insulation and weatherstripping with the best products for the job.

Painting Your House gives you start-to-finish instructions that cover every aspect of the painting process. We discuss paint and painting materials, give thorough preparation instructions, and show you how to apply paint to the many different surfaces and materials you will find on the outside of your house.

Protecting & Maintaining Your Home concludes the book with a variety of exterior projects, from pestproofing to security, that create a safer, more pleasant living environment.

Use this book as a guide for making repairs and improvements to the exterior of your house, and for creating a regular exterior maintenance and evaluation program that will make future exterior projects less frequent and more manageable.

Inspecting Your House

Routine maintenance checks of the exterior of your house do not have to be time-consuming. If you know what to look for and where to look, a semi-annual inspection can be done in 30 minutes—an excellent investment when compared to the cost of fixing problems that could have been prevented with early detection.

By conducting your inspection in a logical sequence, you will save even more time. A good strategy is simply to start at the top, with the roof system, and work your way down and around the house, finishing up with your foundation, driveway, and sidewalks. Do not forget to make important interior inspections, like looking for water damage and checking insulation and weatherstripping.

To assist you in your inspections, we have included an exterior maintenance checklist and some helpful tips on the following pages. Also be sure to refer to the pages cited to the right as you make your evaluation. There, you will find helpful information on what to look for in specific areas of your house, as well as how to plan a strategy for correcting problems.

The following items are helpful when you inspect your house:
• An exterior house maintenance checklist (page 9)
• Binoculars
• A note pad and pencil

6

Flashing: Look for gaps, leaks, damage, rust, and corrosion. Pages 18 to 19.

Chimneys: Examine flashing, mortar joints, and bricks. Check for pests. Pages 18 to 19, 149 to 151.

Security: Check light bulbs, test locks, make sure entry points are unobscured, test alarms. Pages 154 to 157.

Driveway & sidewalks: Check for cracks, holes, spalls, stains. Pages 150 to 151.

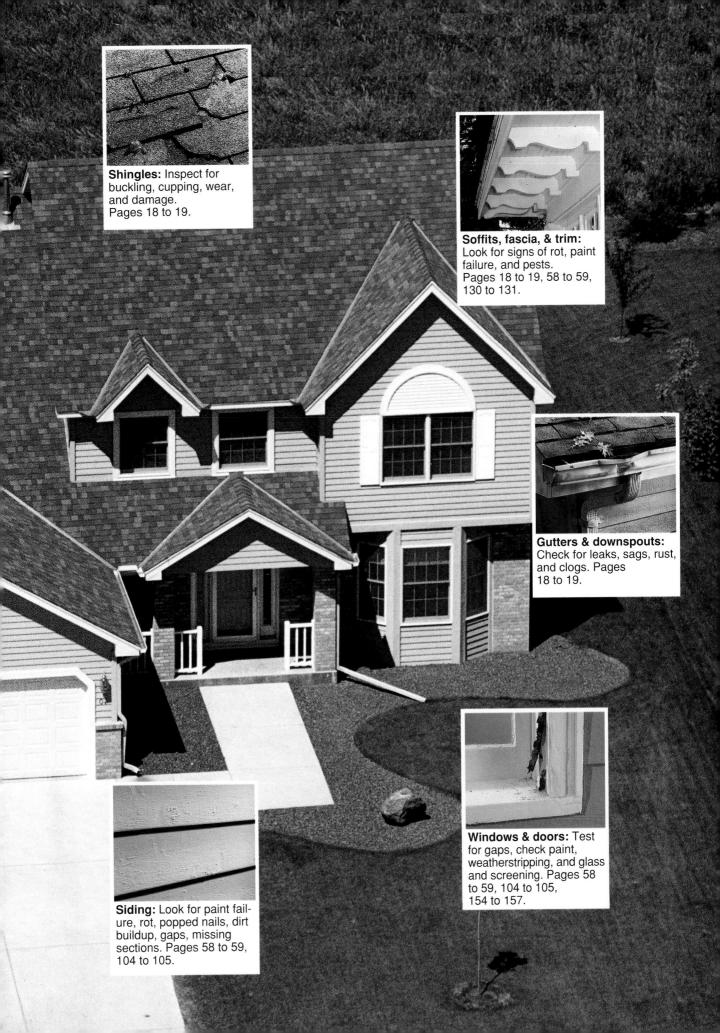

Shingles: Inspect for buckling, cupping, wear, and damage. Pages 18 to 19.

Soffits, fascia, & trim: Look for signs of rot, paint failure, and pests. Pages 18 to 19, 58 to 59, 130 to 131.

Gutters & downspouts: Check for leaks, sags, rust, and clogs. Pages 18 to 19.

Windows & doors: Test for gaps, check paint, weatherstripping, and glass and screening. Pages 58 to 59, 104 to 105, 154 to 157.

Siding: Look for paint failure, rot, popped nails, dirt buildup, gaps, missing sections. Pages 58 to 59, 104 to 105.

Making scheduled inspections

Making scheduled inspections of the exterior of your house is an important responsibility. Make a photocopy of the exterior house maintenance checklist on the following page, and use it to help organize your inspections. Make a check in the box next to any problems you detect, and grade the general condition of each part of your house in the columns to the left.

In moderate and cold climates, inspect your house at least twice a year—once in the spring, and again in the fall. In spring, check to see how well your home weathered the winter. Look for signs of paint failure and damage or wear to your roof system. In the fall, check windows, doors, ventilation, and weatherstripping to make sure the house is well sealed. In warmer climates, it is not as important to divide your inspections into seasonal checkups. But heat and rain can be as harsh on the exterior of a house as ice, snow, and freezing temperatures, so be sure to make inspections at least once a year.

Tips for inspecting your house

• **Look beyond the surface** by probing damaged areas with an awl or a thin-blade screwdriver. Deteriorated wood in need of repair sometimes looks almost normal on the surface.

• **Use binoculars** instead of a ladder for a quick visual inspection of roofs, gutters, chimneys, and second-story areas. If you spot any potential problems, use a ladder for closer inspection (see pages 10 to 13 for tips on ladder safety).

• **Keep permanent records** of your inspection, noting any areas of concern. Monitor the areas carefully, and take action as soon as it becomes clear that a problem is developing.

• **Take photographs** of roofs, walls, and any other parts of your house showing signs of wear. Compare photos from year to year to determine the rate the wear is increasing. Significant changes within a year or two are a sure sign that a problem exists.

• **Check the grounds** near your house for trouble signs, like flakes of paint, roofing-material wash-off, or soil erosion.

Tips for Identifying the Source of a Moisture Problem

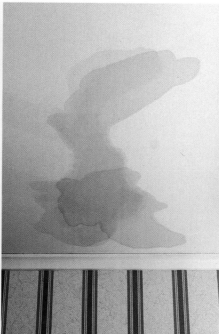

Shown cutaway for clarity

Moisture problems affect houses in all climates. Identifying the source of moisture problems can be tricky because the effects of moisture often appear far from the actual source. *Ice dams* (left) at roof eaves are a common occurrence in colder climates. They result from inadequate attic ventilation (pages 52 to 55), which causes snow to melt higher up the roof. The runoff then freezes when it comes in contact with the colder roof overhang. *Ceiling stains* (center) show up on interior surfaces, but often are caused by leakage from failed roof materials or flashing (pages 18 to 19). *Peeling paint* (right) can occur if your house was improperly prepared for paint, or if the paint was not applied correctly. More likely, there is a condensation problem caused by excess moisture inside the house, or a missing vapor barrier (pages 130 to 131).

Exterior House Maintenance Checklist

Date:

1	2	3	Roof, Gutters, Soffits & Fascia
			Shingles: ❏ buckling ❏ cupping ❏ wear ❏ damage ❏ missing shingles ❏ leaks ❏ exposed nails **Notes:**
			Flashing: ❏ deterioration ❏ loose or detached ❏ bad seals **Notes:**
			Chimney: ❏ loose or crumbling masonry ❏ soot buildup ❏ pests **Notes:**
			Ventilation: ❏ obstructed vents ❏ covers or turbines damaged **Notes:**
			Gutters: ❏ leaks or holes ❏ sags ❏ rust/deterioration ❏ clogs **Notes:**
			Soffits & fascia: ❏ rot ❏ cracks or damage ❏ pests **Notes:**

			Siding & Trim
			Siding: ❏ rot/damage ❏ missing siding ❏ paint failure ❏ buckling **Notes:**
			Trim: ❏ rot/damage ❏ cracks/splits ❏ paint failure **Notes:**

			Doors & Windows
			Weatherstripping: ❏ damaged ❏ missing **Notes:**
			Hardware: ❏ rust/corrosion ❏ paint failure ❏ sticking ❏ misaligned **Notes:**
			Glass & screening: ❏ broken/torn ❏ glazing/retaining strips deteriorated **Notes:**
			Frames, wood: ❏ rot/damage ❏ paint failure **Notes:**

			Foundation
			Leaks: ❏ water in basement ❏ condensation on interior walls **Notes:**
			General condition: ❏ small cracks ❏ large cracks ❏ deterioration **Notes:**

			Decks, Porches & Patios
			Wood surfaces: ❏ rot/damage ❏ paint failure ❏ loose boards **Notes:**
			Masonry surfaces: ❏ cracks ❏ stains ❏ concrete failure **Notes:**
			Railings, trim, accessories: ❏ rust/paint failure ❏ rot/damage **Notes:**

			Driveway & Sidewalks
			Driveway: ❏ cracks ❏ stains ❏ damage **Notes:**
			Sidewalks: ❏ cracks ❏ stains ❏ damage **Notes:**

			Security
			Lighting: ❏ burned-out bulbs ❏ unlit entries **Notes:**
			Locks: ❏ operate smoothly ❏ window locks ❏ strikeplate aligned **Notes:**
			General: ❏ entries unobscured ❏ security system functional **Notes:**

Key:
1=Good condition
2=Fair condition: some wear
3=Needs immediate attention

Comments:

Working Safely

By taking common-sense precautions you can work just as safely outdoors as indoors—even though the exterior presents a few additional safety considerations.

Since many exterior repairs require you to work at heights, learning and following the basic rules of safe ladder and scaffolding use is very important (pages 12 to 13). And any time you are working outside, the weather should play a key role in just about every aspect of how you conduct your work: from the work clothes you select, to the amount of work you decide to undertake.

In addition to the information shown on the following pages, here are some important safety precautions to follow when working outdoors:

• When possible, work with a helper in case there is an emergency. If you have to work alone, inform a friend or family member so they can check on you periodically. If you own a portable telephone, keep it handy at all times.
• Never work at heights, or with tools, if you have consumed alcohol or medication.
• Do not work outdoors in stormy weather. Do not work at heights when it is windy.

Tip for Working Safely

Wear sensible clothing and protective equipment when working outdoors, including: a cap to protect against direct sunlight, eye protection when working with tools or chemicals, a particle mask when sanding, work gloves, full-length pants, and a long-sleeved shirt. A tool organizer turns a 5-gallon bucket into a safe and convenient container for transporting tools.

Set up your work site for quick disposal of waste materials. Old nails, jagged metal from flashing, and piles of old shingles all are safety hazards when left on the ground. Use a wheelbarrow to transfer waste to a dumpster or trash can immediately. NOTE: Disposal of building materials is regulated in most areas. Check with your local waste management department.

Tips for Working Safely

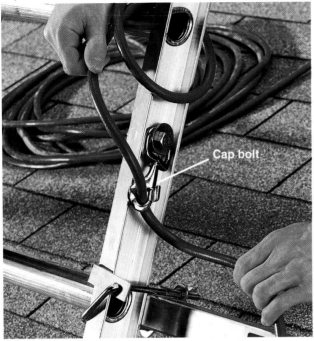

Permanently attach a fastener to the top of your ladder for tying off power cords or air hoses. The weight of a power cord or hose is enough to drag most power tools off the roof. Drill a hole in the ladder and secure a cap bolt (above) to the ladder with a nut and bolt. Do not tie knots in cords and hoses.

Create a storage surface for tools. A sheet of plywood on top of a pair of sawhorses keeps tools off the ground, where they are a safety hazard (and where they can become damaged by moisture). A storage surface also makes it easy to locate tools when you need them.

Stay clear of power cables. Household service cables carry 100 amps or electricity or more. If you must work near a cable, use extreme caution, and use fiberglass or wood ladders only—never use metal ladders near cables.

Use a GFCI extension cord when working outdoors. GFCIs (Ground Fault Circuit Interrupters) shut off power if a short circuit occurs (often from contact with water).

Use cordless tools whenever possible to make your work easier and safer. Power cords, even when properly secured, are a nuisance and create many hazards, including tripping and tangling.

11

Options for Working at Heights

Use an extension ladder for making quick repairs to gutters, fascia, and soffits, and to gain access to roofs. For larger projects, like painting walls, relying solely on ladders is inefficient and dangerous.

Use scaffolding for projects that require you to work at heights for extended periods of time, like preparing walls for paint. If you rent scaffolding, be sure to get assembly-and-use instructions from the rental center.

Tips for Using Ladders and Scaffolds

Provide level, stable footing for ladders and scaffolding. Install sturdy blocking under the legs of ladders (left) if the ground is uneven, soft, or slippery, and always drive a stake next to each ladder foot to keep the ladder from slipping away from the house.

Also insert sturdy blocking under scaffold feet (right) if the ground is soft or uneven. Add more blocking under legs in sloped areas, and use the adjustable leg posts for final leveling. If the scaffold has wheels, lock them securely with the hand brakes.

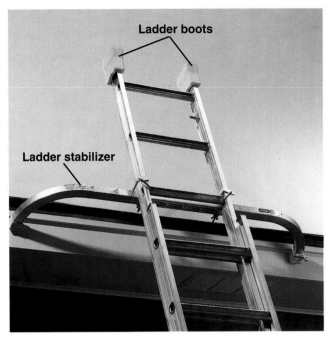

Attach an adjustable ladder stabilizer to your ladder to minimize the chance of slipping. Rest the feet of the stabilizer against broad, flat, stable surfaces only. In addition to making the ladder safer, a stabilizer allows you to work on areas directly in front of the ladder. If you do not use a stabilizer, cover the top ends of the ladder with ladder boots to prevent slipping and protect siding from scratches and dents.

Make sure fly hooks are secure before climbing an extension ladder. The open ends of the hooks should grip a rung on the lower fly extension. Use extra caution when climbing past the fly hooks as you ascend and descend the ladder, and be aware of the points at each fly extension where the doubled rungs end, and single rungs begin.

Anchor ladders and scaffolding by tying them to a secure area, like a chimney—especially if you are not using a ladder stabilizer. If no sturdy anchoring spot exists, create one by driving a #10 screw eye into the fascia. When finished with the ladder, remove the screw eye and cover the hole with caulk.

Ladder Safety Tips:

• Watch out for wires, branches, and overhangs when carrying ladders.

• Position extension ladders so the flat tops of the D-shaped rungs are facing up, parallel to the ground.

• Extend the ladder three feet above the roof edge for greater stability and to provide a gripping point when you mount or dismount the ladder (do not grip too aggressively).

• Do not exceed the work-load rating for your ladder. Limits are listed on the label of any ladder. Read all the safety recommendations.

• Climb on or off a ladder at a point as close to the ground as possible. Move steadily and keep your center of gravity low when crossing between the roof and the ladder.

• Never carry heavy items, like shingle bundles, up an extension ladder. Use a hoist (a simple cord and bucket will do), and pull the items up while you are standing securely on the roof. Lower the items down using the hoist, as well.

Using Caulk & Wood Filler

Apply an even bead of caulk by squeezing the release trigger at regular intervals and moving the caulk gun at a steady pace. Practice drawing beads on scraps until you are comfortable with the technique.

Caulk is one of the most useful materials for repairing and maintaining your house. It is used to fill gaps, cracks, and holes of every variety. It also is useful as a preventative tool—by sealing exterior seams and gaps with caulk, you keep moisture out of wall cavities and other areas that water can damage. For general exterior purposes, use siliconized acrylic or siliconized latex caulk. These products are flexible, long-lasting, paintable, water resistant, and relatively inexpensive. Use special-purpose caulks, like gutter caulk, when the need arises.

Use two-part epoxy wood fillers to patch or repair wood siding and trim. Do not use standard wood putty; it is not rated for exterior use.

Everything You Need:

Tools: caulk gun, utility knife, putty knife, chisel, brush, wooden forms.

Materials: epoxy wood filler, siliconized acrylic caulk, sandpaper, paint, stain.

Choosing Caulk & Wood-repair Products

Epoxy wood filler (A) is an excellent all-purpose product for repairing and patching wood that is exposed to the elements. Most types of epoxy wood filler come with a hardening agent that is mixed in with the product just prior to application. **Wood hardener (B)** is brushed on to damaged or rotted wood to restore strength, often before painting.

Caulking materials include: tinted exterior caulk to match siding color (A); paintable, siliconized acrylic caulk for general exterior use (B); panel adhesive, for attaching rigid insulation (C); clear, peelable acrylic caulk (D) for weatherstripping around glass; and plastic roof cement (E), for repairing and sealing around shingles, flashing, and miscellaneous areas.

How to Apply Caulk

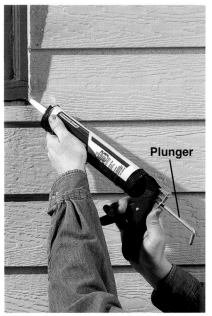

1 Cut out any old caulk with a utility knife, and clean the surface. Cut the tip of the caulk tube at a 45° angle, using a utility knife or scissors. Puncture the seal at the top of the tube, then load the tube into your caulk gun.

2 Squeeze the trigger of the caulk gun to bring caulk to the tip of the tube, then position the tube at an upper end of the gap being caulked. Draw a continuous bead along the gap. Use caulking backer rope (page 107) for cracks wider than ¼".

3 Finish drawing the bead, then release the plunger in the gun immediately, lifting the gun away from the work area. Failure to release the plunger will cause caulk to continue oozing out of the tube, creating a sticky mess.

How to Repair Wood with Wood Filler

1 Remove all damaged or rotted wood from the repair area, using a wood chisel or a utility knife. Clean away debris with a brush, then wash the repair area. For larger repair areas, attach wood forms to help shape the filler.

2 Prepare the filler for application (see manufacturer's directions), then apply it in the repair area with a putty knife (some fillers may be applied in thick layers, other should not exceed ¼"—read the product directions).

3 After the filler has dried completely, sand with 150-grit sandpaper to shape contours and create a smooth surface. Use a wood file for more extensive shaping. Paint or stain the filler to match the surrounding wood.

Replacing & Repairing Roof Systems

The roof system has a greater exposure to the elements than any other part of your house. As a result, it requires the most attention and the most frequent maintenance. This is especially true because problems in the roof system, like leaks or blocked ventilation, lead quickly to damage in other parts of your house.

A roof system is composed of several elements that work together to provide three basic and essential functions for your home: shelter, drainage, and ventilation. The roof covering and the flashing shed water, directing it to the gutters and downspouts to channel it away from the foundation of your house. Air intake and outtake vents keep fresh air circulating below the roof sheathing, preventing moisture buildup and overheating.

Roof system projects range in complexity, from simply caulking a small hole in a shingle, to removing and replacing shingles, building paper, flashing, and sheathing. Whatever the complex-

ity of the repairs your roof system requires, it is very important that you have a thorough understanding of how all the elements of the system work. By understanding your roof system and making timely repairs, you can ensure that your roof system performs for its full, useful life span.

This sections shows:
• Evaluating Roof Systems (pages 18 to 19)
• Planning a Roofing Project (pages 20 to 21)
• Roofing Materials & Tools (pages 22 to 23)
• Removing Roof Coverings & Replacing Sheathing (pages 24 to 25)
• Installing Drip Edge & Building Paper (pages 26 to 27)
• Installing Flashing (pages 28 to 31)
• Shingling a Roof (pages 32 to 37)
• Repairing Shingles & Flashing (pages 38 to 41)
• Repairing Fascia & Soffits (pages 42 to 45)
• Repairing Gutters (pages 46 to 49)
• Installing a Vinyl Snap-together Gutter System (pages 50 to 51)
• Installing Soffit & Roof Vents (pages 52 to 55)

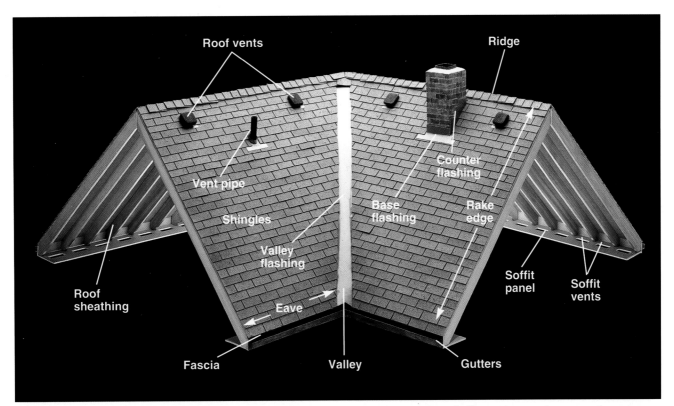

The elements of a roof system work together to provide shelter, drainage, and ventilation. The roof covering is composed of sheathing, building paper, and shingles. Metal flashing is attached in valleys and around chimneys, vent pipes, and other roof elements to seal out water. Soffits cover and protect the eave area below the roof overhang. Fascia, usually attached at the ends of the rafters, supports soffit panels as well as a gutter and downspout system. Soffit vents and roof vents keep fresh air flowing under the roof.

Shown cutaway for clarity

Evaluating Roof Systems

Regular inspections are essential to maintaining a healthy roof system—more can go wrong in the roof area than in just about any other part of your house. Most roof damage is caused by water, either from precipitation or condensation below the roof materials. Because a failed shingle could be caused by a leak somewhere else in the roof, or by inadequate attic ventilation that results in condensation, simply replacing the shingle will not correct the leak. Make sure you eliminate any moisture source outside the damaged area before you repair the damage.

Ice dams occur when melting snow refreezes near the eaves, causing ice to back up under the shingles, where it melts onto the sheathing. To solve the problem, improve roof ventilation (pages 52 to 55).

Finding & Evaluating Roof Leaks

Inspect from inside your attic. Look for discoloration, streaking, or rot on roof sheathing and rafters. Find the highest point of discoloration to pinpoint the source of the leak. Then, measure from the high point to roof vents, chimneys, or other roof elements so you can use their relative locations to help find the leak on the exterior of the roof. If the damage is minimal (left), and no rot has set in, simply repair shingles or flashing (pages 38 to 41). If there is substantial rot (right), tear off the shingles above the rot, replace damaged sheathing (page 25), and reshingle (pages 26 to 36). Fix any moisture problems outside the damaged area.

Common Shingle Problems

Buckled shingles (top) and **cupped shingles** (bottom) usually are caused by lingering moisture beneath the shingle. Likely sources include condensation from poor attic ventilation (pages 52 to 55), or leaky shingles or flashing. If you find and fix the moisture problem, buckled shingles may flatten out by themselves. If they do not flatten out, replace them. Cupped shingles almost always require replacement. See pages 24 to 36 for major damage, or pages 38 to 39 for isolated damage. Do not install new shingles over cupped or buckled shingles.

Damaged shingles (top) and **worn shingles** (bottom) become increasingly common as a roof ages. Damage can occur on any roof, new or old, but it becomes more likely as the shingles age and the protective mineral surfaces wear down. Treat isolated damage or wear by replacing only the problem shingles (pages 38 to 41). Widespread damage and pervasive wear usually require that all the shingles be replaced, either by tearing off and reshingling (pages 24 to 36), or by installing new shingles over the old shingles (page 37—check building codes first).

Gutter Problems

Sagging gutters can be caused by deteriorated fascia or by weight from a blockage. Remove the blockage (page 149), replace damaged fascia (page 43), then raise and refasten gutters (page 46).

Leaking gutters usually result from holes or separated joints (shown). Disassemble leaky joints, then caulk and reassemble the joint (page 48). Patch holes (pages 47 to 48).

Damaged gutter sections should be patched (pages 47 to 48) or replaced (page 49). If damage is widespread, replace with a new gutter system (pages 50 to 51).

Flashing Problems

Loose flashing can be caused by external forces, like high wind, or by failure of sealant or fasteners. To repair, pull back the flashing enough to clean out the old sealant, and resecure with fresh roofing cement and new fasteners (page 38).

Damaged and deteriorated flashing are primary causes of roof leaks. Remove and replace the damaged piece (page 40). If several pieces are damaged or showing signs of wear, remove and replace all the flashing around the affected roof element (page 41).

Fascia & Soffit Problems

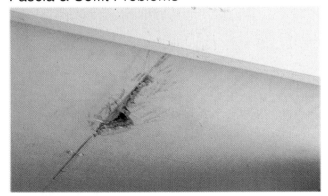

Pest damage and rot are the primary enemies of soffits. Small spots of damage can be repaired by replacing the material (pages 44 to 45). If damage is more widespread, or if your house does not have soffits, and birds or insects are nesting in your eaves, install a new soffit system (page 42).

Rotten fascia is easy to spot from the ground on homes with no gutter system. If your house has gutters, climb up and check for rot behind the gutters, especially if they are sagging. Replace damaged sections of fascia (page 43), removing the gutters where necessary.

Planning a Roofing Project

Dress for protection and safety when working on roof projects. Wear rubber-soled shoes for good traction, knee pads, a nail apron, a tool belt, a long-sleeved shirt, full-length pants, and work gloves. Always wear protective eyewear when nailing or using power tools.

Planning makes any project go more smoothly, and working on your roof is no exception.

Measure the square footage of your roof so you can estimate materials and time. When estimating materials, add 15% to allow for waste. Shop around to compare shingle prices, then make a rough cost estimate for the type you select. Count the number of roof elements, like vent pipes, vent fans, skylights, dormers, and chimneys, that you will need to roof around, and tally up the costs for the flashing needed for these elements. Check your sheathing from the attic side. If replacement is needed, make a cost allowance for it. Add in additional materials costs, like building paper, roof cement, nails, dumpster rental, and tool purchase or rental.

Next, estimate the time your project will demand (see chart, next page). Calculate the slope of the roof so you can determine if you need roof jacks to move around. If so, take that into account when making time estimates. By making reasonable estimates, you can divide the project into manageable portions.

Most building centers will deliver shingles, building paper, and other materials directly to your roof, using a mechanical lift. If you can arrange it, have at least one section of the old roof torn off, with new building paper and drip edge installed, before shingle delivery. This will save time, as well as energy you would use to hoist the heavy shingle bundles up from the ground and reposition them on your roof.

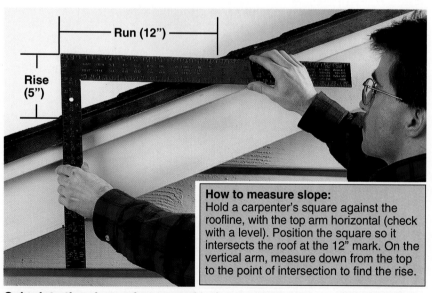

How to measure slope:
Hold a carpenter's square against the roofline, with the top arm horizontal (check with a level). Position the square so it intersects the roof at the 12" mark. On the vertical arm, measure down from the top to the point of intersection to find the rise.

Calculate the slope of your roof before beginning any roofing project. Slope is usually described by the number of inches the roof rises in each foot along a horizontal plane (called the "run"). For example, the roof shown above has a 5-in-12 slope: it rises 5" in 12" of run. Knowing the slope is important for selecting materials, and to help gauge the difficulty of moving on the roof. Use roof jacks if the slope is 7-in-12 or steeper. Roofs with a slope of 3-in-12 or less must have a fully bonded covering.

Tips for Planning a Roofing Project

Estimating time requirements			
Task	**Time Requirement**	**Amount**	**Total Time**
Tear-off	1 hr./square*		•
Install building paper	30 min./square		•
Apply shingles:			
Flat run	2 hrs./square		•
Ridges, hips	30 min./10 ft		•
Dormers**	add 1 hr. ea.		•
•Flashing:			
Chimneys	2 hrs. ea.		•
Vent pipes	30 min. ea.		•
Valleys	30 min./10 ft.		•
Roof vents	30 min. ea.		•
Skylights	2 hrs. ea.		•
Drip edge	30 min./20 ft.		•
TOTAL TIME FOR PROJECT			•

NOTE: All time estimates are based on one worker. Reduce time by 40% if there is a helper.
*One square=100 square feet
**Include area of dormer surface in "flat run" estimate

Protect against damage from falling materials when tearing off old shingles. Hang tarps over the sides of the house, and lean plywood against the house to protect vegetation.

How to Install Roof Jacks

1 Nail roof jacks to the roof at the fourth or fifth course. Position the jacks so the nail slots are in the "dead area" where shingles will not be exposed, then drive a 16d nail into each slot. Install one jack every 4 ft., with 6" to 12" of overhang at the ends of the board.

2 Shingle over the tops of the roof jacks (when installing shingles), then rest a 2 x 8 or 2 x 10 board on the support arms of the jacks—use the widest board the supports will hold. Drive a nail through the hole in the lip of each roof jack to secure the board.

3 Remove boards and roof jacks when the project is complete. Drive in 16d nails by positioning the end of a pry bar over each nail head, then rapping the shank of the pry bar with a hammer.

Choose a roof covering that is a good match for your house and your budget. *Asphalt or fiberglass shingles* (left) are by far the most popular choice because they are relatively inexpensive, durable, easy to install, and available in a wide variety of styles and colors. Look for shingles with a 20-year warranty. *Wood shakes* (center) are usually made from natural split cedar. They are more expensive and more time-consuming to install than shingles. *Clay tiles* (right) create a very distinctive appearance, but they are fairly expensive and should only be installed by a professional.

Roofing Materials & Tools

Most do-it-yourselfers select asphalt or fiberglass shingles because they are inexpensive and simple to install. The most common type are "3-tab" shingles, which contain three 12"-wide tabs, separated by slots. Less common coverings, like cedar shakes and clay tiles, are best installed by a professional, but you can save money by doing the tear-off and preparation work yourself. If your roof has a slope of 3-in-12 (page 20) or less, you need a "fully-bonded" roof covering, usually made of built-up tar or sheets of roll roofing that are bonded to the sheathing with roof cement (also a good job for a professional).

How to estimate shingles:

Shingles are sold in bundles, but estimated in *squares*—the amount needed to cover 100 square feet. Three bundles of shingles cover one square. To estimate how many bundles you need, calculate the square footage of roof area, and add 15% for waste. Divide the total by 100, then multiply by 3 to find the number of bundles needed for your project.

Specialty roofing tools include: roof jacks (A), roofing shovel with slots in the blade for tearing off shingles and prying out nails (B), pneumatic nailer (C), utility knife with hook blade (D), roofing hammer with alignment guides and hatchet-style blade (E), and a release magnet for site cleanup (F).

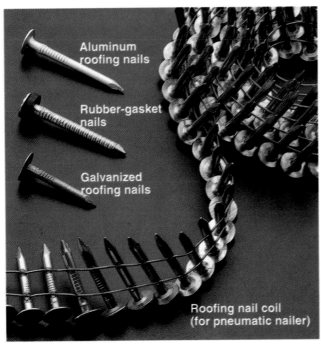

Use the right fastener for the job. Use galvanized roofing nails to hand-nail shingles (buy two pounds of nails per square of shingles); use aluminum nails for aluminum flashing, and rubber-gasket nails for galvanized metal flashing. Use roofing nail coils for pneumatic nailers (check coverage chart on carton).

Common roofing materials include: 30# building paper for shingle underlayment; cartridges of plastic roofing cement; and ice-guard membrane for use as underlayment in the first course or two of roofs in cold climates (page 26).

Roof flashing can be hand-cut or purchased in pre-formed shapes and sizes. Cut rolled flashing material with aviator snips to make longer flashing pieces, like valley flashing (also available pre-formed), or non-standard pieces, like base flashing and top saddles (pages 30 to 31). Most experienced roofers buy step flashing blanks in standard sizes, and bend them to fit their project. Drip edge and vent pipe flashing should be purchased as pre-formed pieces. Skylights usually are sold complete with a flashing kit. Complicated flashing pieces, like chimney crickets (page 31), should be made by a professional metalworker.

Cover unshingled sections overnight, using tarps weighted down with shingle bundles. Tear off only one roof section at a time if you cannot reshingle the entire roof in one day.

Removing Roof Coverings & Replacing Sheathing

Completely remove old shingles, building paper, and flashing if your old roof already has more than one layer of shingles; if shingles are cupped or buckled; or if sheathing is damaged. Replace damaged sheathing after the roof covering is off.

Rent a dumpster from a waste disposal company or your local waste management department, and position it below the roof edge for direct dumping of materials. Or, arrange wheelbarrows on tarps to catch debris. Use extreme caution during tear-off: debris on the roof is a serious hazard.

Everything You Need:

Tools: dumpster, hammer, chisel, pry bar, roofing knife, roofing shovel, broom, release magnet, rake, tin snips, reciprocating saw, drill.

Materials: protective gear, tarps, plywood sheets, 2 × 4 nailing strips, sheathing material, galvanized deck screws.

How to Tear Off Old Roof Coverings

1 Slice through roofing cement around flashing to release it from the shingles. Remove any flashing that you plan to replace. NOTE: Unless the flashing is in exceptional condition, it is easier to remove and replace all the flashing during a full shingle tear-off. Save complicated flashing pieces, like chimney saddles or crickets, and reuse, if practical.

2 Remove the ridge cap, using a pry bar. With the ridge cap out of the way, start prying up the top course of shingles with a roofing shovel or flat pry bar. Work on only one roof section at a time.

3 Remove old shingles and building paper in large sections, using a roofing shovel. Work from top to bottom. NOTE: The tear-off portion of a roofing project is an ideal time to get help. Having another person to dispose of the materials before they can accumulate on the ground is a great time-saver. Make sure your helper is out of the way before you dump materials.

4 After removing shingles and building paper from the entire tear-off section, pry out any remaining nails. Also sweep the roof with a garage broom to prepare it for the building paper. TIP: Clean up nails on the ground with a release magnet (page 22).

How to Replace Damaged Sheathing

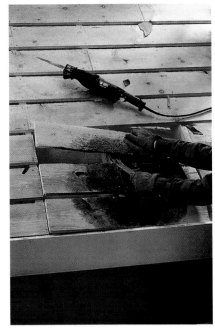

1 Cut out damaged sheathing boards with a reciprocating saw (check inside for wiring first). Cut next to rafters in an area that extends well beyond the damaged material. Pry out the damaged sections.

2 Attach 2 x 4 nailing strips to the rafters at the edges of the cutout sections Using 3" deck screws.

3 Cut sheathing patches from exterior-grade plywood the same thickness as the old sheathing, allowing for a ⅛"-wide expansion gap on all sides. Attach the patch with 2¼" deck screws or 8d ring-shank siding nails, driven into rafters and nailing strips.

Work your way up the roof deck with building paper courses, allowing 4" horizontal overlaps and 12" vertical seams. Roll building paper across valleys from both sides (photo, above), overlapping the ends by 36". Overlap hips and ridges by 6". Attach building paper with a hammer stapler, driving a staple every 6" to 12" at the edges, and one staple per square foot in the field area.

Installing Drip Edge & Building Paper

Drip edge is flashing that is installed at the edges of your roof to direct water flow away from the roof sheathing. Building paper is installed on roof decks as insurance in case leaks develop in shingles or flashing. It is sold in several weights, but 30# paper is a good choice for use under shingles (15# meets code in some areas). Check with your local building inspector.

In colder climates, recent changes to building codes require a special type of underlayment, called "ice guard" or "ice shield," instead of standard building paper for the first course or two of underlayment. An adhesive membrane, the ice guard bonds with the sheathing to create a barrier to runoff from ice dams (page 18).

Everything You Need:

Tools: hammer, pry bar, roofing knife, hammer stapler, chalk line, tape measure, tin snips.

Materials: drip edge, 30# building paper, roofing cement, ice guard, roofing nails.

Tips for Installing Drip Edge

Eave edge

Rake edge

Attach at eaves *before* attaching building paper. Nail a strip of drip edge along the edge of the eaves. Overlap strips by 2" at vertical seams. Miter the ends at a 45° angle to make a miter joint with the drip edge on the rake edge. Install galvanized and vinyl drip edge with galvanized roofing nails. Use aluminum nails for aluminum drip edge. Nail at 12" intervals.

Attach at rake edges *after* attaching building paper. Start at the bottom, forming a miter joint with the drip edge at the eaves. Work toward the ridge, overlapping pieces of drip edge by 2" (make sure the higher strip is on top at overlaps).

Tips for Installing Building Paper & Ice Guard Underlayment

Snap a chalk line 35⅝" up from the eave edge, so the first course of the 36"-wide ice guard membrane (or building paper) overhangs the eaves by ⅜". Install a course of ice guard, using the chalk line as a reference. Peel back the protective backing as you unroll the ice guard. In cold climates, apply as many courses of ice guard as it takes to cover 24" past the roof overhang. In warm climates, ice guard may not be necessary, so check your local codes.

Measure up from the eave edge to a point 32" above the top of the previous course of underlayment, and snap another chalk line. Roll out the next course of building paper (or ice guard, if required), overlapping the first course by 4". Install building paper up to the ridge, ruled side up, snapping horizontal lines every two or three rows to check alignment. Always overlap from above. Trim off courses flush with the rake edge.

Fit a building paper patch over any obstructions, like vent pipes or roof vents. Apply building paper up to the obstruction, then resume laying the course on the opposite side (make sure to maintain the line). Cut a patch that overlaps the building paper by 12" on all sides. Make a cross-hatch cutout for the obstruction. Position the patch, staple in place, then caulk seams with roof cement.

Tuck building paper under siding at the bottoms of dormers and sidewalls, where they intersect with the roof. Also tuck it under counterflashing on chimneys (page 31) and skylights. Carefully pry up the siding, and tuck at least 2" of paper under the siding. Do not refasten siding or counterflashing right away—wait until after you install step flashing (page 30).

Installing Flashing

Bend your own flashing (top). Make a bending jig by driving screws into a piece of scrap wood, creating a line one-half the width of the flashing when measured from the edge of the board. Clamp the bending jig to a worksurface, then press a step flashing blank (page 23) flat on the board. Bend it over the edge. **Use old flashing as a template** (bottom) for making replacement flashing. This is especially useful for reproducing complicated flashing, like saddle flashing for chimneys or dormers.

Tip for Installing Flashing

Replace flashing during shingle installation. Because most roof flashing is interwoven with shingles, you will get better results than if you try to retrofit flashing around existing shingles.

Flashing is a metal or rubber barrier used to protect the seams around roof elements. Many beginning roofers consider flashing installation to be the most difficult element of a roofing project. But once you learn one or two basic principles of installing flashing, the mystery disappears quickly.

The purpose of flashing is to make water flow over shingled surfaces, and away from gaps around roof elements, like vent pipes and chimneys. To accomplish this, pieces of flashing are layered between rows of shingles.

Around roof elements, flashing should be secured to one surface only—usually the roof deck. Use only roof cement to bond the flashing to the roof elements. Flashing must be able to flex as the roof element and the roof deck expand and contract (usually at different rates). If flashing is fastened to both the roof deck and the roof element, it will tear or loosen.

NOTE: In this section, we show you how to install flashing during a shingle-installation project (pages 32 to 36). For information on repairing or replacing flashing, see pages 38 to 41. Also see page 23 for flashing product information.

Everything You Need:

Tools: tape measure, roofing hammer, pry bar, trowel, caulk gun, aviator snips.

Materials: roof cement, roofing nails, rubber gasket nails, galvanized metal flashing, vent pipe flashing, shingles.

How to Install Metal Valley Flashing

8" overlap

Preformed valley flashing

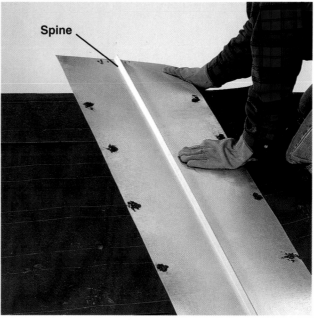

Spine

1 After installing building paper across the valley (page 26), set a piece of valley flashing (preformed or bent from rolled flashing) into the valley, so the bottom of the "V" rests in the crease of the valley. Starting at the eave, nail the flashing near each edge at 12" intervals. Trim the end of the flashing at the eave so it is flush with the drip edges at each side. Add pieces, moving up toward the ridge. Overlap from above by at least 8".

2 Add overlapping pieces, working toward the ridge, until the flashing reaches a few inches past the ridge. Bend the flashing over the ridge, so it lies flat on the opposite side of the roof. If you are installing preformed flashing, make a small cut in the spine for easier bending. Cover nail heads with roof cement (unless you used rubber-gasket nails). Also apply roof cement at the side edges of the flashing.

How to Install Vent Pipe Flashing

Reveal area of shingle

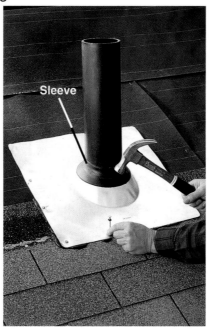

Sleeve

1 Shingle up to the vent pipe. Cut the top shingle to fit around the pipe, so the "reveal area" of the shingle (the exposed portion) is within 5" of the pipe. Apply roof cement to the base of the flashing.

2 Slip the sleeve of the flashing over the vent pipe, making sure the pitch of the flange is sloped in the right direction. Press the flange against the roof deck, then fasten with rubber-gasket nails.

3 Continue installing shingle courses, making cutouts for the pipe. Do not nail through the flashing—attach shingles with roof cement where they cover flashing.

How to Install Step Flashing

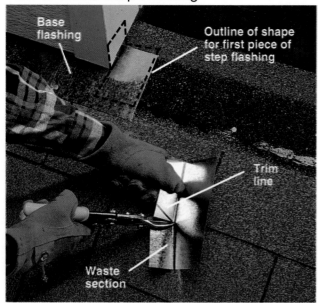

1 Shingle up to the element requiring flashing (here, a dormer) so the tops of the reveal areas are within 5" of the element. Install base flashing (step 1, next page). Bend a piece of step flashing in half, and set the piece next to the lowest corner of the element. Mark a trim line on the flashing, following the vertical edge of the element. Cut off the waste part of the flashing (the area ouside the trim line on the vertical side of the bend), making a starter cut first.

2 Pry out the lower courses of siding and any trim at the base of the element. Insert spacers to prop trim or siding away from the work area. Apply roof cement to the base flashing in the area where the overlap with the step flashing will be formed. Tuck the trimmed piece of step flashing under the propped area, and press the flashing into the roof cement. Fasten the flashing with one rubber-gasket nail driven near the top, and into the roof deck.

3 Apply roof cement to the top side of the first piece of step flashing, where it will be covered by the next shingle course. Install the shingle, setting it firmly into the roof cement. Do not nail through the flashing when attaching shingles. Apply roof cement to the shingle, next to the dormer or other roof element (in the area that will be covered by the next piece of step flashing).

4 Tuck another piece of step flashing under the trim or siding, setting it into the roof cement on the shingle. Overlap the first piece of step flashing by at least 2". Continue flashing in this manner until you reach the top of the element. Trim the last piece of flashing to fit at the top corner of the element. Refasten siding and trim. On chimneys or other elements needing a top saddle (step 3, next page), the saddle should overlap the last piece of step flashing.

How to Install Chimney Flashing

1 Shingle up to the chimney base. Cut base flashing, using the old base flashing as a template (page 28). Bend up counterflashing (the flashing anchored in the chimney to cover the step flashing). Apply roof cement to the base of the chimney and the shingles just below the base. Press the base flashing into the roof cement, and bend the flashing around the edges of the chimney. Drive rubber-gasket nails through the flashing flange and into the roof deck.

2 Apply step flashing and shingles (previous page), working up toward the top of the chimney. Fasten the flashing to the chimney with roof cement only, and fold down counterflashing as you go.

3 Cut and install top flashing (sometimes called a saddle) around the high side of the chimney, overlapping the final piece of step flashing along each side. Attach with roof cement on both the roof deck and the chimney, and rubber-gasket nails driven through the base of the flashing and into the roof deck. Continue shingling past the chimney, using roof cement (not nails) to attach shingles over flashing.

TIP: If your roof originally had a cricket to divert water around the chimney, have a new cricket made by a metalworker. Provide the fabricator with either the old cricket to use as a template, or the roof slope (page 20) and the chimney width to use as a guide. Secure the cricket in place with roof cement on all flanges, and drive rubber-gasket nails through the base flanges and into the roof deck. Bend counterflashing back down, and fill the gap with roof cement.

Stagger shingles for effective protection against leaks. If the tab slots are aligned in successive rows, water forms channels, increasing erosion of the mineral surface of the shingles. Creating a 6" offset between rows of shingles (with the 3-tab shingles shown above) ensures that the tab slots do not align.

Shingling a Roof

If you have the time and the energy, shingling a roof can be a straightforward project that is well within the abilities of most do-it-yourselfers. The most common type of shingles, asphalt 3-tabs, are self-sealing and self-aligning. Installation is mainly a matter of persistence and making sure you follow your lines and shingle pattern.

Because most roof flashing is interwoven into the shingle pattern, be prepared to install all your flashing (pages 28 to 31) during the shingling process. Install building paper and drip edge before you start (pages 26 to 27).

Everything You Need:

Tools: tape measure, roofing hammer, pneumatic nailer (optional), pry bar, roofing knife, chalk line, carpenter's square, straightedge, roof jacks and 2 × 10 lumber, aviator snips.

Materials: roofing nails, nailing cartridges (optional), roof cement, flashing, shingles.

How to Shingle a Roof with 3-tab Shingles

1 Snap a chalk line onto the first course of ice guard or building paper, 11½" up from the eave edge, to create an alignment line for the starter course of shingles. This will result in a ½" shingle overhang past the edge of the roof for standard 12" shingles. TIP: Do not use red chalk—it will stain roofing materials.

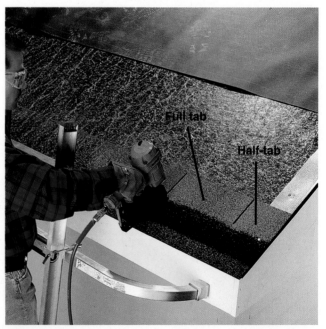

2 Install the starter row: Trim off one-half (6") of an end tab on one shingle. Position the shingle so the tabs are aligned with the chalk line, with the half-tab flush against the rake edge. Drive ⅞" roofing nails near each end, and about 1" down from each slot between tabs. Butt a full shingle next to the trimmed shingle, and nail in place. Fill out the row, trimming the last shingle flush with the opposite rake edge.

3 Apply the first full course of shingles over the starter course, with the tabs pointing down. Begin at the rake edge where you began the starter row. The first shingle should overhang the rake edge by ⅜", and overhang the eave edge by ½". Make sure the tops of the shingles are flush with the tops of the shingles in the starter course, following the chalk line.

4 Snap a chalk line from the eave edge to the ridge to create a vertical shingle alignment line. Choose an area with no obstructions, as close as possible to the center of the roof. The chalk line should pass through a slot or a shingle edge on the first full shingle course. Use a carpenter's square to establish a line that is perpendicular with the eave edge.

NOTE: Do not nail shingles in spots where they do not overlap another shingle. Upper-course shingles must be pulled back to fill in lower courses.

Vertical line

18"
12"
6"
5" reveal

5 Use the vertical line to establish a shingle pattern with slots that are offset by 6" in succeeding courses. Tack down a shingle 6" to one side of the vertical line to start the second course. The bottom of the shingle should be 5" above the bottoms of the first-course shingles. Tack down shingles for the third and fourth courses 12" and 18" away from the vertical line. Start the fifth course against the vertical line.

6 Fill in shingles in the second through fifth courses, working upward from the second course and maintaining a consistent 5" reveal. Slide lower-course shingles under any upper-course shingles left partially nailed, then nail down. NOTE: Install roof jacks, if needed, after filling out the fifth course (page 21).

(continued next page)

TIP: Check the alignment of your shingles after each four-course cycle. In several spots on the top course, measure from the bottom edges of the shingles to the nearest building-paper line. If you discover any misalignment, distribute adjustments over the next few rows until the misalignment is corrected.

7 When you reach obstructions, like dormers, shingle a full course above them so you can retain your shingle offset pattern. On the unshingled side of the obstruction, snap another vertical reference line, using the shingles above the obstruction as a guide.

8 Shingle upward from the eave on the other side of the obstruction, using the vertical line as a reference for reestablishing your shingle slot offset pattern. Fill out the shingle courses past the rake edges of the roof, then trim off the excess (step 15).

9 Trim off some of the excess shingle material at the the "V"s in valley flashing wherever two roof decks join (these edges will be trimmed back farther at a slight taper after both roof decks are shingled). Do not cut into flashing.

10 Install shingles on adjoining roof decks, starting at the bottom edge, using the same offset alignment pattern used on the other roof decks (steps 1 to 6). Install shingles until courses overlap the center of the valley flashing at the joint between roof decks. Trim shingles at both sides of the valley when finished (step 14).

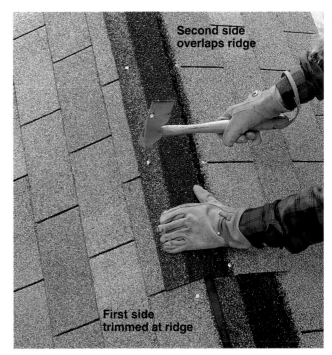

Second side overlaps ridge

First side trimmed at ridge

11 When you reach a hip (any peak where two sections of roof meet) or the ridge (the hip at the top of your roof), shingle up the first roof side until the tops of the uppermost reveal areas are within 5" of the hip or ridge. Trim the excess off along the joint at the peak. Overlap the ridge or hip (no more than 5") with the top shingle course on the other side of the peak.

TIP: Cut three 12"-square ridge/hip caps from each 3-tab shingle. With the top surface facing down, cut the shingles at the tab lines, trimming off both top corners of the 12"-square cap shingles (trimming corners prevents unsightly overlaps in the reveal area).

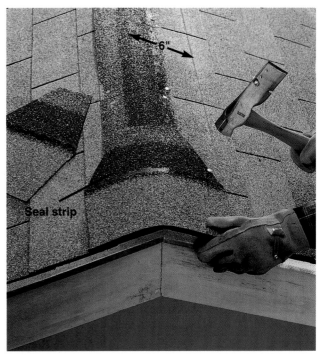

6"

Seal strip

12 Snap a chalk line 6" down from the hip or ridge on one side, parallel to the peak. Begin attaching cap shingles at one end, aligned with the chalk line. Drive two 1¼" roofing nails per cap, about 1" in from each edge, just below the seal strip.

(continued next page)

How to Shingle a Roof with 3-tab Shingles (continued)

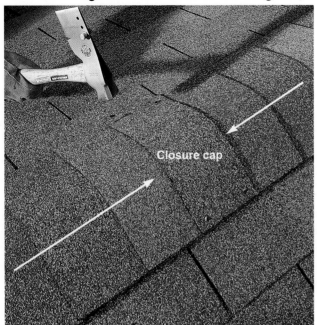

Closure cap

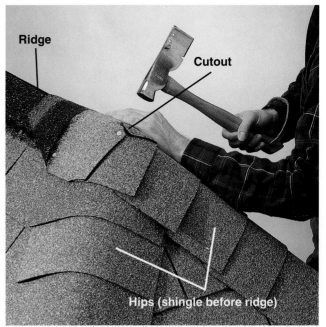

Ridge

Cutout

Hips (shingle before ridge)

13 Install cap shingles halfway along the ridge or hip, creating a 5" reveal for each cap. Follow the chalk line. Then, starting at the opposite end of the ridge or hip, install caps over the other half of the roof. Cut a 5"-wide section from the reveal area of a shingle tab, and use it as a "closure cap" to cover the joint where the caps meet.

VARIATION: Wherever roof hips join with roof ridges, shingle to the top of each hip with cap shingles. Then, make a cutout in the center of a ridge cap, set the cap at the end of the ridge, and bend the corners so they fit over the hips. Secure each corner with a roofing nail, and cover nail heads with roof cement.

14 After all shingles are installed, trim the shingles at the valleys to create a gap that is 3" wide at the ridge, and widens at a rate of ⅛" per foot toward the eave edge. Use a utility knife with a roofing blade and a straightedge (be careful not to cut through the valley flashing). At the valleys, seal the undersides and edges of the shingles with roof cement. Also cover any exposed nail heads with roof cement.

15 Trim the shingles at the rake edges of the roof, using a utility knife with a hooked roofing blade (or you can use aviator snips). Leave a ⅜" overhang. Always use a straightedge to ensure a straight cut.

Variation: How to Shingle Over an Old Roof

1 Cut tabs off shingles and install the remaining strips over the reveal area of the old first course, creating a flat surface for the starter row of new shingles. Use 1¼"-long roofing nails. NOTE: Read the section on shingling a roof (pages 32 to 36) before you start.

2 Trim the tops off shingles for the first course. The shingles should be sized to butt against the bottom edges of the old third course, overhanging the roof edge by ½". Install the shingles so the tab slots do not align with the slots in the old shingles.

3 Using the old shingles to direct your layout, begin installing the new shingles. Maintain a consistent tab slot offset (page 33, step 5). Shingle up toward the roof ridge, stopping before the final course. Install flashing as you proceed (see next step). If valley flashing is in good condition, it does not need to be replaced.

4 Replace old flashing during the shingling sequence (pages 28 to 31). A "roofover" is flashed using the same techniques and materials used for shingling over building paper, except you need to trim or fill in shingles around vent pipes and roof vents to create a flat surface for the base flange of the flashing pieces.

5 Tear off old hip and ridge caps before shingling the hips and ridge. Replace old hip and ridge caps after all other shingling is completed (pages 35 to 36).

Repairing Shingles & Flashing

Roof materials that have sustained minimal damage or wear can be patched or repaired, avoiding the expense and work of replacing some or all of your roof. Plastic roof cement and rolled, galvanized flashing can be used for many simple roof repairs. TIP: Heat brittle shingles with a hair dryer to make them easier to handle.

Everything You Need:

Tools: hammer, pry bar, caulk gun, utility knife with roofing blade, pointed trowel, hacksaw, rubber mallet.

Materials: flashing, roof coverings, roof cement, roofing nails, 30# building paper.

Use plastic roof cement for a variety of minor repairs, like reattaching loose shingles. Wipe down the building paper and the underside of the shingle, let them dry, then apply roof cement liberally. Seat the shingle in the bed of cement.

Tips for Making Repairs with Roof Cement

Tack down buckled shingles by cleaning out below the buckled area, filling with roof cement, and pressing the shingle in the cement. Also use roof cement to patch cracks or other minor shingle problems. See page 18 for more information on buckled shingles.

Seal gaps around flashing by cleaning out the old roof cement and replacing it with fresh roof cement. Joints around flashing are common places for roof leaks to occur.

How to Replace a Section of Shingles

1 Pull out damaged shingles in the repair area, beginning with the uppermost shingle. Be careful not to damage any surrounding shingles that are in good condition.

2 Remove old nails with a flat pry bar. Exposed nail heads will cause punctures in new shingles. Important: remove nails in the shingle above the repair area to enable you to nail new shingles. Cover holes or damage in the building paper with roof cement.

3 Install replacement shingles, beginning with the lowest shingle in the repair area. Nail above tab slots with ⅞" or 1" roofing nails. TIP: Asphalt shingles can be aged to match surrounding shingles by wiping the surface with mineral spirits. Rinse before installing.

Seal line

4 Install all but the top shingle with nails (pages 32 to 33), then apply roof cement to the underside of the top shingle, above the seal line.

5 Slip last shingle into place under the overlapping shingle. Press the shingle into the roof cement. Lift up the shingle above the repair area, and nail the top replacement shingle in place.

How to Replace Wood Shakes & Shingles

1 Split the damaged shake (shown) or shingle, using a hammer and chisel, and remove the pieces. Pry out (cut nails in overlapping shingles with a hacksaw blade slipped underneath the shingle).

2 Gently pry up shingles or shakes above the repair area. Cut new shingles or shakes for the lowest course, leaving about ⅜" for expansion. Nail replacement pieces in place with ring-shank siding nails. Fill in all but the top course.

3 Cut pieces for the top course, slip them beneath the overlapping shingles, and face-nail them in place near the tops. Cover all exposed nail heads with roof cement, then wipe off the excess. TIP: Apply wood sealer or stain to "weather" new material.

How to Patch Damaged Flashing

1 Measure the damaged area and cut a patch from flashing material of the same type as the original flashing. The patch should be wide enough to slip under the shingles at each side of the repair area. Break the seal between the valley flashing and the shingles around the damaged area. Scrub the damaged flashing with a wire brush, and wipe clean.

2 Apply a bed of roof cement to the back side of the patch, then slip the patch under the shingles on each side of the repair area. Press the patch securely into the roof cement. Add cement at the seams and the shingle joints. Feather out the cement to prevent damming of water. NOTE: New flashing material will blend in quickly as natural forces cause the metal to discolor.

How to Replace Step Flashing

1 Carefully bend up counterflashing (or pry out siding) covering the damaged step flashing. Cut roof cement seals, and pull back the shingles covering damaged step flashing. Remove the damaged piece or pieces of flashing with a flat pry bar.

2 Cut new step flashing from the same type of metal (aluminum or galvanized steel) used for the old flashing. Apply roof cement to the flashing on both unexposed sides. Slip the flashing into place, making sure it is overlapped by the flashing above it, and that it overlaps the flashing below. It also must overlap the shingle beneath it. Drive one roofing nail through the flashing at the bottom corner, and into the roof deck. Do not fasten to the roof element.

3 Bend counterflashing back down, and seal the counterflashing seams with roof cement.

4 Lift shingles next to the repair area, then apply fresh roof cement to the undersides and to any exposed nail heads. Press the shingles down against the flashing to create a bond. Do not nail flashing when attaching shingles.

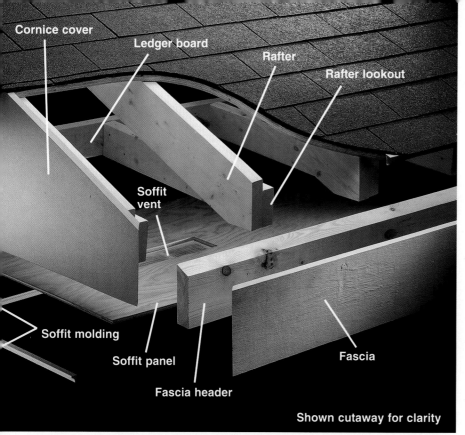

Cornice cover
Ledger board
Rafter
Rafter lookout
Soffit vent
Soffit molding
Soffit panel
Fascia header
Fascia

Shown cutaway for clarity

Fascia and soffits close off the eave area beneath the roof overhang. The fascia covers the ends of rafters and rafter lookouts, and provides a surface for attaching gutters. Soffits are protective panels that span the area between the fascia and the side of the house. Some soffit types attach to fascia headers (above), while others fit into grooves cut in the back sides of the fascia. Soffit moldings and ledger boards are used to mount the soffit panels at the side of the house.

Option: Install a New Soffit System

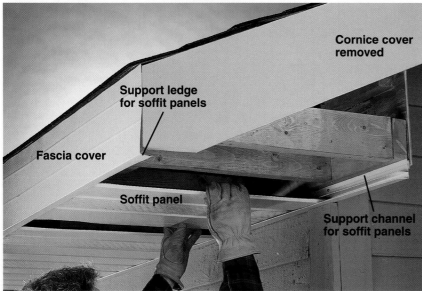

Cornice cover removed
Support ledge for soffit panels
Fascia cover
Soffit panel
Support channel for soffit panels

Install a new soffit system if your old system has failed, or pests have infested the open eave areas of your roof overhang. A complete soffit system consists of fabricated fascia covers, soffit panels (nonventilated or ventilated), and support channels that hold the panels at the sides of your house. Most soffit systems sold at building centers are made of aluminum or vinyl. Follow manufacturer's instructions for installation.

Repairing Fascia & Soffits

Fascia and soffits add a finished look to your roof, and promote a healthy roof system. A well-ventilated fascia/soffit system prevents moisture from building up under the roof and in the attic. A secure system keeps pests, like birds and bats, from nesting in the eaves.

Usually fashioned from dimension lumber, fascia is attached to rafters or rafter lookouts (photo, left). While enhancing the appearance of your home, it also provides a stable surface for hanging gutters.

Repairing fascia and soffits is easy. Most problems can be corrected by cutting out the damaged material and replacing it with new material. Joints between fascia boards are lock-nailed (page 43), so you should remove whole sections of fascia to make accurate miter cuts for patches. Soffits usually are not removed for repairs (pages 44 to 45).

Fasten soffit and fascia material with ring-shank siding nails, or use galvanized deck screws. Nails are easier to work with in some cases, but screws provide more holding power.

Whenever repairing soffits, take a moment to inspect vents in the system for sufficient air flow (pages 52 to 54).

Everything You Need:

Tools: circular saw, jig saw, drill, hammer, flat pry bar, chisel, nail set.

Materials: replacement materials to match damaged parts, nailing strips, nails or screws, caulk, primer, paint.

How to Repair Fascia

1 Remove gutters, shingle moldings, and any other material that prevents removal of the damaged section of fascia.

2 Using a flat pry bar, remove the entire damaged section all the way to the next fascia board. Remove old nails.

3 Cut off the damaged portion of the fascia board. Set your circular saw to make a miter cut, and saw at a rafter location (look for nail holes to identify the rafter location).

4 Attach the undamaged original fascia, using 2" galvanized deck screws driven into rafter lookouts or rafters. Cut a patch board with a matching miter at the mating end to replace the damaged section.

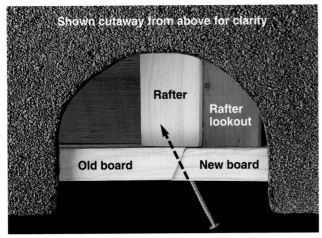

5 Attach the patch board. Drill pilot holes, then drive nails at an angle through the mitered ends of both boards, creating a lock-nail joint.

6 Reattach the shingle moldings and trim, using 4d galvanized finish nails. Set nail heads. Prime and paint the patch to match the fascia. Reattach gutters.

How to Repair Wood-panel Soffits

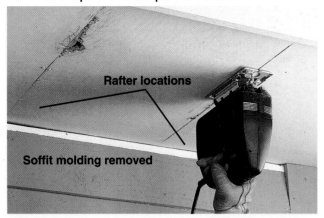

1 Remove the support molding in the damaged area. Drill entry holes for a jig saw blade, then cut out the soffit area that contains the damage. Saw as close as possible to the rafter or lookout locations. If necessary, finish the cut with a wood chisel.

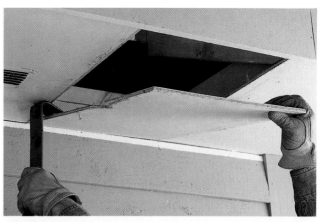

2 Remove the damaged soffit section, using a flat pry bar if necessary. Cut nailing strips and attach them to the rafters or rafter lookouts at the edges of the opening (step 2, next page).

3 Measure the opening, and cut a soffit patch to fit from material similar to the original soffit. Allow ⅛" on all sides for expansion gaps. Make cutouts for existing soffit vents, or for new soffit vents (page 54).

4 Install the soffit patch by driving 1¼" galvanized deck screws into the nailing strips or rafter lookouts. NOTE: If you do not plan to paint the entire soffit, you may find it easier to prime and paint the patch before installing.

5 Reattach the soffit molding, using 4d galvanized casing nails.

6 Fill nail holes, screw holes, and gaps with siliconized acrylic caulk. Smooth out the caulk so it is even with the surface. Prime and paint to match. Install vent covers if needed.

How to Repair Tongue-and-groove Soffits

1 Remove the soffit molding. Locate the closest rafter lookout on each side of the damaged area. Drill an entry hole for a jig saw, then cut out the damaged section, cutting as close as possible to the lookout. Pry the damaged section loose. NOTE: To remove width-run tongue-and-groove soffits (inset), cut across the ends of boards near the fascia.

2 Cut a nailing strip from 2 × 2 stock, and fasten it to the rafter lookout at each end of the opening, using 2½" galvanized deck screws.

3 Cut patch boards to fit, using similar tongue-and-groove stock. Fasten all but the final board by driving 8d galvanized casing nails through pilot holes in the tongues of the boards, and into the nailing strips. Set the nail heads so the next patch board will fit cleanly over the tongue of the first board.

Top lip removed

4 Trim the top lip from grooved edge of the final board in the installation sequence. Position the board in the opening. Face-nail ring-shank siding nails through the last patch board and into the nailing strips. Prime and paint to match. Attach soffit vents covers, if needed.

Rehanging sagging gutters is a common gutter repair. Before rehanging, snap a chalk line that follows the original slope (usually about ¼" per 10 ft. toward the downspouts). To rehang gutters, remove the hangers in and near the sag, and lift the gutter until it is flush with the chalk line. Reattach the hangers (replace them if they are in bad condition), shifting their location slightly so you do not use the original holes. If the hangers are more than 24" apart, or there is no hanger within 12" of a seam, add hangers.

Repairing Gutters

Gutters channel water away from your home. Clogged, sagging, or leaky gutters can cause extensive damage to your siding, foundation, or landscaping. They can also result in water buildup in your basement.

Evaluate the type and extent of gutter damage to select the appropriate repair method. Often, small leaks and minor damage can be repaired with easy-to-use gutter repair products (next page). Moderate damage to metal gutters can be patched with flashing (pages 48 to 49). TIP: Prevent corrosion by patching with the same type of metal (usually aluminum or galvanized steel) from which the gutters are made.

If the damaged area is more than 2 ft. in length, replace the entire section of gutter with new material (page 49). To locate a section of gutter for making repairs, trace the profile of your existing gutters and take it with you to the building center. Also measure the gutter at the widest

point—if your gutters are more than 15 years old, they likely are a little larger than gutters made today. Check salvage yards, or have a new section custom-bent by a metal fabricator.

If your gutters are beyond repair, remove and replace them. Snap-together vinyl gutters (pages 50 to 51) are popular with today's homeowners.

If your house has wood gutters, patch small holes or rot with epoxy wood filler (pages 14 to 15). If damage is more serious, contact a professional carpenter.

Everything You Need:

Tools: utility knife, stiff-bristled or wire brush, abrasive pads, aviator snips, screwdriver, pry bar, hammer, portable drill, hacksaw, caulk gun.

Materials: gutter caulk, gutter patching kit, roof cement, flashing material, gutter fasteners.

Gutter Accessories

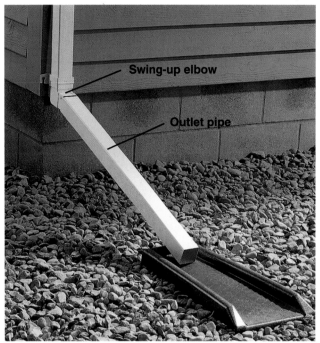

Install gutter guards to prevent buildup of debris in the gutters. Buy guards that match the size and style of your gutters. Common mesh gutter guards (above) usually require mesh supports. **Downspout strainers** at the outlets prevent debris from collecting in downspouts, where clogs are hard to remove.

Install a swing-up elbow at the end of each drain pipe, allowing the outlet pipe to be lifted out of the way when you are working near the foundation of the house. Add a **splash block** to prevent erosion and help direct runoff away from your house.

Tips for Using Gutter Repair Products

Use gutter caulk to fill small holes and seal minor leaks. Usually made with a butyl-rubber base, gutter caulk flexes without losing its seal. It is also resistant to the elements.

Use gutter patching kits for temporary repairs to gutters with minor damage. Read the manufacturer's recommendations and directions before purchasing and using repair products. For long-term repairs, see pages 48 to 49.

How to Patch Metal Gutters

1 Clean the area around the damage with a wire brush. Scrub with an abrasive pad to loosen residue, then clean the area with water.

2 Apply a ⅛"-thick layer of roof cement evenly over the damage, and spread it a few inches beyond the damaged area on all sides.

3 Cut and bend a patch from flashing made from the same material as the gutters. Bed the patch in the roof cement, and feather the cement so it will not cause significant damming.

How to Repair Leaky Joints

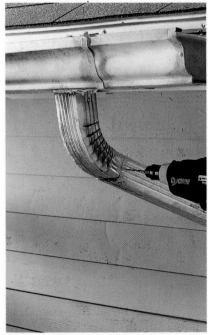

1 Drill out rivets or remove metal screws that secure the joint. Disassemble the damaged joint. With downspouts, you may need to disassemble the entire downspout to get the bad joint apart.

2 Scrub both parts of the joint, using a stiff-bristled brush (for vinyl gutters) or a wire brush (for metal gutters). Clean the damaged area with water.

3 When dry, apply caulk to the joining parts, then reassemble the joint. Reinforce with new fasteners, adding new hangers if the originals need replacing.

How to Replace a Section of Metal Gutter

1 Remove gutter hangers in or near the damaged area. TIP: Insert wood spacers in the gutter, near each hanger, before putting pressure on the gutter. This helps protect gutters from damage.

2 Slip spacers between the gutter and fascia, near each end of the damaged area, so you do not damage the roof when cutting the gutter. Cut out the damaged area with a hacksaw.

3 Cut a gutter patch from material similar in type, size, and profile to the original gutter. The patch should be at least 4" longer than the damaged section.

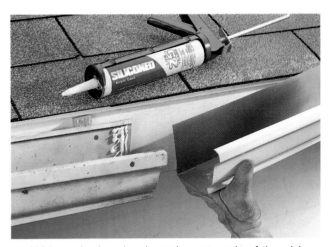

4 With a wire brush, clean the cut ends of the old gutter. Caulk the ends, then center the gutter patch over the damage and press into caulk.

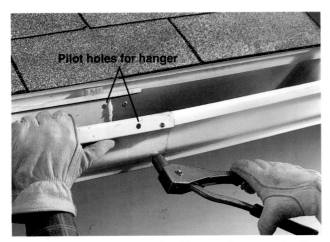

5 Secure the gutter patch with pop rivets or sheet metal screws. Use at least three or four fasteners at each joint. On the inside surfaces of the gutter, caulk over the heads of the fasteners.

6 Install the gutter hangers, using new hangers if necessary (do not use old holes). Prime and paint the patch to match.

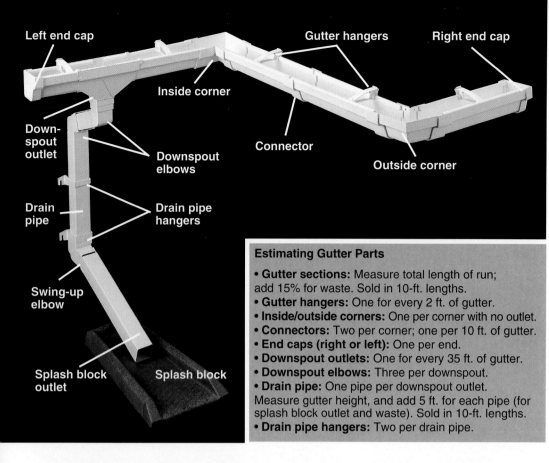

Left end cap

Gutter hangers

Right end cap

Inside corner

Downspout outlet

Downspout elbows

Connector

Outside corner

Drain pipe

Drain pipe hangers

Swing-up elbow

Splash block outlet

Splash block

Vinyl snap-together gutter systems are becoming increasingly popular. Easy to install and relatively inexpensive, they will not rot or deteriorate. The slip joints allow for expansion and contraction. Before you purchase and install new gutters, make a cost estimate. Do not base the estimate solely on the advertised prices of gutter and drain pipe sections, which make up only a fraction of the final cost of the system.

Estimating Gutter Parts

• **Gutter sections:** Measure total length of run; add 15% for waste. Sold in 10-ft. lengths.
• **Gutter hangers:** One for every 2 ft. of gutter.
• **Inside/outside corners:** One per corner with no outlet.
• **Connectors:** Two per corner; one per 10 ft. of gutter.
• **End caps (right or left):** One per end.
• **Downspout outlets:** One for every 35 ft. of gutter.
• **Downspout elbows:** Three per downspout.
• **Drain pipe:** One pipe per downspout outlet. Measure gutter height, and add 5 ft. for each pipe (for splash block outlet and waste). Sold in 10-ft. lengths.
• **Drain pipe hangers:** Two per drain pipe.

Installing a Vinyl Snap-together Gutter System

Installing a new gutter system is a manageable task for most homeowners. Snap-together gutter systems are designed for ease of installation, requiring no fasteners other than the screws used to attach the gutter hangers to the fascia.

Draw a detailed plan before purchasing and installing new gutters. See the chart above for tips on planning and estimating. If you have never installed gutters before, you may find it

helpful to test-fit all the pieces on the ground, following your plan, before you begin the actual installation.

Everything You Need:

Tools: chalk line, tape measure, drill, hacksaw.

Materials: 1¼" deck screws, gutters and drain pipes, connectors, and fittings (see above).

How to Install Vinyl Snap-together Gutters

Slope= ¼" per 10 ft.

Fascia

1 Mark a point at the high end of each gutter run, 1" down from the top of the fascia. Snap chalk lines that slope ¼" per 10 ft. toward downspout outlets. For runs longer than 35 ft., mark a slope from a high point in the center toward downspouts at each end.

2 Install downspout outlets near the ends of gutter runs (at least one outlet for every 35 ft. of run). The tops of the outlets should be flush with the slope line, and they should align with end caps on the corners of your house, where drain pipes will be attached.

3 Attach hangers or support clips for hangers (some models) for a complete run, following the manufacturer's directions. Attach to fascia at 24" intervals, using 1¼" deck screws. Follow the slope line.

4 Attach outside and inside corners at corner locations that do not have downspout outlets or end caps. Follow the slope line.

5 Cut gutter sections to fit between outlets and corners, using a hacksaw. Attach end cap, and connect gutter section to outlet. Cut gutter sections to fit between outlets, allowing for expansion gaps. Test-fit.

6 On the ground, join the gutter sections together using connectors. Attach gutter hangers to the gutters (for models with support clips mounted on fascia). Hang the gutters, connecting to the outlets.

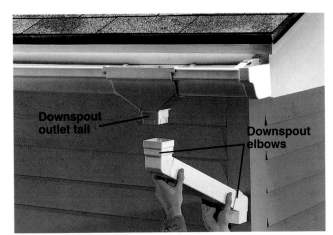

7 Cut a section of drain pipe to fit between two downspout elbows—one elbow should fit over the tail of the downspout outlet, the other fits against the wall. Assemble the parts, slip the top elbow onto the outlet, and secure the other with a drain pipe hanger.

8 Cut a piece of drain pipe to fit between the elbow at the top of the wall (step 7) and the end of the drain pipe run (at least 12" above the ground). Attach an elbow to the end of the pipe, and secure to the wall with a drain-pipe hanger. Add accessories (page 47).

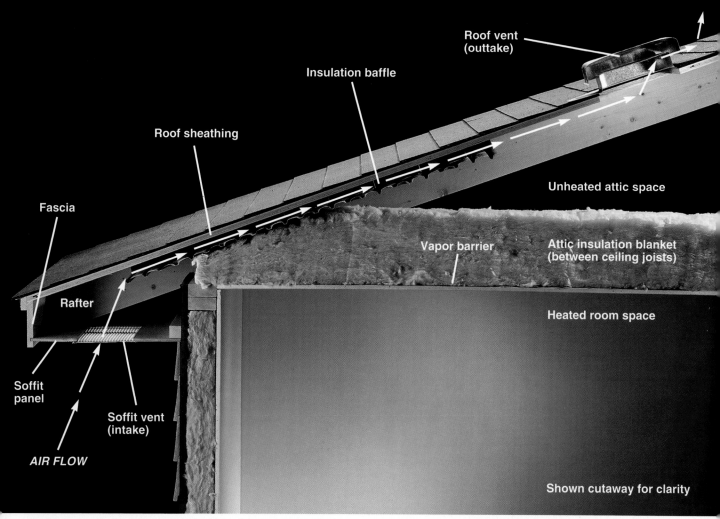

Roof vent (outtake)

Insulation baffle

Roof sheathing

Unheated attic space

Fascia

Vapor barrier

Attic insulation blanket (between ceiling joists)

Heated room space

Rafter

Soffit panel

Soffit vent (intake)

AIR FLOW

Shown cutaway for clarity

Sufficient air flow prevents heat build-up in your attic, and helps protect your roof from damage caused by condensation or ice. A typical ventilation system has vents in the soffits to admit fresh air, which flows upward beneath the roof sheathing and exits through roof vents.

Installing Soffit & Roof Vents

An effective ventilation system equalizes temperatures on both sides of the roof, which helps keep your house cooler in the summer and prevents ice dams at the roof eaves in cold climates.

The best strategy for increasing roof ventilation is to add more of the existing types of vents. If you are reroofing, however, consider replacing all your roof vents with a continuous ridge vent (next page). You can increase outtake ventilation by replacing a standard roof vent with an electric turbine vent, but an easier solution is simply to add another standard roof vent.

Everything You Need:

Tools: hammer, caulk gun, drill, jig saw, tape measure, pry bar, pencil, utility knife.

Materials: roofing nails, roof cement, stainless steel screws, soffit vent covers, roof vents.

Determining Ventilation Requirements

Measure attic floor space to determine how much ventilation you need. You should have one square foot each of intake and outtake vents for every 150 square feet of unheated attic floor space.

Common Intake Ventilation Types

Soffit vents can be added to increase air flow into attics on houses with a closed soffit system. Make sure there is an unobstructed air passage from the soffit area to the roof before you install new soffit vents (page 54).

Continuous soffit vents provide even air flow into attics. They are usually installed during new construction, but they can be added as retrofits to unvented soffit panels.

Common Outtake Ventilation Types

Roof vents can be added near the ridge line when you need to increase outtake ventilation. Fixed roof vents are easy to install (page 55) and have no mechanical parts that can break down.

Gable and dormer vents generally are installed instead of soffit vents—especially on houses with open eaves. Covers come in a variety of styles and colors to match siding.

Continuous ridge vents create an even outtake air flow because they span the entire ridge. Barely noticeable from the ground, ridge vents are usually installed during roof construction, but can be added during a reroofing project.

How to Install a Soffit Vent

1 Examine the eave area from inside your attic to make sure there is nothing obstructing air flow from the soffits. If insulation is blocking the air passage, install insulation baffles (page 108).

2 Draw a cutout for the soffit vent cover on the soffit panel. Center the vents between the fascia and the side of the house. The cover outline should be ¼" smaller on all sides than the soffit vent cover.

3 Drill a starter hole, then cut the vent openings with a jig saw.

4 Caulk the flanges of the vent cover with siliconized acrylic caulk. Screw the vent cover to the soffit.
TIP: For visual effect, install all of the new vent covers with the louvers pointing in the same direction.

How to Install a Roof Vent

Ridge pole

1 Mark the location for the roof vent by driving a nail through the roof sheathing. The nail should be centered between rafters, and between 16" and 24" from the ridge pole.

Shingles removed

2 Locate the marker nail, and center the vent cover over the nail. Outline the base flange of the vent cover on the shingles, then remove shingles in an area 2" inside the outline. Mark the roof-vent hole using the marker nail as a centerpoint. Cut the hole with a reciprocating saw or jig saw.

3 Apply roof cement to the underside of the base flange. Set the vent cover in position, slipping the base flange under the shingles, centered over the vent-hole cutout.

4 Secure the roof vent to the sheathing with rubber gasket nails on all sides of the flange. Tack down any loose shingles. Do not nail through the base flange when attaching shingles.

Repairing Siding & Trim

The materials we use to cover the outside of our home have changed dramatically in recent years. But even with the advances, one fact has not changed: all types of siding and trim need some maintenance or repair from time to time.

Traditional wood lap siding can be repaired quite easily if, like most homeowners, you have some experience repairing wood. Epoxy-based wood fillers and long-lasting caulk products make the task easy. And replacing missing or damaged wood shakes is one of the simplest exterior home repairs.

Repairing masonry siding, like brick veneer and stucco, no longer requires a skilled mason. It can be repaired with a few easy-to-apply products (pages 65, 150 to 151).

But perhaps the most significant change in siding maintenance and repair has come with "low-maintenance" or "no-maintenance" manufactured siding products. Once viewed as gimmicks sold door-to-door, aluminum, vinyl, and steel siding products have become commonplace in the past few decades. When they first hit the market, repair of these products was the exclusive terrain of licensed contractors, but now most building centers carry a range of replacement parts and repair products. As a result, simple repairs can be done by do-it-yourselfers.

However, there are still some repairs you should think twice about attempting. If the damage to your siding (whatever its type) is so extensive that it appears to require full replacement, you should consider hiring a contractor. Few home improvement projects are more time-consuming than applying new siding—especially if you are installing products that you have never worked with before. There is a lot of competition among siding contractors, and you can usually come up with a range of bids. But do not look only at the cost—whenever hiring a contractor, check references and licenses, and get estimates in writing.

This section shows:
• Evaluating Siding & Trim (pages 58 to 59)
• Repairing Siding (pages 60 to 67)
  Repairing Wood Siding (pages 62 to 64)
  Repairing Stucco (page 65)
  Repairing Vinyl & Metal Siding (pages 66 to 67)
• Repairing Trim (pages 68 to 69)

Evaluating Siding & Trim

The first step in inspecting and evaluating siding and trim is to identify with certainty the material types (photos, below). Once you have determined the material, take a closer look for any potential problems (photos, right). If your siding is under warranty, read the warranty document closely before attempting any repairs. Making repairs yourself could invalidate the product warranty.

CAUTION: many homes built in the 1940s and 1950s were covered with milled asbestos shingles. Asbestos shingles have the same general appearance as fiberglass, usually with a rough, heavily ridged surface. Because asbestos is classified as a hazardous material, its handling and disposal are regulated. Contact your local waste management department before handling asbestos shingles.

Siding damage, like the water damage caused by the leaky hose bib shown above, often requires replacement of the affected siding pieces. Identify and eliminate the cause of the damage before you replace or repair siding and trim (pages 8 and 131).

Common Siding Types

Wood lap siding is usually made of cedar, pine, or hardwood particle board. Beveled boards are the most common. Wood lap is very easy to repair (pages 62 to 64).

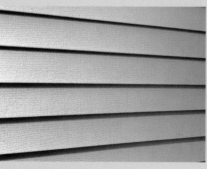

Vinyl siding is virtually maintenance-free. Minor repairs can be made with caulk or patches (pages 66 to 67). Contact a siding contractor before making major repairs.

Metal siding: Minor patching and caulking can take care of many common problems affecting metal siding (pages 66 to 67). Contact a contractor for major repairs.

Shakes & shingles: Shakes (shown) and shingles usually are cut from cedar or pine. Basic repairs are easy on wood shakes and shingles (pages 64).

Brick: Small problems in brick veneer can be repaired with quick-fix concrete repair products (pages 150 to 151). For major repairs, contact an expert.

Stucco: Minor repairs, like filling thin cracks or small holes, can be made with concrete or stucco repair products (page 65). For wide cracks and major damage, call an expert.

Common Siding Problems

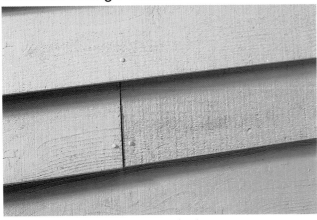

Separated joints can occur in any type of lap siding, but are most common in wood lap. Gaps between ⅛" and ¼" thick can be filled with caulk. Gaps ⅜" or wider could mean that your house has a serious moisture or shifting problem: consult a professional inspector.

Buckling occurs most frequently in manufactured siding, when expansion gaps are too small at the points where the siding fits into trim and channels. If possible, move the channel slightly. If not, remove the siding (page 64), trim length slightly, then reinstall.

Minor surface damage to metal siding is best left alone in most cases—unless damage has penetrated the surface (page 61). With metal products, cosmetic surface repairs often look worse than the damage.

Missing siding, like the cedar shakes that have been blown from the wall shown above, should be replaced immediately (pages 60 to 67). Check the surrounding siding to make sure it is secure.

Tips for Inspecting Trim

Check window and door trim for rot, especially on horizontal surfaces and at joints. Try to make repairs without removal (pages 68 to 69).

Remove decorative trim, like the gingerbread trim above, if you suspect damage. Inspecting and repairing it is easier in a workshop.

Evaluate broad trim pieces, like the end cap trim shown above, and make repairs using the same techniques used for siding.

Stagger vertical seams to make your siding repairs less visible. Where possible, drive fasteners into framing members. Siding sheathing or underlayment, if present at all, is often made from soft composite boards that do not hold fasteners well.

Repairing Siding

Repairing common types of siding damage is a manageable project for most homeowners. Small to medium-size holes, cracks, and rotted areas can be repaired by filling with repair products or by replacing the damaged sections with matching siding.

As with most exterior repair projects, the primary goal of siding repair is to make sure minor or moderate damage does not turn into major damage. But a well-executed siding repair also will add to the visual appeal of your home, especially if the repair materials are a good blend with the surrounding siding.

If you cannot find new matching siding for patches at building centers, check with salvage yards or siding contractors. When repairing aluminum or vinyl siding, contact the manufacturer or the contractor who installed the siding to help you locate matching materials and parts. If you cannot find an exact match, remove original siding from a less-visible area of your house, like the back of the garage, and use it as the patch. Patch the gap in the less-visible area with the near-match siding.

Tips for Repairing Siding

Create an expansion gap at each seam between wood siding panels or lap siding. Use a nail as a guide to set the width of the gaps (for most siding types, ⅛" is an adequate expansion gap). Fill the gaps with exterior caulk (pages 14 to 15).

Repair small holes with the appropriate filler product. For *wood siding* (top), fill holes with epoxy wood filler. Paint to match. For *metal and vinyl siding* (bottom), use tinted exterior caulk to fill holes. If you cannot find a matching color at a building center, check with the siding manufacturer.

Number the siding pieces as you remove them from your house to simplify reinstallation. You can also use the boards as templates for replacement pieces.

Patch damaged building paper before attaching new siding. When applying a patch, loosen the building paper above the damaged area, and slip the top of the patch underneath. Attach the patch with staples. Use roof cement to patch small holes or tears.

Insert spacers between the siding and sheathing above the work area while you make repairs to lap siding. This creates better access, simplifying the repair process. **CAUTION:** Metal siding will buckle if bent too far.

Repairing Wood Siding

Wood siding is the easiest type to repair. Fixing cracks, replacing damaged sections, and filling holes requires only basic carpentry tools and inexpensive materials. Only use wood and wood repair products that are suitable for exterior use.

Everything You Need:

Tools: hammer, chisel, trowel, screwdrivers, hacksaw, circular saw, keyhole saw, pry bar, nail set, electronic stud finder, paint brush.

Materials: epoxy wood filler, epoxy glue, nails and deck screws, siliconized acrylic caulk, plastic roof cement, building paper, lumber crayon, sheathing, wood preservative, primer, paint or stain.

Repair cracks and splits in wood siding with epoxy wood glue. Apply the glue to both sides of the crack, then press the board back together. For best results, position a board under the bottom edge of the damaged board and press it upward to create even pressure until the glue sets (if working near the ground, wedge a 2 × 4 under the board). After the glue sets, drive galvanized deck screws on each side of the crack to reinforce the repair. Clean off excess glue, and touch up the repair with paint.

How to Replace a Section of Wood Lap Siding

1 Using an electronic stud finder, locate and mark framing members around the repair area. Mark cutout lines over the centers of framing members on each side of the repair area. Stagger the lines so vertical joints do not align (page 60, top photo).

2 Insert spacers beneath the board above the repair area. Make entry cuts at the tops of the cutting lines with a keyhole saw, then saw through the boards with the saw in an upright position. Remove the boards. Pry out any nails, or cut off the heads with a hacksaw blade.

TIP: Trace cutouts for any fixtures, wall openings, or other obstructions using the old siding board as a template. Also mark the end lines if the template board is still intact (make sure there will be a ⅛"-wide expansion gap at each end). Make the cutouts with a jig saw or coping saw, then cut to length.

3 Measure and cut all replacement siding boards to fit, leaving an expansion gap of ⅛" at each end. Apply wood preservative/sealer or primer to the ends and back sides of the boards before installation.

4 Nail the new boards in place with ring-shank siding nails, starting with the lowest board. Drive nails into framing members using the original nailing pattern (normally at 12" intervals through the bottom of the exposed board and the top of the board below).

5 Fill expansion joints with caulk (use paintable caulk for painted wood, and tinted caulk for stained wood), then prime and paint or stain the replacement siding boards to match the surrounding boards.

How to Replace Wood Shakes & Shingles

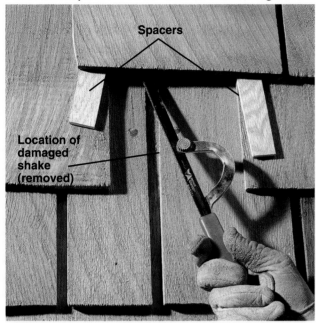

Spacers

Location of damaged shake (removed)

1 Split damaged shakes or shingles with a hammer and chisel, and remove. Insert wood spacers under the shakes or shingles above the repair area, then slip a hacksaw blade under the top board to cut off any nail heads remaining from the old shake or shingle.

2 Cut replacement shakes or shingles to fit, leaving a ⅛" to ¼"-wide expansion gap at each side. Coat all sides and edges with wood preservative. Slip the patch pieces under the siding above the repair area (start on lower courses if patching a large area). Attach with ring-shank siding nails, driven near the top of the exposed area on the patch. Cover nail heads with caulk, wiping off any excess. Remove spacers.

How to Replace Siding Panels

1 Remove battens or trim securing the damaged panels. Pry out the entire damaged panel. Inspect the building paper under the panels, and patch as needed.

2 Cut replacement panels from matching material, allowing a ⅛"-wide expansion gap at side seams. Prime or seal the edges and back side of the replacement boards before installing.

3 Nail the new boards in place with ring-shank siding nails. Caulk all seams and expansion joints, then replace battens and other trim. Prime and paint or stain to match.

Repairing Stucco

Stucco is a very long-lasting siding product. But, over time, it will crumble and crack. Making permanent repairs to extensively damaged stucco walls is a job for a professional, but most homeowners can make smaller repairs with simple repair products.

Use premixed stucco repair compound for patching small holes or crumbled areas in stucco walls. Use concrete or stucco repair caulk for filling small cracks. For other masonry repair products, see pages 150 to 151.

Everything You Need:

Tools: wire brush, putty knife, whisk broom.

Materials: concrete caulk, stucco repair compound.

Fill thin cracks with concrete caulk. Overfill the crack with caulk, and feather until it is flush with the stucco. Allow the caulk to set, then paint to match. Concrete caulk stays semiflexible, preventing further cracking.

How to Patch Stucco Walls

1 Clean out loose material from the repair area with a wire brush. Remove rust from any exposed metal lath, and treat the lath with metal primer.

2 Trowel premixed stucco repair compound into the repair area with a putty knife or pointed trowel, overfilling slightly (read manufacturer's directions—drying times and application techniques vary).

3 Smooth out the repair with a putty knife or trowel, feathering it even with the surrounding surface. Use a whisk broom to create a matching texture on the stucco patch. Touch up with masonry paint to blend in the repair.

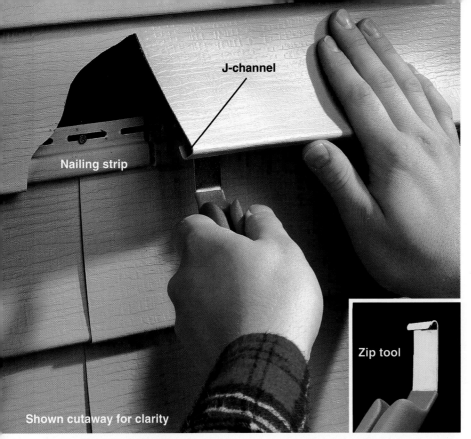

J-channel

Nailing strip

Zip tool

Shown cutaway for clarity

Repairing Vinyl & Metal Siding

Vinyl and metal siding are popular with homeowners because they are inexpensive and can last for decades. However, the materials are susceptible to dents, holes, and fading. Minor repairs can be done by do-it-yourselfers. For major work, and to help find replacement parts, contact the contractor that installed your siding, or the siding manufacturer.

Everything You Need:

Tools: hammer, tape measure, drill, aviator snips, utility knife, caulk gun, zip tool, pry bar, straightedge.

Materials: nails; caulk; roof cement or exterior panel adhesive; end caps, trim, and siding panels as needed.

Vinyl and metal siding pieces have a locking J-channel that fits over the bottom of the nailing strip on the piece below. Use a zip tool (inset) to separate siding panels. Insert the zip tool at the overlapping seam nearest the repair area. Slide the zip tool over the J-channel, pulling outward slightly, to unlock the joint from the siding below.

How to Patch Vinyl Siding

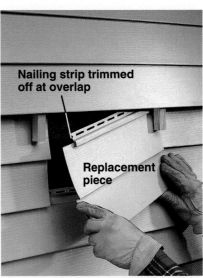

Nailing strip trimmed off at overlap

Replacement piece

Top of nailing strip on replacement piece

Nail location

1 Unlock interlocking joints with the siding above the repair area, using a zip tool (photo above). Start unlocking at the seam nearest the damaged area. Install spacers below the piece above, then pry out fasteners in the top piece of damaged siding, using a flat pry bar.

2 Cut out the damaged area, using a straightedge and utility knife; then cut a replacement piece 4" longer than the open area, from similar siding material. Before installing, trim off 2" of the nailing strip from each end of the replacement piece in the overlap area. Slide the piece into position.

3 Attach the replacement siding. Because the nailing strip is difficult to reach with a hammer, press ring-shank siding nails in the slots of the nailing strip, then position the end of a flat pry bar over each nail head. Drive nails by rapping on the neck of the pry bar with a hammer. Slip the J-channel over the nailing strip (photo, top left).

How to Patch Metal Siding

1 Cut out the damaged area with aviator snips and a hacksaw blade. Leave some exposed surface area at the top of the uppermost piece you remove to serve as a bonding surface for the top siding patch.

2 Cut a patch or patches 4" wider than the repair area, using matching material. Cut off the nailing strip from the top of the top patch piece. Make sure all edges are smooth, deburring with metal sandpaper if necessary.

3 Nail lower patches in place by driving ring-shank siding nails through the nailing strips, starting with the lowest piece. To install the top piece, apply roof cement to the back, and press the patch in place, slipping the J-shaped locking channel over the nailing strip below. Caulk the seams.

How to Replace Aluminum End Caps

1 Remove the damaged end cap. If end caps cannot be removed easily, pry the bottom loose, then cut along the top with a hacksaw.

2 Attach replacement end caps, starting at the bottom. Drive ring-shank siding nails through the nailing tabs, and into framing members.

3 Trim the nailing tabs off the top replacement cap, then apply roof cement to the back. Snap the cap over the J-shaped locking channels of the siding courses. Press the top cap securely in place.

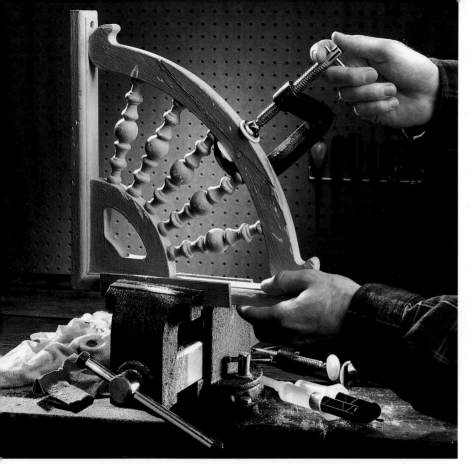

Repairing Trim

Some exterior trim serves as decoration, like gingerbread and ornate cornice moldings. Other trim, like brick molding and end caps, works with siding to seal your house from the elements. Damaged brick molding and corner boards should be patched with stock material similar to the original. If you cannot find matching replacement parts for decorative trim, check salvage shops or contact a custom millworker.

Everything You Need:

Tools: hammer, chisel, circular saw, nail set, putty knife, utility knife, paint brush, flat pry bar.

Materials: epoxy wood filler, epoxy glue, caulk, nails and screws, sandpaper, paint, building paper, drip edge.

Repair delicate or ornamental trim molding in your workshop. You will get better results more easily than if you try repairing it while it is still attached. Leave decorative trim in place if you must remove siding to gain access to it.

Tips for Repairing & Replacing Trim

Reattach loose trim with new ring-shank siding nails driven near old nail locations. Fill old nail holes with paintable caulk, and touch up caulk and new nail heads with paint to match the surrounding surface.

Repair decorative trim molding with epoxy glue or wood filler (page 14). For major repairs, make your own replacement parts, or take the trim to a custom millwork shop.

How to Replace Brick Molding

1 Pry off old brick molding around windows and doors using a flat pry bar. Remove any old drip edge. Inspect and repair the building paper (page 61). NOTE: Drip edge that fits above doors and windows is a different product from roof-style drip edge (page 23).

2 Hold a replacement piece of brick molding, slightly longer than the original piece, across the opening. Mark cutting lines to fit the opening. Cut the replacement brick molding at the cutting lines, matching any miter cuts.

3 Cut a 3"-wide piece of flashing to fit between the jambs, then bend it in half lengthwise to form the new drip edge (preformed drip edge is available). Slip it between the siding and the building paper, above the door or window. Do not nail the drip edge in place.

4 Test-fit the replacement piece of brick molding, then apply exterior-grade panel adhesive to the back side. Follow the manufacturer's directions for allowing the adhesive to set.

5 Nail the brick molding to the door header with 10d galvanized casing nails. Lock-nail the miter joints, and set all nail heads. Seal joints, and cover nail holes with caulk. Prime and paint when the caulk dries.

Good repairs restore both the appearance and the function to failing concrete structures and surfaces. Careful work can produce a well-blended, successful repair, like the one shown above.

Repairing Concrete

Concrete is one of the most durable building materials, but it still requires repair and maintenance occasionally. Freezing and thawing, improper finishing techniques, a poor subbase, or lack of reinforcement all can cause problems with concrete. By addressing problems as soon as you discover them, you can prevent further damage that may be difficult or impossible to fix.

Concrete repair projects fall into a wide range, from simple cleaning and sealing, to completely removing and replacing sections of concrete. Filling cracks and repairing surface damage are the most common concrete repairs.

Another effective repair is resurfacing—covering an old concrete surface with fresh concrete. It is a good option for spalling, crazing, or popouts—minor problems that affect the appearance more than the structure. These problems often result from inadequate preparation or incorrect finishing techniques.

As with any kind of repair, the success of the project depends largely on good preparation

and use of the best repair products for the job. Specially formulated repair products are manufactured for just about every type of concrete repair. Be sure to read the product-use information before purchasing any products; some products need to be used in combination with others.

A good repair can outlast the rest of the structure in some cases, but if structural damage has occurred, repairing the concrete is only a temporary solution. By using the right products and techniques, however, you can make cosmetic repairs that improve the appearance of the surface and keep damage from worsening.

This section shows:

- Identifying Concrete Problems (pages 72 to 73)
- Filling Cracks (pages 76 to 77)
- Patching Holes (pages 78 to 79)
- Resurfacing Concrete (pages 80 to 81)
- Repairing Steps (pages 82 to 83)
- Miscellaneous Concrete Repairs (pages 84 to 85)
- Sealing & Maintaining Concrete (pages 86 to 87)

Concrete Repair Products

Concrete repair products include: vinyl-reinforced concrete patch (A) for filling holes, popouts, and larger cracks; hydraulic cement (B) for repairing foundations, retaining walls, and other damp areas; quick-setting cement (C) for repairing vertical surfaces and unusual shapes; anchoring cement (D) for setting hardware in concrete; concrete sealing products (E); concrete recoating product (F) for creating a fresh surface on old concrete; masonry paint (G); joint-filler caulk (H); pour-in crack sealer (I); concrete cleaner (J); concrete fortifier (K) to strengthen concrete; bonding adhesive (L) to prepare the repair area; and concrete sand mix (M) for general repairs and resurfacing.

Tips for Disguising Repairs

Add concrete pigment to concrete patching compound to create a color that matches the original concrete. Experiment with different mixtures of pigment and repair cement until you find the right mixture. Samples should be dry to show the actual colors.

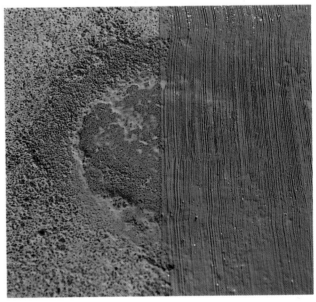

Use masonry paint to cover concrete repairs. Paint can be used on vertical or horizontal surfaces, but high-traffic surfaces will require more frequent touchup or repainting.

Widespread cracks all the way through the surface, and other forms of substantial damage, are very difficult to repair effectively. If the damage to the concrete is extensive, remove and replace the structure.

Identifying Concrete Problems

There are two general types of concrete failure: structural failure usually resulting from outside forces like freezing water; and surface damage most often caused by improper finishing techniques or concrete mixtures that do not have the right ratio of water to cement. Surface problems sometimes can be treated with permanent repairs if the correct products and techniques are used. More significant damage can be patched for cosmetic purposes and to resist further damage, but the structure may eventually need to be replaced.

Common Concrete Problems

Sunken concrete is usually caused by erosion of the subbase. Some structures, like sidewalks, can be raised to repair the subbase, then relaid. A more common (and more reliable) solution is to hire a mudjacking contractor to raise the surface by injecting fresh concrete below the surface.

Frost heave is common in colder climates. Frozen ground forces concrete slabs upward, and sections of the slab can pop up. The best solution is to break off and remove the affected section or sections, repair the subbase, and pour new sections that are set off by isolation joints.

Moisture buildup occurs in concrete structures, like foundations and retaining walls, that are in constant ground contact. To identify the moisture source, tape a piece of foil to the wall. If moisture collects on the outer surface of the foil, the source likely is condensation, which can be corrected by installing a dehumidifier. If moisture is not visible on the foil, it is likely seeping through the wall. Consult a professional mason.

Staining can ruin the appearance of a concrete surface or structure. Stains can be removed with commercial-grade concrete cleaner or a variety of other chemicals (page 100). For protection against staining, seal masonry surfaces with clear sealant (pages 86 to 87).

Isolated cracks occur on many concrete building projects. Fill small cracks with concrete caulk or crack-filler (page 76), and patch large cracks with vinyl-reinforced patching material (pages 77 to 79).

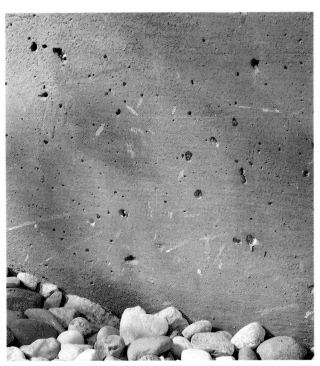

Popouts can be caused by freezing moisture or stress, but very often they occur because the concrete surface was improperly floated or cured, causing the aggregate near the surface of the concrete to loosen. A few scattered popouts do not require attention, but if they are very large or widespread, you can repair them as you would repair holes (pages 78 to 79).

Spalling is surface deterioration of concrete. Spalling is caused by overfloating, which draws too much water to the surface, causing it to weaken and peel off over time. When spalling occurs, it is usually widespread, and the structure may need resurfacing.

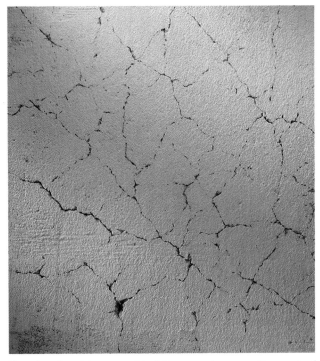

Crazing is widespread hairline cracks, usually caused by overfloating. Clean and seal the surface to help prevent further crazing. For a long-term solution, resurface (pages 80 to 81).

Safety & Tools

Concrete products must be handled with care and disposed of properly. Concrete and mortar mix contains silica, which is a hazardous substance in large quantities, so always wear a particle mask when handling or mixing dry mix, and read and follow the manufacturer's safety precautions. Because these products will irritate your skin, always wear gloves when handling masonry products.

Concrete products are heavy, and lifting and moving them is hard work. For added protection, and when lifting, always wear a lifting belt and take care to use safe lifting techniques.

Most waste-removal companies will not accept masonry waste in regular curbside pickup. You will need to make special pickup arrangements—call your waste-disposal company for information. Where possible, use old masonry waste as clean fill for new projects.

Wear protective equipment, including a particle mask, eyewear, and gloves when mixing masonry products. Concrete products can be health hazards, and they will irritate skin upon contact. Also wear a mask to protect yourself from dust when cutting concrete, brick, or block.

Tip for Working Safely

Tip for Disposal

Wear a lifting belt to help prevent lower back strain when stacking brick and block, and when hand-mixing concrete products. Always lift with your legs, not your back, and keep the items being lifted as close to your body as you can.

Save old broken-up concrete for use as clean fill in building and landscaping projects.

Masonry Tools

Specialty masonry tools for handling concrete, mortar, and masonry units include: a magnesium float (A) for setting exposed aggregate or smoothing concrete to a hard, glossy finish; a wood float (B) for smoothing most exterior masonry surfaces; a groover (C) for cutting control joints into concrete; a stair edger (D) for creating smooth, even noses on steps; an edger (E) for rounding off edges in concrete at form locations; a jointer (F) for smoothing mortar joints; a power drill (G) with masonry bits (H) and a masonry grinding disc (I); a masonry-cutting blade for a circular saw (J); a masonry trowel (K) for building with brick or block; a pointing trowel (L) for repairing masonry; a brickset (M) for cutting brick and block; a cold chisel (N) for chipping out and breaking apart masonry; a bricklayer's hammer (O) with a claw for cutting masonry units; a maul (P) for driving form stakes and for use with a cold chisel and brickset.

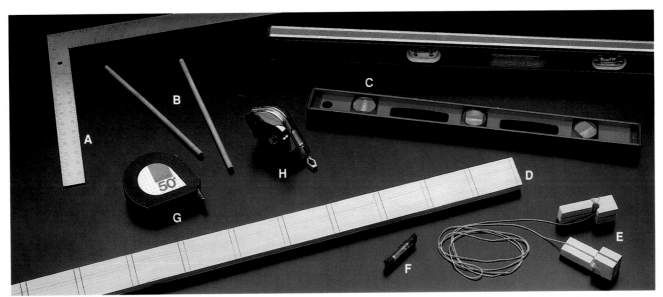

Alignment and measuring tools for masonry projects include: a carpenter's framing square (A) for setting project outlines; ⅜" dowels (B) for use as spacers between dry-laid masonry units; levels (C) for setting forms and for use when stacking masonry units; a story pole (D) that can be calibrated for stacking masonry units; line blocks and mason's string (E) for stacking brick and block; a line level (F) for making layouts and setting slope; a tape measure (G); and a chalk-line (H) for marking layout lines on footing or slabs.

Use concrete repair caulk for quick-fix repairs to minor cracks. Although convenient, repair caulk should be viewed only as a short-term solution to improve appearance and help prevent further damage from water penetration.

Filling Cracks

The materials and methods you will use for repairing cracks in concrete depend on the location and size of the crack. For small cracks (less than ¼" wide), you can use gray-tinted concrete caulk for a quick fix. For more permanent solutions, use pourable crack filler or fortified patching cements (page 71). The patching cements are polymer compounds that significantly increase the bonding properties of cement, and also allow some flexibility. For larger cracks on flat surfaces, use fortified sand-mix concrete, and for cracks on vertical surfaces, use hydraulic or quick-setting cement. Thorough preparation of the cracked surface is essential for creating a good bonding surface.

Everything You Need:

Tools: wire brush, drill with wire wheel attachment, cold chisel, hand maul, paint brush, trowel.

Materials: vinyl-reinforced patching compound, concrete caulk, sand-mix concrete.

Tips for Preparing Cracked Concrete for Repair

Clean loose material from the crack using a wire brush, or a portable drill with a wire wheel attachment. Loose material or debris left in the crack will result in a poor bond and an ineffective repair.

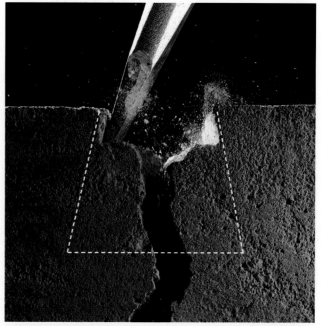

Chisel out the crack to create a backward-angled cut (wider at the base than at the surface), using a cold chisel and hammer. The angled cutout shape prevents the repair material from pushing out of the crack.

How to Repair Small Cracks

1 Prepare the crack for the repair (see previous page), then apply a thin layer of bonding adhesive to the entire repair area, using a paint brush. The bonding adhesive helps keep the repair material from loosening or popping out of the crack.

2 Mix vinyl-reinforced patching compound, and trowel it into the crack. "Feather" the repair with a trowel, so it is even with the surrounding surface.

Variations for Repairing Large Cracks

Sand

Shown cutaway

Horizontal surfaces: Prepare the crack (previous page), then pour sand into the crack to within ½" of the surface. Prepare sand-mix concrete, adding a concrete fortifier, then trowel the mixture into the crack. Feather until even with the surface, using a trowel.

Vertical surfaces: Prepare the crack (previous page). Mix vinyl-reinforced concrete or hydraulic cement, then trowel a ¼" to ½"-thick layer into the crack until the crack is slightly overfilled, and let it dry. Feather even with surface. If the crack is deep (over ½" thick), trowel in consecutive layers, ¼" to ½" thick. Pack in the concrete, let it dry, then pack in more.

Patching Holes

Large and small holes are treated differently when repairing concrete. The best product for filling in smaller holes (less than ½" deep) is vinyl-reinforced concrete patcher. Because reinforced repair products should be applied only in layers that are ½" thick or less, use sand-mix concrete with an acrylic or latex fortifier for holes more than ½" deep. Sand mix can be applied in layers up to 2" thick.

Patches in concrete will be more effective if you create clean, backward-angled cuts (page 76) around the damaged area, so the repair will bond. For extensive cutting of concrete, use power tools with masonry blades.

Use hydraulic cement or quick-setting cement for repairing holes and chip-outs in vertical surfaces. Because they set up in just a few minutes, these products can be shaped to fill in holes without the need for forms. If the structure is exposed constantly to moisture, use hydraulic cement.

Everything You Need:
Tools: trowels, drill with masonry-grinding disc, circular saw with masonry-cutting blade, cold chisel, hand maul, paint brush, screed board, wood float.
Materials: gloves, hydraulic cement, concrete bonding adhesive, vinyl-reinforced patching compound, sand-mix, concrete fortifier.

Tips for Preparing Holes for Repair

For small holes: Cut out around the damaged area with a masonry-grinding disc mounted on a portable drill (or use a hammer and cold chisel). The cuts should bevel about 15° away from the center of the damaged area. Chisel out any loose concrete within the repair area. Always wear gloves and eye protection.

For large holes: Mark straight cutting lines around the damaged area, then cut with a circular saw equipped with a masonry-cutting blade. Set the foot of the saw so the cut bevels away from the damage at a 15° angle. Chisel out any remaining concrete within the repair area. TIP: Set the foot of the saw on a thin board to protect it from the concrete.

How to Repair Small Holes

1 Prepare the damaged area (previous page), then apply a thin layer of bonding adhesive to help create a sturdy bond with the patch.

2 Fill the damaged area with vinyl-reinforced patching compound, applied in layers no thicker than ¼ to ½". Add layers of patching mixture until the hole is filled just above surface level, waiting about 30 minutes between coats. Feather out the surface and let the repair cure.

How to Repair Large Holes

1 Prepare the damaged area (previous page). Mix sand-mix concrete with concrete acrylic fortifier, and fill the damaged area slightly above the surrounding surface.

2 Smooth out and feather the repair with a wood float until the repair is level with the surrounding surface. Re-create any surface finish, like brooming used on the original surface.

Resurfacing Concrete

Concrete that has surface damage but is still structurally sound can be preserved by resurfacing—applying a thin layer of new concrete over the old surface. If the old surface has deep cracks or extensive damage, resurfacing will only solve the problem temporarily. A bonding agent helps the new surface adhere to the old. Because new concrete will bond to the old surface better if it is packed down, use a dry, stiff concrete mixture that can be compacted with a shovel.

Everything You Need:

Tools: wood float, spade, broom, circular saw, hand maul, drill, paint brush, paint roller and tray, wheelbarrow, screed board, groover, edger.

Materials: gloves, 2 × 4s, sand-mix concrete, bonding adhesive, plastic sheets.

New surface

Old surface

Shown cutaway

Resurface concrete that has extensive surface damage, like spalling or popouts. Because the new surface is so thin (1" to 2"), use sand-mix concrete. If you are having ready-mix concrete delivered by a concrete contractor, make sure they do not use aggregate larger than ½" in the mixture.

How to Resurface Concrete

1 Clean the surface thoroughly. If the surface is flaking or spalled, scrape it with a spade to dislodge as much loose concrete as you can, then sweep the surface clean.

2 Dig a 6"-wide trench around the surface on all sides to create room for 2 × 4 forms.

3 Stake 2 × 4 forms flush against the sides of the concrete slabs, 1" to 2" above the surface (make sure height is even). Drive stakes every 3 ft., and at every joint in forms. Mark control joint locations onto the outside of the forms, directly above existing control joints. Coat the inside edges of the forms with vegetable oil.

4 Apply a thin layer of bonding adhesive over the entire surface. Follow the directions on the bonding adhesive product carefully. Instructions for similar products may differ slightly.

5 Mix concrete using sand-mix concrete. Make the mixture slightly stiffer (drier) than normal concrete. Spread the concrete, then press down on the concrete with a shovel or 2 × 4 to pack the mixture into the forms. Smooth the surface with a screed board.

6 Float the concrete with a wood float, then tool with an edger. Recreate any surface treatment, like brooming, used on the original surface. Cut control joints in the original locations. Let the surface cure for one week, covered with plastic.

Repairing Steps

Steps require more maintenance and repair than other concrete structures around the house because heavy use makes them more susceptible to damage. Horizontal surfaces on steps can be treated using the same products and techniques used on other masonry surfaces (pages 76 to 79). For vertical surfaces, use quick-setting cement, and shape it to fit.

Everything You Need:

Tools: trowel, wire brush, paint brush, circular saw with masonry-cutting blade, chisel, wood float, edger.

Materials: gloves, bonding adhesive, vinyl-reinforced patching compound, quick-setting cement.

Wear and tear on the surfaces of steps, like the deep popout being repaired above, can be fixed successfully to renew your steps. If you have extensive damage, you may need to replace the steps.

How to Replace a Step Corner

1 Retrieve the broken corner, then clean it and the mating surface using a wire brush. Apply bonding adhesive to both surfaces. If you do not have the broken piece, you can rebuild the corner with quick-setting cement (see next page).

2 Spread a heavy layer of fortified patching cement on the surfaces to be joined, then press the broken piece into position. Lean a heavy brick or block against the repair until the patching compound sets (about 30 minutes). Protect the repair from traffic for at least one week.

How to Patch Step Treads

1 Make a cut in the stair tread just outside the damaged area, using a circular saw with a masonry-cutting blade. Make the cut so it angles toward the back of the step (page 76). Make a similar cut on the riser below the damaged area, then chisel out the area in between the two cuts.

2 Cut a form board the same height as the step riser. Press it against the riser of the damaged step, and brace it in position with heavy blocks. Make sure the top of the form is flush with the top of the step tread.

3 Apply bonding adhesive to the repair area, then press a stiff mixture of quick-setting cement into the damaged area with a trowel.

4 Smooth off the concrete with a wood float, and let it set for a few minutes. Round over the front edge of the nose with an edger. Use a trowel to slice off the sides of the patch, so it is flush with the side of the steps. Wait at least overnight before allowing traffic on the step.

Reset loose masonry anchors by removing the anchors, filling the old holes with anchoring cement (anchoring cement expands as it dries, creating a tighter repair), then pressing the anchors into the fresh cement. Make sure the anchors are not disturbed while the cement sets up (usually about 1 hour).

Miscellaneous Concrete Repairs

There are plenty of concrete problems you may encounter around your house that are not specifically addressed in many repair manuals. These miscellaneous repairs include such tasks as resetting posts and post anchors, patching contoured objects that have been damaged, and repairing masonry veneer around the foundation of your house. You can adapt basic concrete-repair techniques to make just about any type of concrete repair.

Everything You Need:

Tools: putty knife, trowel, hand maul, chisel, wire brush, aviator snips, drill, whisk broom.

Materials: gloves, anchoring cement, quick-setting cement, emery paper, wire lath, concrete acrylic fortifier, sand-mix.

How to Repair Shaped Concrete

1 Scrape all loose material and debris from the damaged area, then wipe down with water. Mix and trowel quick-setting cement into the area. Work quickly—you only have a few minutes before the concrete sets up.

2 Use the trowel or putty knives to mold the concrete to follow the form of the object being repaired. Smooth the concrete as soon as it sets up. Buff with emery paper to smooth out any ridges after the repair dries.

How to Repair Masonry Veneer

1 Chip off the crumbled, loose, or deteriorated veneer from the wall, using a cold chisel and hammer. Chisel away damaged veneer until you have only good, solid surface remaining. Use care to avoid damaging the wall behind the veneer. Clean the repair area with a wire brush.

2 Clean up any metal lath in the repair area if it is in good condition. If not, cut it out with aviator snips. Add new lath where needed, using masonry anchors to hold it to the wall.

3 Mix fortified sand-mix concrete (or specialty concrete blends for wall repair), and trowel it over the lath until it is even with the surrounding surfaces.

4 Recreate the surface texture to match the surrounding area. For our project, we used a stiff-bristled brush to stipple the surface. OPTION: To blend in the repair, add pigment to the sand mixture or paint the repair area after it dries (page 71).

Use waterproof concrete paint to paint concrete surfaces. Concrete paint is formulated to resist chalking and efflorescence. It is sold in several stock colors, or you can have custom colors mixed from a tint base.

Sealing & Maintaining Concrete

Protect concrete that is exposed to heavy traffic or constant moisture by sealing it with a clear concrete sealer. In addition to sealer, there are other special-purpose products designed for concrete surfaces. Specially formulated concrete paints, for example, help keep minerals in the concrete from leeching through paint and hardening into a white, dusty film (called efflorescence).

Regular cleaning is an important element of concrete maintenance to prevent deterioration from oils and deicing salts. Use concrete cleaner products for scheduled cleanings, and special solutions (page 100) for specific types of stains.

Everything You Need:

Tools: paint brush, paint roller and tray, dust brush and pan, caulk gun, paint pad.

Materials: masonry paint, paint thinner, repair caulk, sealer, concrete recoating product.

Tips for Cleaning & Maintaining Concrete

Clean oil stains by dampening sawdust with paint thinner, then applying the sawdust over the stain. The paint thinner will break apart the stain, allowing the oil to be absorbed by the sawdust. Wipe up with a broom when finished, and reapply as necessary.

Fill control joints in sidewalks, driveways and other concrete surfaces with concrete repair caulk. The caulk fills the joint, preventing water from accumulating and causing damage to the concrete.

Exposed-aggregate sealer is specially formulated to keep aggregate from loosening. It should be applied about 3 weeks after the concrete surface is poured. To apply, wash the surface thoroughly and allow it to dry. Pour some sealer into a roller tray. Make a puddle of sealer in the corner and spread it out evenly with a paint roller and extension pole.

Clear concrete sealer helps create a water-resistant seal on the surface. The more popular concrete sealing products today are acrylic based and do not attract dirt. Some types of sealer, like the product shown (right), also help the concrete cure evenly.

Masonry recoating products are applied like paint, but they look like fresh concrete when they dry. They are used frequently to improve the appearance of walls, although they generally have little value as waterproofing agents.

Choose the best materials and techniques for repairing problems with brick and block structures. A simple chip or popout, like the one shown above, can be fixed easily by packing the damaged area with latex-fortified mortar. More extensive problems require more complicated solutions.

Repairing Brick & Block Structures

Brick, block, and mortar are very durable building materials. But when they are combined in a permanent structure, stress and the forces of nature can lead to damage that requires attention. Common examples of brick and block structural problems include walls with failing mortar joints, cracked or crumbling bricks or blocks, and worn or discolored surfaces.

Many common brick and block problems can be corrected with simple repairs. These require just a few basic masonry tools (see opposite page) and a minimal investment of time and money. The completed repair job will result in a dramatic improvement in the appearance and strength of the structure. With regular maintenance and cleaning, the repaired structure will provide many years of productive use.

Brick and block are used frequently in the construction of foundation walls, retaining walls, and other load-bearing structures. Some simple repairs, like filling cracks, can be done with a low level of risk. But always get a professional evaluation from a masonry contractor before you attempt to make any major repairs to structures of this type.

This section shows:
- Identifying Brick & Block Problems (pages 90 to 91)
- Repairing Brick & Block Walls (pages 92 to 97)
- Repairing & Replacing Chimney Caps (pages 98 to 99)
- Cleaning & Painting Brick & Block (pages 100 to 101)

Tools for Repairing Brick & Block Structures

Basic tools for repairing brick and block include: a masonry chisel (A) for cutting new brick or block; a cold chisel (B) for breaking up and repairing masonry structures; a raking tool (C) for cleaning mortar out of joints; a mason's trowel (D) for applying mortar to con- crete block; a pointing trowel (E) for applying mortar to brick or block, and for smoothing out fresh repairs; a bricklayer's hammer (F); a ½"-wide (G) and ⅜"-wide (H) joint filler for packing fresh mortar into joints; and a V-shaped mortar tool (I) for finishing mortar joints.

Tips for Working with Mortar

Add concrete fortifier to mortar for making repairs. Fortifier, usually acrylic or latex based, increases overall strength and bondability of mortar.

Add mortar pigment to plain mortar so repairs blend in better. Compare pigment samples, available from concrete products suppliers, to match mortar colors.

Identifying Brick & Block Problems

Inspect damaged brick and block structures closely before you begin any repair work. Accurately identifying the nature and cause of the damage is an important step before choosing the best solution for the problem.

Look for obvious clues, like overgrown tree roots, or damaged gutters that let water drain onto masonry surfaces. Also check the slope of the adjacent landscape; it may need to be regraded to direct water away from a brick or block wall (see *Landscape Construction & Design,* Black & Decker Home Improvement Library), or consult a landscape architect.

Repairs fail when the original source of the problem is not eliminated prior to making the repair. When a concrete patch separates, for example, it means that the opposing stresses causing the crack are still at work on the structure. Find and correct the cause (often a failing subbase or stress from water or freezing and thawing), then redo the repair.

Deteriorated mortar joints are common problems in brick and block structures—mortar is softer than most bricks or blocks, and is more prone to damage. Deterioration is not always visible, so probe surrounding joints with a screwdriver to see if they are sound. Tuckpoint deteriorated joints (page 93).

Major structural damage, like the damage to this brick porch, usually requires removal of the existing structure, making subbase improvements, and reconstruction of the structure. Projects of this nature should only be attempted by professional masons.

Damage to concrete blocks often results from repeated freezing and thawing of moisture trapped in the wall or in the blocks themselves. Instead of replacing the whole block, repair the damaged concrete block or blocks by chipping out the face of the block and replacing it with a concrete paver with the same dimensions as the face of the block (pages 96 to 97).

Spalling occurs when freezing water or other forces cause enough directional pressure to fracture a brick. The best solution is to replace the entire brick (pages 94 to 95) while eliminating the source of the pressure, if possible. Spalled blocks can be refaced (previous photo). TIP: Chip off a piece of the damaged brick to use as a color reference when looking for a replacement.

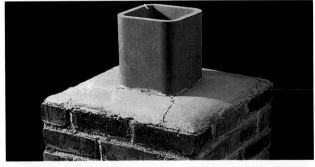

Damaged mortar caps on chimneys allow water into the flue area, where it can damage the chimney and even the roof or interior walls. Small-scale damage (top photo) can be patched with fire-rated silicone caulk. If damage is extensive (bottom photo), repair or replace the mortar cap (page 98).

Stains and discoloration can be caused by external sources or by minerals leeching to the surface from within the brick or block (called efflorescence). If the stain does not wash away easily with water, use a cleaning solution (page 100).

Before

After

Make timely repairs to brick and block structures. Tuckpointing deteriorated mortar joints (photos above) is a common repair that, like other types of repair, improves the appearance of the structure or surface and helps prevent further damage.

Repairing Brick & Block Walls

The most common brick and block wall repair is tuckpointing—the process of replacing failed mortar joints with fresh mortar. Tuckpointing is a highly useful repair technique for any homeowner. It can be used to repair walls, chimneys, brick veneer, or any other structure where the bricks or blocks are bonded with mortar.

Minor cosmetic repairs can be attempted on any type of wall, from free-standing garden walls to block foundations. Filling minor cracks with caulk or repair compound, and patching popouts or chips are good examples of minor repairs. Consult a professional before attempting any major repairs, like replacing brick or blocks, or rebuilding a structure—especially if you are dealing with a load-bearing structure.

Basement walls are a frequent trouble area for homeowners. Constant moisture and stress created by ground contact can cause leaks, bowing, and paint failure. Small leaks and

cracks can be patched with hydraulic cement. Masonry-based waterproofing products can be applied to give deteriorated walls a fresh appearance. Persistent moisture problems are most often caused by improper grading of soil around the foundation or a malfunctioning downspout and gutter system.

NOTE: The repairs shown in this section feature brick and block walls. The same techniques may be used for other brick and block structures.

Everything You Need:

Tools: raking tool, mortar hawk, joint filler, jointing tool, mason's trowel, mason's chisel, pointing trowel, drill with masonry disc and bit, stiff-bristled brush.

Materials: mortar, gravel, concrete fortifier, replacement bricks or blocks.

How to Tuckpoint Mortar Joints

Joint filler

Mortar hawk

1 Clean out loose or deteriorated mortar to a depth of ¼" to ¾". Use a mortar raking tool (top) first, then switch to a masonry chisel and a hammer (bottom) if the mortar is stubborn. Clear away all loose debris, and dampen the surface with water before applying fresh mortar.

2 Mix the mortar, adding concrete fortifier. Also add pigment if old mortar joints have discolored (page 89). Load mortar onto a mortar hawk, then push it into the horizontal joints with a joint filler. Apply mortar in ¼"-thick layers, and let each layer dry for 30 minutes before applying another. Fill the joints until the mortar is flush with the face of the brick or block.

3 Apply the first layer of mortar into the vertical joints by scooping mortar onto the back of a joint filler, and pressing it into the joint. Work from the top downward.

4 After the final layer of mortar is applied, smooth the joints with a jointing tool that matches the profile of the old mortar joints. Tool the horizontal joints first. Let the mortar dry until it is crumbly, then brush off the excess mortar with a stiff-bristled brush.

How to Replace a Damaged Brick

1 Score the damaged brick so it will break apart more easily for removal: use a power drill with a masonry-cutting disc to score lines along the surface of the brick and in the mortar joints surrounding the brick.

2 Use a mason's chisel and hammer to break apart the damaged brick along the scored lines. Rap sharply on the chisel with a hammer, being careful not to damage surrounding bricks. TIP: Save fragments to use as a color reference when you shop for replacement bricks.

3 Chisel out any remaining mortar in the cavity, then brush out debris with a stiff-bristled or wire brush to create a clean surface for the new mortar. Rinse the surface of the repair area with water.

4 Mix the mortar for the repair, adding concrete fortifier to the mixture, and pigment if needed to match old mortar (page 89). Use a pointing trowel to apply a 1"-thick layer of mortar at the bottom and sides of the cavity.

5 Dampen the replacement brick slightly, then apply mortar to the ends and top of the brick. Fit the brick into the cavity and rap it with the handle of the trowel until the face is flush with the surrounding bricks. If needed, press additional mortar into the joints with a pointing trowel.

6 Scrape away excess mortar with a masonry trowel, then smooth the joints with a jointing tool that matches the profile of the surrounding mortar joints. Let the mortar set until crumbly, then brush the joints to remove excess mortar.

Tips for Removing & Replacing Several Bricks

For walls with extensive damage, remove bricks from the top down, one row at a time, until the entire damaged area is removed. Replace bricks using the techniques shown above and in the section on building with brick and block. CAUTION: Do not dismantle load-bearing brick structures like foundation walls; consult a professional mason for these repairs.

For walls with internal damaged areas, remove only the damaged section, keeping the upper layers intact if they are in good condition. Do not remove more than four adjacent bricks in one area—if the damaged area is larger, it will require temporary support, which is a job for a professional mason.

How to Reface a Damaged Concrete Block

1 Drill several holes into the face of the deteriorated block at the cores (hollow spots) of the block, using a masonry bit. Wear protective eye covering when drilling or breaking apart concrete.

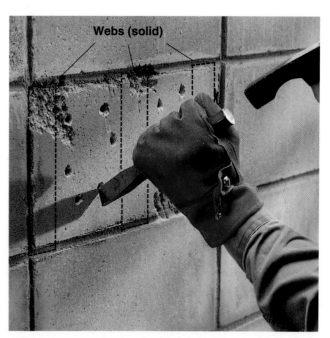

2 Using the holes as starting points, chip away the face of the block over the core areas with a cold chisel and hammer. Be careful to avoid damaging surrounding blocks. Try to leave the block face intact in front of the solid web areas.

3 Use a cold chisel to carefully chip out a 2"-deep recess in the web areas. Mark and score cutting lines 2" back from the block face, then chisel away the block in the recess area. Avoid deepening the recess more than 2" because the remaining web sections provide a bonding surface for the concrete paver that will be installed to replace the face of the concrete block.

4 Mix mortar (page 89), then apply a 1"-thick layer to the sides and bottom of the opening, to the webs, and to the top edge and web locations on the paver (use an 8 × 16" paver to fit standard blocks). Press the paver into the cavity, flush with the surrounding blocks. Add mortar to the joints if needed, and finish joints with a jointing tool. Prop a 2 × 4 against the paver until the mortar sets.

How to Reinforce a Section of Refaced Blocks

1 Reinforce repair areas with two or more adjacent block faces. Start by drilling a few holes in a small area over a core in the block located directly above the repair area. Chip out the block face between the holes with a cold chisel.

2 Prepare a thin mortar mix made from 1 part dry gravel and 2 parts dry mortar. Add water. The mixture should be thin enough to pour easily, but not soupy. NOTE: Gravel increases the strength of the mortar, as well as the yield from mixing.

3 Pour the mortar/gravel mixture into the hole above the repair area, using a piece of metal flashing as a funnel. Continue mixing and filling the hole until it will not accept any more mortar. The mortar will dry to form a reinforcing column that is bonded to the backs of the pavers used to reface the blocks.

4 Patch the hole above the repair area by using a pointing trowel to fill the hole with plain mortar mix. Smooth the surface with the pointing trowel, then finish the joint below the patch with a jointing tool.

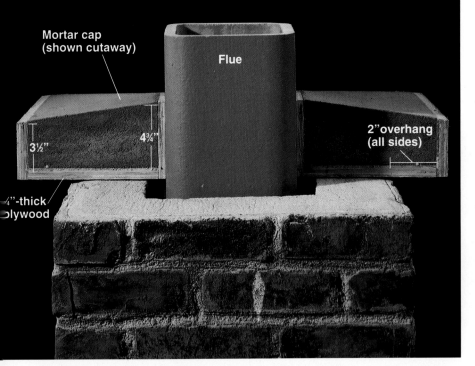

Mortar cap
(shown cutaway)

Flue

4¾"

3½"

2" overhang
(all sides)

¾"-thick
plywood

Build and install a "floating" chimney cap to put an end to annual treks up to the roof to fix a cracked mortar cap on your chimney. A floating chimney cap is cast in a form, using mortar or sand-mix concrete, then placed on the top of the chimney. It is not permanently bonded to the chimney or flue, so it can move independently as the chimney temperature changes.

Repairing & Replacing Chimney Caps

Chimney caps undergo stress because the temperature of the cap and chimney flue fluctuates dramatically. Use fire-rated silicone caulk to patch minor cracks in chimney caps. For more extensive repairs, reapply fresh mortar over the cap, or replace the old cap for a permanent solution.

Everything You Need:

Tools: hammer, cold chisel, drill, wood float, pointing trowel, tape measure.

Materials: mortar, concrete fortifier, ¾"-thick plywood for form construction, ¼" dowel, 1½" wood screws, fire-rated silicone caulk.

How to Repair a Chimney Cap

1 Carefully break apart and remove the deteriorated sections of the chimney cap, using a cold chisel and hammer. Be very careful when chiseling around the flue.

2 Mix a batch of latex-fortified mortar (page 89). Trowel an even layer of mortar all the way around the chimney cap, following the slope of the existing cap. Mortar should cover the chimney from the outside edges of the chimney bricks to the flue. Smooth out the mortar with a wood float, trying to recreate the original slope of the chimney cap. Inspect mortar annually.

How to Cast & Install a Replacement Chimney Cap

1 Measure the chimney and the chimney flue and build a form from ¾"-thick plywood (see form dimensions on page 98, top). Attach the form to a plywood base, using 1½" wood screws to connect all form parts. Make a frame from ⅜" dowels, 1" inside the form. Glue the dowel frame to the base of the form to cast a drip edge into the cap.

2 Prepare a stiff (dry) mixture of mortar to cast the cap—for average-sized chimneys, two 60-lb. bags of dry mix should yield enough mortar. Fill the form with mortar. Rest a wood float across the edges of the form, and strike off the mortar. Keep angles sharp at the corners. Let the cap cure for at least two days, then carefully disassemble the form.

3 Chip off the old mortar cap completely, and clean the top of the chimney with a wire brush. With a helper, transport the chimney cap onto the roof and set it directly onto the chimney, centered so the overhang is equal on all sides. For the new cap to function properly, do not bond it to the chimney or the flue.

4 Shift the cap so the gap next to the flue is even on all sides, then fill in the gap with fire-rated rope or mineral wool. Caulk over the fill material with a very heavy bead of fire-rated silicone caulk. Also caulk the joint at the underside of the cap. Inspect caulk every other year, and refresh as needed.

Use a pressure washer to clean large brick and block structures. Pressure washers can be rented from most rental centers. Be sure to obtain detailed operating and safety instructions from the rental agent.

Solvent Solutions for Common Brick & Block Stains

- **Egg splatter:** dissolve oxalic acid crystals in water, following manufacturer's instructions, in a nonmetallic container. Brush onto the surface.

- **Efflorescence:** scrub surface with a stiff-bristled brush. Use a household cleaning solution for surfaces with heavy accumulation.

- **Iron stains:** spray or brush a solution of oxalic acid crystals dissolved in water, following manufacturer's instructions. Apply directly to the stain.

- **Ivy:** cut vines away from the surface (do not pull them off). Let remaining stems dry up, then scrub them off with a stiff-bristled brush and household cleaning solution.

- **Oil:** apply a paste made of mineral spirits and an inert material like sawdust (see page 86).

- **Paint stains:** remove new paint with a solution of trisodium phosphate (TSP) and water, following manufacturer's mixing instructions. Old paint can usually be removed with heavy scrubbing or sandblasting.

- **Plant growth:** use weed killer according to manufacturer's directions.

- **Smoke stains:** scrub surface with household cleanser containing bleach, or use a mixture of ammonia and water.

Cleaning & Painting Brick & Block

Check brick and block surfaces annually for stains or discoloration. Most problems are easy to correct if they are treated in a timely fashion. Refer to the information below for cleaning tips that address specific staining problems.

Painted brick and block structures can be spruced up by applying a fresh coat of paint. As with any other painting job, thorough surface preparation and the use of a quality primer are critical to a successful outcome.

Regular maintenance will keep brick and block structures around your house looking their best, helping them last as long as possible.

Tips for Cleaning Masonry
- Always test cleaning solutions on a small area of the surface to evaluate the results.

- Some chemicals and their fumes may be harmful. Be sure to follow manufacturer's safety and use recommendations. Wear protective clothing.

- Soak the surface to be cleaned with water before you apply any solutions. This keeps solutions from soaking in too quickly. Rinse the surface thoroughly after cleaning to wash off any remaining cleaning solution.

Tips for Cleaning Brick & Block Surfaces

Mix a paste made from cleaning solvents (see chart, previous page) and talcum or flour. Apply paste directly to stain, let it dry, then scrape it off with a vinyl or plastic scraper.

Use a nylon scraper or a thin block of wood to clean up spilled mortar that has hardened. Avoid metal scrapers since they are likely to damage masonry surfaces.

Mask off windows, siding, decorative millwork, and other exposed nonmasonry surfaces before cleaning brick and block. Careful masking is essential if you are using harsh cleaning chemicals like muriatic acid.

Tips for Painting Masonry

Clean mortar joints, using a drill with a wire wheel attachment before applying paint. Scrub off loose paint, dirt, mildew, and mineral deposits so the paint will bond better.

Apply masonry primer before repainting brick or block walls. Primer helps to eliminate stains and prevent problems like efflorescence.

Insulating & Weatherizing

Whether you live in a warm or cold climate, adequately weatherizing and insulating your house has many benefits. It saves money—even in homes with average insulation, heating and cooling costs account for over half of the total energy bill. And because most insulating and weather-stripping products are relatively inexpensive, an investment in them can be recovered through energy savings in a short amount of time.

Also, by reducing energy use, you help reduce pollution and slow the depletion of irreplaceable natural resources. In an average home in a cold climate, it is estimated, reducing energy usage by only 15% can save the equivalent of 500 pounds of coal each year.

And finally, a tightly sealed, well-insulated house not only saves money and resources, it eliminates drafts and cold spots, creating a more comfortable home for your family to enjoy.

This section shows:

- Detecting Energy Loss (pages 104 to 105)
- Insulating & Weatherizing Products (pages 106 to 107)
- Improving Insulation (pages 108 to 111)
- Weatherizing Your House (pages 112 to 119)
- Maintaining Storm Doors & Windows (pages 120 to 126)
- Replacing Storm Windows (page 127)

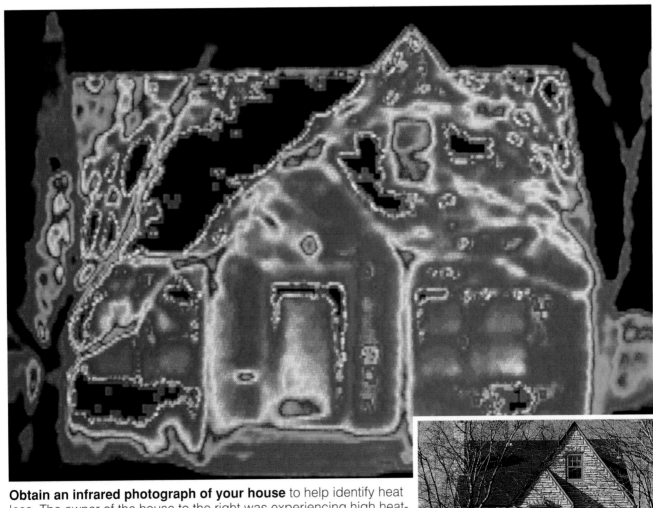

Obtain an infrared photograph of your house to help identify heat loss. The owner of the house to the right was experiencing high heating bills, and contacted his local public utility company. He was referred to an infrared inspection service, which took the infrared photograph shown above. The photo clearly showed high heat loss (seen as red and yellow in the photo) around his entry door and second-floor window. With this information, he was able to make efficient weatherstripping improvements that paid off quickly.

Detecting Energy Loss

Some signs that your home is not energy efficient are very obvious: for example, general draftiness; windows that are constantly frosted; a roof that loses its snow cover well before other roofs in the neighborhood; and high heating bills. Other signs are trickier to detect; for example, inadequate wall insulation; warm air loss around chimneys; and heat transfer through glass. The tips on these pages will help you detect and solve energy-loss problems.

Some energy-loss problems can be expensive and time-consuming to correct: for example, removing interior wall surfaces to improve wall insulation. Check with a contractor, and compare potential savings to the project cost before you undertake any large projects, like adding insulation to finished walls.

Measure insulation between joists in unheated attics to see if amounts meet recommended standards (page 108). Multiply the number of inches of loose insulation by 3.7 to find the total current R-value. For fiberglass insulation, multiply by 3.1 per inch. If the total amounts are substandard, add enough insulation to meet the recommendation (pages 104 to 111).

Tests for Detecting Energy Loss

Measure the temperature in different parts of a room. Differences of more than one or two degrees indicate that the room is poorly sealed. Update weatherstripping around doors and windows (pages 114 to 119).

Check for drafts around windows and doors by holding a tissue next to gaps at the door or window on a windy day. Fluttering indicates weatherstripping is inadequate, and it should be replaced or upgraded (pages 114 to 119). Also look for light coming from the outside around door and window jambs.

Conduct an energy audit with the assistance of your local public utility company. Most power companies will provide an energy audit kit, or conduct the audit for you (sometimes free of charge). Some audits include the use of a blower door (above), which measures air flow and detects leakage.

Tips for Identifying Energy Loss

Frost buildup on windows is a sign of poor weather-stripping and an inadequate storm window. If a tight seal is not made, cold air surrounds the window, causing moisture in the warm inside air to condense on the surface of the cold glass. As moisture builds up, it turns to frost or even ice. Upgrade weatherstripping and add a layer of plastic sheeting on the interior or exterior side of the window (page 106).

Condensation or frost between windows indicates that moisture is building up in the space between the window and the storm window. Fix the problem by updating interior weatherstripping to keep warm, moist air inside (pages 114 to 116). Also check the storm window to make sure there is an outlet for moisture. If not, drill one or two small holes in the lower rail of the storm window so moisture can escape (page 116).

Inspect weatherstripping and insulation. Look for signs of deterioration: crumbling foam or rubber; hardening of flexible products, like felt or foam rubber; or damaged metal stripping. Replace the products as needed. Most weatherstripping products will last only a few years.

Monitor energy usage and costs and compare them year-to-year, taking into account any changes in the rate structures or general weather conditions. Significant increases may indicate that weatherstripping or insulation needs replacement or improvement. Make further evaluations to determine where energy loss is occurring—like having an infrared photo taken of your home (page 103).

Insulating & Weatherizing Products

(A) A vapor barrier prevents condensation from occurring around insulation. Use 6-mil poly as a vapor barrier for rigid insulation boards or unfaced fiberglass insulation (page 108).

(B) Faced fiberglass insulation has an attached vapor barrier. More expensive than unfaced insulation, it is especially useful in areas, like crawl spaces, where the vapor barrier must be on the opposite side from which the insulation is installed.

(C) An attic blanket is a common type of unfaced fiberglass insulation. Unfaced insulation is less costly than faced insulation and, when used with a solid poly vapor barrier, it provides better protection from mois-

ture. Sold in rolls and flat batts sized to fit standard stud cavities.

(D) Rigid insulation boards are attached directly to basement walls, usually with panel adhesive. Urethane foam insulation (shown) is sturdy and a good insulator. Inexpensive open-cell foam boards can be used, but they are harder to work with. Rigid boards are sold in thicknesses ranging from ½" to 2".

(E) Baffles are attached to the rafters at the sill plate in your attic. Usually made of plastic or polystyrene, they ensure that attic insulation does not obstruct the air flow across the underside of the roof.

(F) A door sweep attaches to the inside of the door bottom to seal out drafts. Felt (shown) and bristle sweeps work well with uneven floors or low thresholds. Vinyl and rubber versions are also sold.

(G) A threshold insert seals the gap between the door and the threshold. Usually made from vinyl or rubber, most can be replaced easily. **A door bottom** fits around the bottom of the door. Most have a sweep on the interior side and a drip edge on the exterior to direct water away from the threshold.

(H) Metal v-channel forms a seal between sliding window sash (shown), in sash channels, or between doors and jambs. Metal v-channel is similar to tension stripping (page 118).

(I) A garage-door sweep creates a continuous barrier between the garage door and the garage floor.

(J) Tubular gasket flexes to cover gaps between moving parts, like window sash. It also can be used on door and window stops because it is compressible.

(K) Switch and receptacle sealers fit behind cover plates on exterior walls to block drafts in these heat-loss areas.

(L) Self-adhesive foam strips are attached to sash and window or door frames where contact occurs with windows and doors.

(M) Reinforced felt strips have a metal spine to add rigidity for high-impact areas, like door stops.

(N) Plastic sheeting adds an extra storm window layer. Interior and exterior types are sold. Interior (shown) can be made wrinkle-free by warming with a hair dryer.

(O) Peelable caulk is applied in gaps around windows and doors, on the interior side. It can be peeled off easily at the end of the heating season.

(P) Caulk can be applied on interior or exterior surfaces to fill narrow gaps. See pages 14 to 15.

(Q) Caulking backer rope fills large voids and gaps that are difficult to caulk. It can be used alone to fill wider gaps.

(R) Sprayable foam is sprayed into hard-to-reach areas, like siding cutouts and baseboard gaps. For best control, use foam with a 1:1 expansion rate.

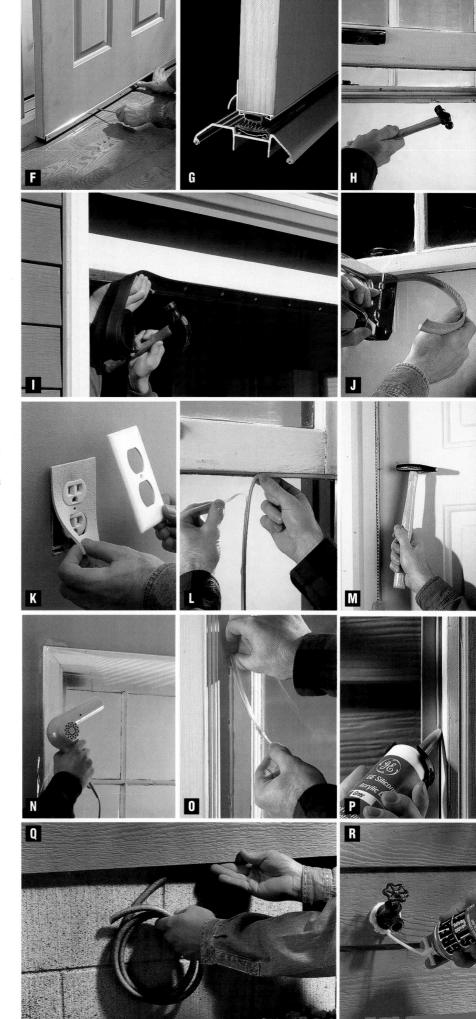

Install baffles to keep new attic insulation from blocking the flow of air through your attic. You can purchase and install ready-made baffles, or make your own from plywood or rigid insulation board. For more information on ventilation, see pages 52 to 55.

Improving Insulation

Adding insulation to attics or basement walls is a quick and easy do-it-yourself project that has an immediate payback in energy savings.

Most local building codes require minimum amounts of insulation for new construction. Check with your building inspector—these minimum requirements make good guidelines for owners of older homes as well. Guidelines for insulation are given in terms of total "R-value," which measures the ability of materials to resist the flow of heat (see chart below).

In this section we show you how to install a fiberglass attic blanket. For most homeowners this is a simpler and cleaner type of attic insulation than loose, blown insulation. Attics with existing insulation should have a vapor barrier in place: use unfaced insulation. Rigid boards are good for basement walls because they pack greater R-value into smaller spaces, and they can be attached directly to walls with panel adhesive.

Everything You Need:

Tools: tape measure, utility knife, straightedge, plumb line, insulation board saw, staple gun.

Materials: 6-mil poly vapor barrier, baffles, insulation, 2 × 2 furring strips, construction adhesive, rigid foam insulation, panel adhesive.

Tips for Planning Your Insulation Project

Recommended insulation amounts		
	Cold climate	**Moderate climate**
Attic:	R38	R26
Wall:	R19	R19
Floor:	R22	R11

Insulation thickness chart:

Fiberglass		**Open-cell foam:**	
R11 (faced)	3½"	R4	1"
R13 (unfaced)	3½"	R6	1½"
R19 (unfaced)	6"	R8	2"
R21 (high density)	5¼"	**Urethane foam:**	
R25 (unfaced)	8"	R5	1"
R30 (unfaced)	10"	R10	2"

Resistance value (R-value) measures the ability of a material to resist heat flow. The charts above show minimum R-values for different areas (often obtained by combining two layers). Use the lower chart to determine how much insulation you can install in a specific area (never compress insulation).

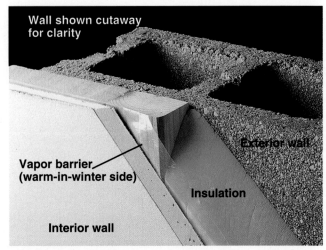

Wall shown cutaway for clarity

Vapor barrier (warm-in-winter side)

Exterior wall

Insulation

Interior wall

Install vapor barriers made of 6-mil (recommended) or 4-mil poly on the warm-in-winter side of insulation. Vapor barriers protect the insulation and the structural members of your house from condensation that can occur when warm, humid air meets cold air. When layering insulation, install one vapor barrier only.

Tips for Insulating Your House

SAFETY TIP: Always wear a long-sleeved shirt, gloves, and a particle mask or respirator when handling fiberglass insulation.

Install fiberglass insulation between floor joists over crawl spaces or unheated basements. Make sure the vapor barrier faces up, and install chicken wire or insulation support rods below to hold the insulation in place.

Insulate the rim joist at the top of your foundation walls by filling it loosely with fiberglass insulation. Pack the insulation just tightly enough that it does not fall out.

Insulate garage walls in attached garages. Use faced fiberglass insulation, with the vapor barrier facing into the garage. Cover with wall covering, like wallboard, especially in areas that are vulnerable to damage.

Tips for Installing Insulation

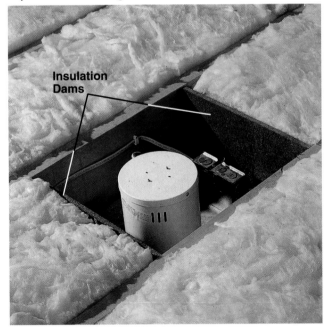

Insulation Dams

Make insulation dams from rigid boards and install them between ceiling joists to keep attic insulation at least 6" away from recessed lights, vents fans, and other electrical fixtures that generate heat. Check the fixture to see if it is "IC" rated for insulation contact. If it is IC rated, no dams are needed.

Do not compress insulation to fit a spot. Insulation needs air space within the material to be effective in resisting heat transfer. If the insulation you want to install is too thick, trim or tear it to match the depth of the wall, ceiling, or floor cavity.

How to Insulate Your Attic

1 Measure the depth of existing insulation, and calculate how much additional insulation, if any, is required (see page 104 top left, and page 108, chart). TIP: When working over exposed joists, lay a sheet of plywood across the joists to create a stable working surface.

2 Attach baffles to the roof sheathing or rafters to keep new insulation from blocking the air flow along the roof sheathing. Baffles should extend past the bottoms of the ceiling joists.

3 Cut rolls of unfaced fiberglass insulation to length in a well-ventilated work area, using a straightedge and a utility knife. For attics with uneven joist spacing, you will need to trim a few pieces for width as well.

4 Roll out insulation, starting at the farthest point from the attic access. NOTE: Attic blankets may be piled higher than the tops of the joists as long as you do not plan to use your attic for storage.

OPTION: For greater insulation (especially in colder climates), roll out a second attic blanket layer perpendicular to the first layer. Do not use faced insulation or another layer of vapor barrier.

How to Insulate Basement Walls

1 Use a plumb line to mark vertical reference lines for furring strips. Space the furring strips to conform to the width of the rigid insulation boards (do not space them more than 24" apart). Use construction adhesive to attach the furring strips to the foundation walls. OPTION: If you plan to install wallboard over furring strips, attach top and sole plates above and below the furring strips.

2 Cut the rigid panels to fit from floor to ceiling, between furring strips. Use an insulation-board saw. Mark and make cutouts for receptacles, windows, and any other obstructions. For our project, we used 2"-thick urethane foam insulation boards.

3 Attach the insulation panels to the wall with panel adhesive (check the manufacturer's recommendations to make sure the adhesive is compatible with the type of insulation you purchase).

4 Staple a 6-mil poly vapor barrier to the furring strips. For extra vapor barrier protection, tape over seams and staples with clear plastic tape. Attach wallcovering, if desired.

Cover window wells with preformed window-well covers to minimize heat loss through basement windows (and keep out pests). Most window well covers have an upper flange designed to slip under siding. Fasten them to foundation walls with masonry anchors, and weight down the bottom flange with stones. Caulk around edges for extra protection. Before purchasing window well covers, measure the widest point of your window well, and note whether it is rectangular or semicircular.

Weatherizing Your House

Most weatherizing projects involve windows and doors, because these are the primary heat-loss areas in most homes. Caulk and weatherstripping are the principal tools used to weatherize windows and doors. Storm windows and storm doors also play an important role in weatherizing your home, and similar products, like the plastic window well cover shown above, can make a significant contribution.

Choose weatherstripping materials that meet your specific needs—there are many different types sold, and most are designed for specific applica-tions (page 107). Generally, metal or metal reinforced weatherstripping is more durable than products made from only plastic, rubber, or foam. But even with plastic, rubber, and foam weatherstripping, there is a wide quality range. Neoprene rubber is considered the best type of rubber, and should be used whenever it is available.

Weatherizing your house is an ideal project for homeowners because it can be done a little at a time, according to your schedule. The best time to weatherize is in the fall, just before the weather turns too cold to work outdoors.

Tips for Weatherizing Your House

Seal between baseboards and floorboards. Remove the base shoe and spray 1:1-expansion sprayable foam into the gap. While preventing drafts, the foam barrier also stops insects from entering your living areas.

Caulk around dryer vents, exhaust vents from vent fans, and any other fittings mounted to the side of your house.

Insulate around spigots, television cable jacks, telephone lines, and other entry points to your house, using sprayable foam insulation. **CAUTION:** Do not work around or near power service cables.

Seal the sill plate gap between the house sill and the siding by stuffing it with ⅜"-diameter plastic or foam caulking backer rope.

The primary heat loss areas in windows (shown highlighted) should be sealed with the appropriate weatherstripping material. This can increase the energy efficiency of a window by 100% or more.

Weatherizing Windows

The secret to energy-tight windows is blocking air movement, creating a sealed-off dead air space between interior and exterior glass panes.

Modern double and triple-paned windows often contain inert gases between panes to help create dead air spaces. You can create dead air spaces in older windows by using weatherstripping and a good storm window (or plastic window sheeting) to block air movement. Weatherstripping the inside gaps helps keep warm, moist air on the interior side of a window, minimizing condensation and frosting between the window and the storm.

Everything You Need:

Tools: tack hammer, aviator snips, putty knife, hair dryer, staple gun.

Materials: metal v-channel, compressible foam, tubular gasket, reinforced felt, brads, clear silicone caulk, siliconized acrylic caulk, peelable caulk, plastic sheeting (interior and exterior).

How to Weatherstrip Windows

1 Cut metal v-channel to fit in the channels for the sliding sash, extending at least 2" past the closed position for each sash (do not cover sash-closing mechanisms). Attach the v-channel by driving wire brads (usually provided by the manufacturer) with a tack hammer. Drive the fasteners flush with the surface so the sliding sash will not catch on them.

2 Flare out the open ends of the v-channels with a putty knife so the channel is slightly wider than the gap between the sash and the track it fits into. Avoid flaring out too much at one time—it is difficult to press v-channel back together without causing buckling.

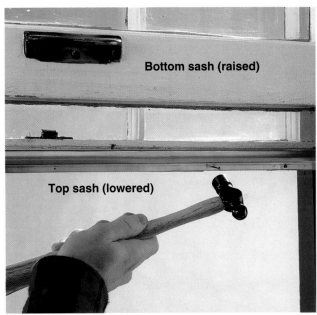

3 Wipe down the underside of the bottom window sash with a damp rag, and let it dry; then, attach self-adhesive compressible foam or rubber to the underside of the sash. Use high-quality hollow neoprene strips, if available. This will create an air-tight seal when the window is locked in position.

4 Seal the gap between the top sash and the bottom sash on double-hung windows. Lift the bottom sash and lower the top sash to improve access, and tack metal v-channel to the bottom rail of the top sash using wire brads. TIP: The open end of the "v" should be pointed downward so moisture cannot collect in the channel. Flare out the v-channel with a putty knife to fit the gap between the sash.

Tips for Weatherizing Windows

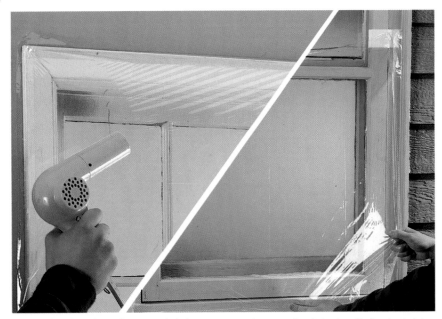

Apply caulk around the interior window casing with clear silicone caulk. For added protection, lock the window in the closed position, and caulk the gaps around the interior edges of the sash with clear, peelable caulk (which can be removed easily when the heating season is over).

Add plastic sheeting or shrink-wrap product to the interior (left photo) to block drafts and keep moisture away from the window surfaces. Follow the manufacturer's installation directions, which often include using a hair dryer to tighten the plastic and remove wrinkles, making it almost invisible. Install exterior plastic sheeting (right photo) on the outside of your window, following the manufacturer's directions (rolls of tacking or stapling strips are often included with the product).

(continued next page)

Tips for Weatherizing Windows (continued)

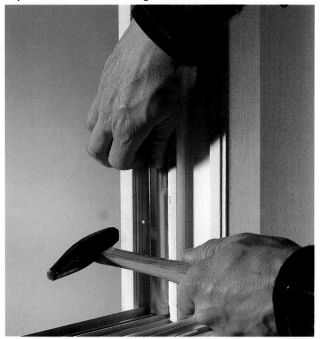

Sliding windows (side by side): Treat side-by-side sliding windows as if they were double-hung windows (pages 114 to 115) turned 90°. For greater durability, substitute metal tension strips for self-adhesive compressible foam in the sash track that fits against the edge of the sash when the window is closed.

Casement windows: Attach self-adhesive foam or rubber compression strips on the outside edges of the window stops.

Tips for Weatherizing Storm Windows

Storm windows: Create a tight seal by attaching foam compression strips to the outside of the storm window stops (left photo). After installing the storm window, fill any gaps between the exterior window trim and the storm window with caulk backer rope. Check the inside surface of the storm window during cold weather for condensation or frost buildup (page 105). If moisture is trapped between the storm window and the permanent window, drill one or two small holes through the bottom rail of the storm window (right photo) to allow moist air to escape. Drill at a slight upward angle.

116

Weatherizing Doors

Door weatherstripping is prone to failure because it undergoes constant stress. Use metal weatherstripping that is tacked to the surfaces whenever you can—especially around door jambs. It is much more durable than self-adhesive products. If your job calls for flexible weatherstripping, use products made from neoprene rubber, not foam. Replace old door thresholds or threshold inserts as soon as they begin to show wear.

Everything You Need:

Tools: putty knife, tack hammer, screwdriver, backsaw, flat pry bar, chisel and mallet, tape measure, drill.

Materials: metal v-channel or tension strips, reinforced felt strips, door sweep, nails or brads, wood filler, caulk, threshold and insert.

The primary heat loss areas in doors (shown highlighted) are around jambs and at the threshold. Install weatherstripping on jambs, and update the threshold and threshold insert to cut down on drafts.

Tips for Weatherizing Doors

Install a storm door to decrease drafts and energy loss through entry doors. Buy an insulated storm door with a continuous hinge and seamless exterior surface.

Adjust the door frame to eliminate large gaps between the door and the jamb. Remove the interior case molding and drive new shims between the jamb and the framing member on the hinge side. Close the door to test the fit, and adjust as needed before reattaching case molding. For added home security, install plywood spacers between shims (page 156).

How to Weatherize an Exterior Door

1 Cut two pieces of metal tension strip or v-channel the full height of the door opening, and cut another to full width. Use wire brads to tack the strips to the door jambs and door header, on the interior side of the door stops. TIP: Attach metal weatherstripping from the top down to help prevent buckling. Flare out the tension strips with a putty knife to fill the gaps between the jambs and the door when the door is in closed position (do not pry too far at one time).

2 Add reinforced felt strips to the edge of the door stop, on the exterior side. The felt edge should form a close seal with the door when closed. TIP: Drive fasteners only until they are flush with the surface of the reinforcing spine—overdriving will cause damage and buckling.

3 Attach a new door sweep to the bottom of the door, on the interior side (felt or bristle types are better choices if the floor in your entry area is uneven). Before fastening it permanently, tack the sweep in place and test the door swing to make sure there is enough clearance.

TIP: Fix any cracks in wooden door panels with epoxy wood filler or caulk (page 14) to block air leaks. If the door has a stain finish, use tinted wood putty, filling from the interior side. Sand down and touch up with paint or stain.

How to Replace a Door Threshold

1 Cut the old threshold in two, using a backsaw. Pry out the pieces, and clean the debris from the sill area below the threshold. Note which edge of the threshold is more steeply beveled; the new threshold should be installed in the same way.

2 Measure the opening for the new threshold, and trim it to fit, using the pieces of the old threshold as templates, if possible. If the profile of the new threshold differs from the old threshold, trace the new profile onto the bottoms of the door stops. Chisel the stops to fit.

3 Apply caulk to the sill. Position the new threshold, pressing it into the caulk. Drive the screws provided with the threshold through the pre-drilled holes in the center channel, and into the sill. Install the threshold insert (see manufacturer's directions).

Tips for Weatherizing Doors

Patio door: Use rubber compression strips to seal the channels in patio door jambs, where movable panels fit when closed. Also install a patio door insulator kit (plastic sheeting installed similarly to plastic sheeting for windows—page 115) on the interior side of the door.

Garage door: Attach a new rubber sweep to the bottom, outside edge of the garage door if the old sweep has deteriorated. Also check the door jambs for drafts, and add weatherstripping, if needed.

Maintaining Storm Doors & Windows

Build a storage rack for removable screens and storm windows. Simply attach a pair of 2 × 4s to the rafters of your garage or the ceiling joists in your basement. Attach window-hanger hardware to the top rails of the screen and storm windows, if they do not already have them. Space the hangers uniformly. Then, attach screw eyes to the 2 × 4s in matching rows to fit the window hangers.

Removable storm windows are excellent insulators when they are in good condition, and removable screens provide full ventilation. For these reasons, many homeowners still prefer them over combination storm and screen windows—even though they must be changed with the seasons.

Simple wood-sash construction and a lack of moving parts make removable storm and screen windows easy to repair and maintain. Replacing screening or glass, tightening loose joints, and applying fresh paint are the primary maintenance jobs.

Combination storm and screen windows offer convenience, and can be repaired simply if you have a little know-how and the right replacement parts.

Tools & Materials

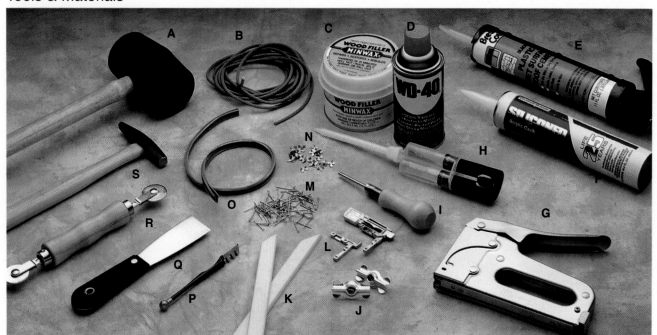

Tools and materials for repairing and maintaining storm windows include: rubber mallet (A), spline cord for metal sash (B), epoxy wood filler (C), penetrating lubricant (D), roof cement (E), siliconized acrylic caulk (F), staple gun (G), epoxy glue (H), brad pusher (I), turnbuttons (J), retaining strips for wood sash (K), metal sash replacement hardware (L), wire brads (M), glazier's points (N), rubber window gasket for metal sash (O), glass cutter (P), putty knife (Q), spline roller (R), tack hammer (S).

Tips for Maintaining Storm Doors & Windows

Tighten storm door latches by redriving loose screws in the strikeplate. If the latch does not catch on the strikeplate, loosen the screws on the strikeplate, insert thin wood shims between the plate and the jamb, and retighten the screws.

Add a wind chain if your storm door does not have one. Wind chains prevent doors from blowing open too far, causing damage to the door hinges or closer. Set the chain so the door will not open more than 90°.

Adjust the door closer so it has the right amount of tension to close the door securely, without slamming. Most closers have tension-adjustment screws at the end of the cylinder farther from the hinge side of the door.

Replace turnbuttons and window clips that do not hold storm windows tightly in place. Fill old screw holes with wood putty or toothpicks and glue before driving screws.

Lubricate sliding assemblies on metal-framed combination storm windows once a year, using penetrating lubricant.

Replace deteriorated glazing around glass panes in wood-framed windows. Sound glazing makes windows more energy-efficient and more attractive.

Repairing Wood Storm Windows & Screens

Because they are installed, removed, transported, and stored so frequently, removable wood storm windows need repair and maintenance regularly. Broken glass, torn screens, loose joints or hangers, dry or missing glazing, and failed paint are the primary problems. Fortunately, fixing wood storm windows is simple, and maintaining them well has a high payback in the appearance and efficiency of your house.

Everything You Need:

Tools: utility knife, clamps, drill, mallet, putty knife, staple gun, tack hammer, scissors.

Materials: epoxy glue, dowels, caulk, replacement glass, glazier's points, glazing compound, screening, wire brads.

Clean out recesses for glass and screening by carefully removing old glass, glazing compound, and glazier's points (or screening and retaining strips). Scrape residue from the recess with an old chisel, then paint with a coat of primer or sealer before installing new glass or screen.

How to Repair Loose Joints in Wood Sash Frames

1 Remove the glass or screening, then carefully separate the loose joint, using a flat pry bar if necessary. Scrape the mating surfaces clean. Inject epoxy glue into the joint (plain wood glue should not be used for exterior work). Press the mating surfaces back together and clamp with bar clamps, making sure the frame is square.

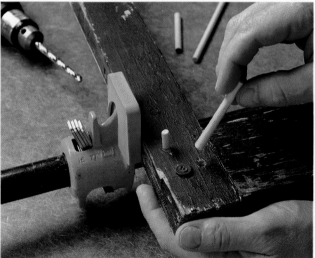

2 After the glue is dry, reinforce the repair by drilling two ³⁄₁₆"-diameter holes through the joint (mortise-and-tenon joints are common). Cut two ³⁄₁₆"-diameter dowels about 1" longer than the thickness of the frame, and round over one end of each dowel with sandpaper. Coat the dowels with epoxy glue, and drive them through the holes. After the glue dries, trim the ends of the dowels with a backsaw, then sand until they are flush with the sash. Touch up with paint.

How to Replace Glass in a Wood Storm Window

1 Clean and prepare the glass recess (top photo, previous page). Measuring from the outside shoulders of the glass recess, measure the full width and height of the opening, subtract ⅛" from each dimension, and have new glass cut to fit. Apply a thin bead of caulk in the recess to create a bed for the new pane of glass.

2 Press the new glass pane into the fresh caulk. Use a putty knife or screwdriver blade to push glazier's points into the frame every 8" to 10" to hold the glass in place.

3 Roll glazing compound into ⅜"-diameter "snakes" and press the snakes into the joint between the glass and the frame. Smooth the compound with a putty knife held at a 45° angle to create a flat surface. Strip off the excess. Let the compound dry for several days before painting.

How to Replace Screening in a Wood Storm Window

1 Completely clean and prepare the recess (top photo, previous page). Cut a new piece of screening at least 3" longer in height and in width than the opening. Tɪᴘ: Use fiberglass screening for residential windows—it is easy to work with, and will not rust or corrode.

2 Tack the top edge of the screening into the recess with a staple gun. Stretch the screen tightly toward the bottom. Tack the bottom into the recess. Tack one side in place. Then, stretch the screening tightly across the frame, and tack the other side.

3 Attach retaining strips over the edges of the screening. Do not use old nail holes: drill 1/32"-diameter pilot holes in the retaining strips, then drive 1" wire brads. Trim off excess screening with a sharp utility knife.

Slide tab

Repairing Metal Storm Windows

Compared to removable wood storm windows, repairing combination storms is a little more complex. But there are several repairs you can make without too much difficulty, as long as you find the right parts. Bring the old corner keys, gaskets, or other original parts to a hardware store that repairs storm windows so the clerk can help you find the correct replacement parts (page 126, step 3). If you cannot find the right parts, have a new sash built.

Everything You Need:

Tools: tape measure, scissors, utility knife, spline roller, drill, screwdriver, hammer, nail set.

Materials: spline cord, rubber gasket, glass, screening, replacement hardware.

Remove metal storm window sash by pressing in the release hardware in the lower rail (like the slide tabs above), then lifting the sash out. Sash hangers on the corners of the top rail (see step 2, next page) should be aligned with the notches in the side channels before removal.

How to Replace Screening in a Metal Storm Window

1 Remove the spline cord holding the damaged screening in the frame. Also remove the old screening material, and clean any debris from the spline-cord tracks in the frame.

2 Cut the new screening material at least 3" wider and longer than the frame opening, and lay it over the frame. Set the spline cord over the screening so it is aligned with the spline-cord track.

3 At the top of the window, press the spline cord into the spline-cord track with a spline roller. Stretch the screening across the opening and continue setting the cord all the way around the frame. Trim off the excess screening with a utility knife.

How to Replace Glass in a Metal Storm Window

1 Remove the sash frame from the window, then completely remove the broken glass from the sash. Remove the rubber gasket that framed the old glass pane and remove any glass remnants. Find the dimensions for the replacement glass by measuring between the inside edges of the frame opening, then adding twice the thickness of the rubber gasket to each measurement.

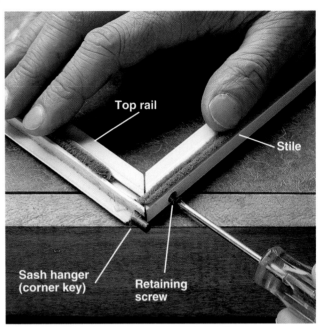

Top rail

Stile

Sash hanger (corner key)

Retaining screw

2 Set the frame on a flat surface, and disconnect the top rail. Normally, you need to remove the retaining screws in the sides of the frame stiles where they join the top rail. After unscrewing the retaining screws, pull the top rail loose, pulling gently in a downward motion to avoid damaging the L-shaped corner keys that join the rail and the stiles. For glass replacement, you need only disconnect the top rail.

3 Fit the rubber gasket (buy a replacement if the original is in poor condition) around one edge of the replacement glass pane. At corners, cut the spine of the gasket partway so it will bend around the corner. Continue fitting the gasket around the pane, cutting at the corners, until all four edges are covered. Trim off any excess gasket material.

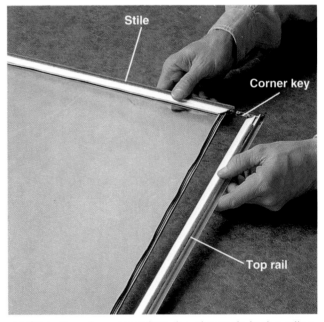

Stile

Corner key

Top rail

4 Slide the glass pane into the channels in the stiles and the bottom rail of the sash frame. Insert the corner keys into the top rail, then slip the other ends of the keys into the frame stiles. Press down on the top rail until the mitered corners are flush with the stiles. Drive the retaining screws back through the stiles and into the top rail to join the frame together. Insert the frame back into the window.

How to Disassemble & Repair a Metal Sash Frame

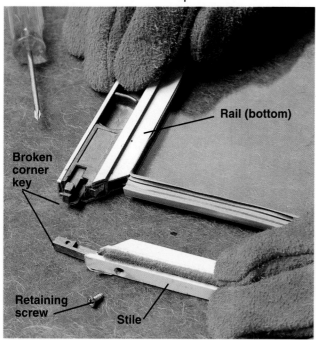

Rail (bottom)

Broken corner key

Retaining screw

Stile

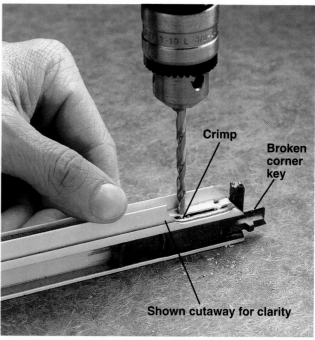

Crimp

Broken corner key

Shown cutaway for clarity

1 Metal window sash are held together at the corner joints by L-shaped pieces of hardware that fit into grooves in the sash frame pieces. To disassemble a broken joint, start by disconnecting the stile and rail at the broken joint—there is usually a retaining screw driven through the stile that must be removed.

2 Corner keys are secured in the rail slots with crimps that are punched into the metal over the key. To remove keys, drill through the metal in the crimped area, using a drill bit the same diameter as the crimp. Carefully knock the broken key pieces from the frame slots with a screwdriver and hammer.

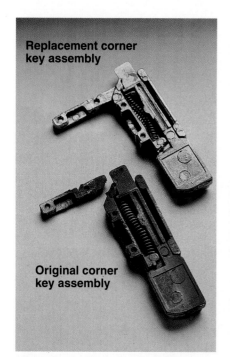

Replacement corner key assembly

Original corner key assembly

3 Locate matching replacement parts for the broken corner key (page 124), which is usually an assembly of two or three pieces. There are dozens of different types, so it is important that you save the old parts for reference.

4 Insert the replacement corner key assembly into the slot in the rail. Use a nail set as a punch, and rap it into the metal over the corner key, creating a new crimp to hold the key in place.

5 Insert the glass and gasket into the frame slots (see previous page), then reassemble the frame and drive in retainer screws (for screen windows, replace the screening).

Replacing Storm Windows

As old removable storm windows wear out, many homeowners elect to replace them with modern combination storm windows. Designed to mount permanently in the existing opening, "retrofit" combination storm windows are very easy to install, and fairly inexpensive.

Most retrofit storm windows attach to the outside edges of the window stops on the sides and top of the window opening. Most windows do not have a bottom stop. Secure the bottom rail of the new window with caulk. Common window sizes are stocked at most building centers, but you may need to order custom-made windows. Bring exact measurements (photo, right) when you order the windows. You also will be asked to choose a finish color and a style. If you have operating double-hung windows, choose 3-sash windows so you have the option of opening the top storm sash.

"Retrofit" storm windows attach to the window stops in the existing window opening. The easiest way to size them is to use the dimensions of old storms. Otherwise, measure the narrowest point between side jambs to find the width, and measure the shortest point from the header to the sill (where it meets the front edges of the stops) to find the height.

Everything You Need:

Tools: screwdriver, drill, tape measure.

Materials: replacement storm windows, caulk or panel adhesive, screws.

How to Install New Combination Storm Windows

1 Buy replacement storm windows to fit your window openings (photo, above). Test-fit windows before installing them. To install, first apply a bead of exterior-grade panel adhesive or caulk to the outside edges of the window stops at the top and sides.

2 Predrill pilot holes for fasteners in the mounting flanges, spaced 12" apart, making sure they will be centered over the stops. Press the new storm window into the opening, centered between the side stops, with the bottom rail resting on the window sill.

3 Drive fasteners (#4 × 1" sheet-metal screws work well), starting at the top. Make sure the window is squarely in the opening, then fill in the fasteners on the side stops. Apply caulk along the bottom rail, leaving a ¼"-wide gap midway to function as a weep hole.

Painting Your House

Painting your house yourself greatly reduces the cost and, if done with care and patience, the finished product will look as good as that produced by a professional contractor.

A house-painting project breaks naturally into two stages: preparing the surfaces, and applying the paint. In most cases, the preparation work is more time-consuming than the application. But the investment of time is reflected in an even and long-lasting painted finish.

Planning and timing are critical elements in a painting project. Try to tackle only one side of your house at a time. Scraping and sanding the old paint exposes your siding to the elements, which can cause wood pores to become plugged—resulting in a poor bond with the paint. Cover the siding with primer and paint as soon as you finish the preparation.

When applied correctly over a well-prepared, primed surface, paint can last 10 years or more, especially with regular maintenance. By touching up minor problems, like chips or localized flaking, you can prevent water from building up beneath the surface. Cracks and alligatoring should be sanded, primed, and painted as soon as they occur. Left uncorrected, they invite mildew formation, leading to staining and the eventual failure of the paint. Pressure washing your siding should be the cornerstone of your annual maintenance program.

Like any project that involves the use of ladders or scaffolding, painting your house requires good safety practices. Read the section on safety (pages 10 to 13) before you start.

This section shows:
• Evaluating Painted Surfaces (pages 130 to 131)
• Tools & Materials (pages 132 to 133)
• Preparing Surfaces for Paint (pages 134 to 139)
• Applying Primer & Paint (pages 140 to 147)

Safety Warning:

Lead-based paint is a hazardous material: its handling and disposal are strictly regulated. Especially if your home was built before 1960, you should test the paint for lead using a lead-testing kit (available at building centers and paint stores). Call your local building inspector or waste management department for information on handling and disposing of lead paint.

Evaluating Painted Surfaces

Two primary factors work against painted surfaces: moisture and age. A simple leak or a failed vapor barrier inside the house can ruin even the most carefully executed paint job. If you notice signs of paint failure, like blistering or peeling, take action to correct the problem right away. If the damage to the surface is caught in time, you may be able to correct it with just a little bit of touch-up painting.

Evaluating the painted surfaces of your house can help you identify problems with siding, trim, roofs, and moisture barriers. Before you begin a thorough inspection of the painted surfaces, read pages 6 to 9 and the evaluation information at the beginning of each section in this book.

Check sheltered areas first. Initial signs of paint failure in areas that receive little or no direct sunlight are a warning sign that neighboring areas may be in danger of similar paint failure.

Common Forms of Paint Failure

Blistering describes paint that bubbles on the surface. It is an early sign that more serious problems, like peeling, may be forming.

Causes: Blistering can result from poor preparation or hasty application of primer or paint. The blisters are caused by trapped moisture as it forces its way through the surface.

Solution: Scrape and touch up localized blistering. For widespread damage, remove paint down to bare wood, then apply new primer and paint.

Peeling occurs when paint disengages entirely from the surface, falling away in flakes.

Causes: Peeling is most often associated with persistent moisture problems, generally from a leak or a failed vapor barrier.

Solution: Identify and correct any moisture problems. If the peeling is localized, scrape and sand the damaged area only, then touch up with new primer and paint. If peeling is widespread, remove the old paint down to bare wood. Apply new primer and paint.

Alligatoring is widespread flaking and cracking of surfaces, typically seen on old paint and surfaces with many built-up layers of paint.

Causes: Alligatoring can be caused by excessive layers of paint, inadequate surface preparation, or insufficient drying time for a primer.

Solution: Repainting will not permanently cover significant alligatoring. Remove the old paint down to bare wood, then prime and repaint.

Detecting the Source of Moisture Beneath a Painted Surface

Localized blistering and peeling indicates that moisture, usually from a leaky roof or gutter system, is trapped under the paint. Check roofing and gutter materials to find the source of the leak. Also look for leaking pipes inside the wall. Correct the moisture problem before you repaint.

Clearly defined blistering and peeling occurs when a humid room, like a bathroom, has an insufficient vapor barrier (page 108). If there is a clear line where an interior wall ends, you probably will need to remove the wall coverings and replace the vapor barrier. In some cases, you may be able to solve the problem by increasing ventilation or adding a dehumidifier.

Identifying Common Surface Problems

Mildew forms in cracks and in humid areas that receive little direct sunlight. Wash the areas with a 1:1 solution of household chlorine bleach and water, or with trisodium phosphate (TSP) to kill the mildew.

Rust occurs when moisture penetrates failed paint on iron or steel. Remove the rust and any loose paint with a wire brush attachment and portable drill, then prime and repaint the affected area.

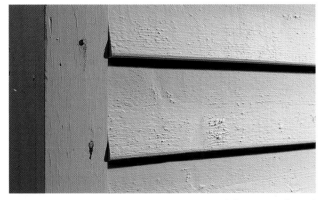

Bleeding spots occur when nails in siding "pop" and turn rusty. Remove the nails, sand out the rust, and drive in new ring-shank siding nails. Apply metal primer, then paint to blend in.

Efflorescence occurs in masonry when minerals leech through the surface, forming a crystalline or powdery layer. Use muriatic acid to remove efflorescence before priming and painting.

Materials for painting include: tarps, masking tape, sandpaper, caulk, primers (tinted to match paint color), house paint, trim paint, and special-task paints.

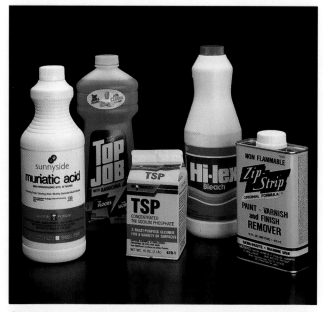

Chemicals and cleaners for paint maintenance and for surface preparation include (from left): muriatic acid for cleaning rust from metal, household detergent and TSP (trisodium phosphate) for general washing of surfaces, household chlorine bleach for cleaning mildew, and chemical stripper for removing thick layers of paint from delicate surfaces.

Tools & Materials

An investment in quality primer and house paint will make your hard work last for years longer than if you use cheaper products. High-quality preparation and application tools are also a good investment because they produce better results with less work.

Traditionally, almost all house paint was oil-based. But new latex-based products now rival oil-based products in durability and appearance, without the hazards, odors, and disposal problems of oil-based paints.

How to Estimate Your Paint Needs

Add:
square footage of walls (length × height)
square footage of soffit panels
15% allowance for waste
Subtract:
square footage of doors and windows

Find the coverage rate on the labels of the paint you will use (350 square feet per gallon is an average rate). Divide the total square footage by the coverage rate to determine the number of gallons you will need for each coat.

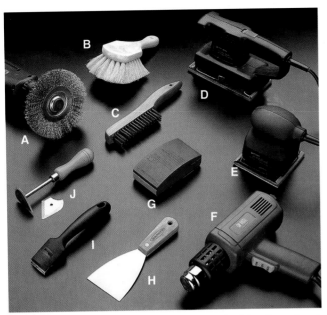

Tools for paint removal include: drill with wire-wheel attachment (A), stiff-bristled scrub brush (B), wire brush (C), ⅓-sheet finishing sander (D), ¼-sheet finishing sander (E), heat gun (F), sanding block (G), putty knife (H), paint scraper (I), and detail scraper with interchangeable heads (J).

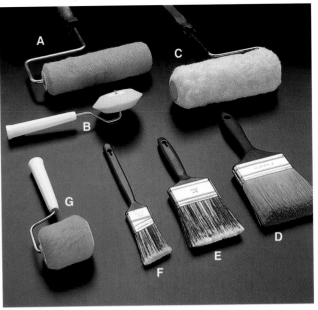

Tools for applying paint include: roller and sleeve with ⅜" nap for smooth or semi-smooth surfaces (A), corner roller for corners and trim (B), roller with ⅝" nap for rough surfaces (C), 4" paint brush for lap siding (D), 3" paint brush for siding and trim (E), 2" sash brush for trim and window frames (F), 3"-wide roller for painting trim (G). NOTE: All brushes shown have synthetic bristles for use with latex-based paint.

Rent a pressure washer and attachments for the surface-preparation process. A pressure washer cleans siding thoroughly, and removes old, flaky paint. A nozzle with an extension pole attaches to the hose from the pressure washer. Accessories, like the rotating scrub brush shown, clean hard-to-reach areas.

Sanded to bare wood

Scraped and spot-sanded

Pressure-washed only

Preparation defines the final appearance. For the smoothest finish, sand all the way to bare wood with a power sander (top). For a less time-consuming (but rougher) finish, scrape off loose paint, then spot-sand the rough edges (middle). Pressure-washing alone removes some flaky paint, but it will not create a satisfactory finish (bottom).

Preparing Surfaces for Paint

Preparing the surface is a crucial part of the house-painting process. Generally, the more preparation work you do, the smoother and more long-lasting the finished surface will be. But anyone who paints his or her house learns quickly that there is a point of diminishing return when it comes to preparation. You must decide for yourself how much sanding and scraping is enough for you to obtain a finish that meets your demands. But whether you are attempting to create a glass-smooth finish with a professional look or you simply want to freshen up the look of your house, always remove and spot-sand all paint that has lost its bond with the surface.

Everything You Need:

Tools: pressure washer, paint scrapers, finishing sander, wire brush, stiff-bristled brush, file, sanding blocks, hammer, putty knife.

Materials: sandpaper, epoxy wood filler, caulk, colored push pins, tape.

Tips for Pressure-washing

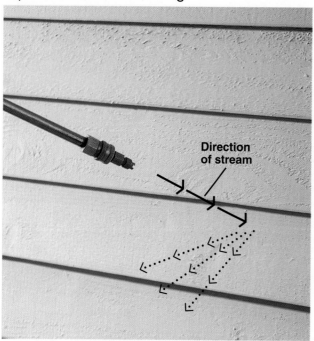

Direction of stream

Direct the water stream at a downward angle when pressure-washing siding. Avoid getting too close to the surface with the sprayer head, because the force of the stream can damage siding and trim. When pressure-washing high on the wall, use an extension attachment (page 133).

Attach a rotating scrub brush attachment to clean hard-to-reach areas, like cornices and soffits. Check with the rental store for available pressure-washer accessories.

Tips for Protecting Your House & Yard

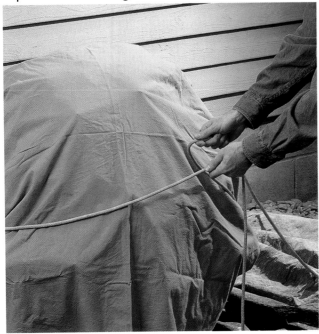

Protect delicate plants and shrubs with tarps when you are working near them. Also lay tarps on the ground around your house to collect debris. Turn off air conditioners and other appliances, and cover them with plastic sheets to protect them from debris and paint.

Remove shutters and decorative trim to protect them from damage and to give you better access to the surface of your house. Inspect the shutters and trim to see if they are in good repair, and fix them if necessary (pages 68 to 69). Prepare, prime, and paint them before reinstalling.

Options for Removing Paint

Use a heat gun to loosen thick layers of paint. Aim the gun at the surface, and move it constantly. Follow with a scraper once the paint releases. Read the manufacturer's directions and precautions.

Use chemical stripper to remove paint from delicate trim. Work in a well-ventilated area, wearing heavy-duty rubber gloves. Read the stripper manufacturer's directions and precautions.

Rent a siding sander to remove large areas of paint on wood lap siding. Rent a sander with a disk the same diameter as the width of the reveal area on your siding. Get instructions from the rental store.

How to Prepare Surfaces for Paint

1 Pressure-wash your house (page 134). Pressure-washing cleans the surface and dislodges loose paint. Allow the house to dry thoroughly before continuing with the preparation work.

2 Scrape off loose paint that was not removed during pressure-washing, using a paint scraper. Be careful not to damage the surface with overly aggressive scraping.

3 Remove loose paint in hard-to-reach areas with detail scrapers (available at building centers and woodworker's stores). Some have interchangeable heads that match common trim profiles.

4 Use a finishing sander with 80-grit sandpaper to smooth out rough paint.

5 Use sanding blocks and 80 to 120-grit sandpaper to remove paint and smooth out ridges in hard-to-reach areas of trim. Sanding blocks are available at building centers in a variety of shapes and sizes, like the teardrop design shown here. Or, you can make your own blocks from dowels, wood scraps, garden hose, or other household materials.

6 Inspect all surfaces for cracks, rot, or other damage. Mark damaged areas with colored push pins or tape so you can locate them easily when making repairs.

7 Repair all the damaged areas (pages 60 to 64 and 68 to 69).

8 Use a finishing sander with 120-grit sandpaper to sand down ridges and hard edges left from the scraping process, creating a smooth surface. Also sand repaired areas.

(continued next page)

How to Prepare Surfaces for Paint (continued)

9 Scuff-sand glossy surfaces on doors, window casings, and any surfaces painted with enamel paint, using a coarse abrasive pad or 150-grit sandpaper. Scuffing creates a better bonding surface for primer and paint.

10 Fill cracks in siding and gaps around window and door trim with paintable siliconized acrylic caulk. The caulk makes a tight, long-lasting seal.

Tips for Removing Clear Finishes

Pressure-wash stained or unpainted surfaces that have been treated with a wood preservative or protectant (page 134) before recoating with fresh sealant. Clear topcoats and sealants can flake and peel, just like paint.

Use a stiff-bristled brush to dislodge any flakes of loosened surface coating not removed by pressure-washing. Do not use a wire brush on wood surfaces.

Tips for Removing Paint from Metal & Masonry

Use a wire brush to remove loose paint and rust from metal hardware, like railings and ornate trim. Cover the surface with metal primer immediately after brushing to prevent new rust from forming.

Scuff-sand metal siding and trim with medium-coarse steel wool or a coarse abrasive pad. Wash the surface before priming and painting.

Use a drill with a wire-wheel attachment to remove loose mortar, mineral deposits, or paint from mortar lines in masonry surfaces. Clean broad, flat surfaces with a wire brush. Correct any minor damage with masonry repair products (pages 150 to 151).

Remove rust from metal hardware with diluted muriatic acid solution. CAUTION: When working with muriatic acid, wear safety equipment, work in a well-ventilated area, and follow the manufacturer's directions and precautions.

Paint downward from the top of your house, covering as much surface as you can reach comfortably without moving your ladder or scaffolding. After the primer or paint dries, return to each section and touch up any un-painted areas that were covered by the pads of the ladder or ladder stabilizer.

Applying Primer & Paint

Like doing preparation work, applying primer and paint requires good planning and execution. If you use a quality primer that is tinted to match the color of your house paint as closely as possible, you can often achieve good coverage with only one coat of house paint.

Keep an eye on the weather when you are planning to paint. Damp weather or rain that falls within an hour or two of application will ruin your paint job. Do not apply paint when the temperature is below 50°F, or above 90°F. And avoid working during high winds—it is unsafe, and dust and dirt are likely to blow onto the freshly painted surface.

TIP: Apply primer and paint in the shade or in indirect sunlight. Direct sunlight dries primers and paints too rapidly, causing moisture to become trapped below the dried surface. This can result in blistering, peeling, and other types of paint failure. Also, lap marks and brush marks are more likely to show up if paint is applied in direct sunlight.

Tips for Applying Primer & Paint

Use the best type of primer or paint for the job. For best results, use a metal primer with rust inhibitor for metal surfaces, and use masonry primer with an anti-chalking additive for masonry surfaces. Always read the manufacturer's recommendations for use.

Follow a logical painting sequence. For example, priming and painting wood stairs and porch floors *after* walls, doors, and trim prevents the need to touch up spills.

Options for Applying Primer & Paint

Use paint brushes for maximum control of the materials. Have clean 4" and 2½" or 3" brushes on hand, as well as a tapered sash brush (page 133). Using brushes that fit the area helps you create a professional-looking finish.

Use paint rollers to paint smooth surfaces quickly. Use a roller with an 8" or 9" roller sleeve (top) for broad surfaces. Use a 3"-wide roller to paint flat-surfaced trim, like end caps (bottom).

Use a power sprayer to apply paint to porch railings, ornate trim, shutters, and other hard-to-paint metal hardware. Read the manufacturer's directions before you start. NOTE: Professional-quality airless sprayers can be rented for large spray-painting projects.

Tips for Painting with a Paint Brush

Load your paint brush with the correct amount of paint for the area you are painting. Use a full load for broad areas, a moderate load for smaller areas and feathering strokes, and a light load when painting or working around trim.

Hold the paint brush at a 45° angle when painting broad, flat areas. Apply just enough downward pressure to flex the bristles and "squeeze" the paint out of the brush. Load your brush properly (photo, left), use good brushing technique, and avoid overbrushing to achieve smooth, pleasing results.

How to Apply Paint to Flat Surfaces

1 Load your paint brush with a full load of paint. Starting at one end of the surface, make a long, smooth stroke until the paint begins to "feather" out.

2 As you finish the stroke, lift the brush gradually from the surface so you do not leave a definite ending point. If the paint appears uneven or contains heavy brush marks, smooth it out with the brush. Be careful to avoid overbrushing.

3 Reload your brush and make another stroke from the other direction, painting over the feathered end of the first stroke to create a smooth, even surface. If the area where the two strokes meet is noticeable, rebrush it with a light load of paint. Feather out the starting point of the second stroke to avoid lap marks.

Tips for Working with Paint

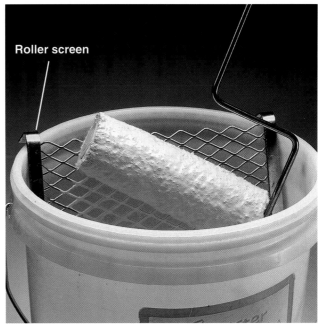

Mix cans of paint together, called boxing, in a large bucket. Stir thoroughly with a stir stick or paint-stirring attachment for your power drill. This ensures that the paint is uniform in color. Pour the mixed paint back into the cans after it is blended (if you are painting with a paint brush). If you are painting with a roller, leave the paint in the larger container.

Use a roller screen inside a five-gallon paint bucket when painting with a roller. Before starting, wet the roller nap with water (if using latex-based paint), then squeeze out any excess water. Dip the roller in the paint, and roll back and forth across the roller screen. The roller sleeve should be full, but not dripping, when lifted from the container.

Tips for Cleaning Painting Tools

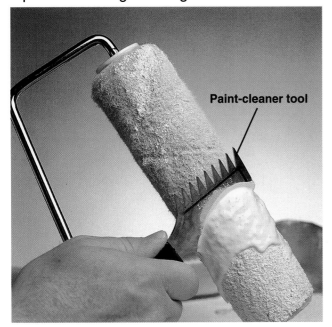

Clean roller sleeves with the curved side of a paint-cleaner tool. Remove as much paint as possible, then clean the roller with a solution of warm water and household soap. Continue squeezing paint and water solution from the roller with the cleaning tool until all of the paint is removed. Rinse thoroughly and hang roller sleeves to dry.

Clean paint brushes in a solution of warm water and dish soap (for latex-based paints—use paint thinner for oil-based paints). Rinse thoroughly, then comb the bristles of the brush with the spiked edge of a paint-cleaner tool (photo, left).

How to Apply Primer & Paint to Your House

Of all the steps involved in painting your house, applying paint is perhaps the most satisfying. Prime all surfaces to be painted, then go back and apply the paint. Allow ample drying time for primers before applying paint.

If you use quality primer that is tinted in the color range of your house paint or trim paint, you should get sufficent paint coverage with just one coat.

Everything You Need:

Tools: 4" paint brush, 2½" or 3" paint brush, sash brush, scaffolding or ladder.

Materials: primers, house paint, trim paint, cleanup materials.

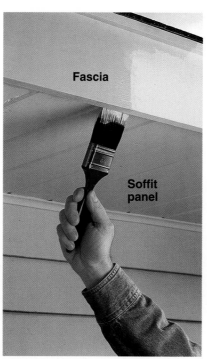

1 Paint the face of the fascia first, then cut in paint at the bottom edges of soffit panels. NOTE: Fascia and soffits are usually painted the same color as the trim.

TIP: Paint gutters and downspouts after painting the fascia, beginning with the back sides and working toward the front. If you use metal primer, you can paint gutters and downspouts with trim paint.

2 Paint the soffit panels and trim with a 4" paint brush. Start by cutting in around the edges of the panels using the narrow edge of the brush, then feather in the broad surfaces of the soffit panels with full loads of paint. Make sure to get good coverage in the groove areas.

TIP: Paint any decorative trim near the top of the house at the same time you paint soffits and fascia. Use a 2½" or 3" paint brush for broader surfaces, and use a sash brush for more intricate trim areas.

3 Paint the bottom edges of lap siding with the paint brush held flat against the wall. Paint the bottom edges of several siding pieces before returning to paint the faces of the siding boards.

4 Paint the broad faces of the siding boards with a 4" brush. Use the painting technique shown on page 142. Working down from the top, paint only as much surface as you can reach comfortably.

5 Paint all the siding all the way down to the foundation, working from top to bottom. Shift the ladder or scaffolding, and paint the next section. NOTE: Paint up to the edges of end caps and window and door trim that will be painted later. If trim will not be painted, mask it off or use a paint shield.

VARIATION: On board-and-batten or any vertical-panel siding, paint the edges of the battens or top boards first. Paint the faces of the battens before the sides dry, then paint the large, broad surfaces between the battens, feathering in at the edges of the battens. Rollers are good tools for panel siding (use a ⅝"-nap sleeve for rough-textured panels).

(continued next page)

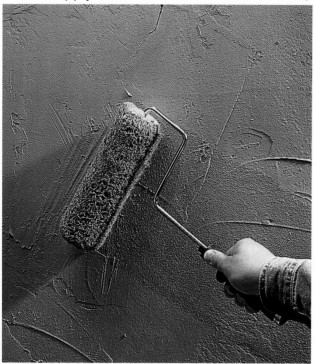

VARIATION: On stucco siding, paint the walls with a paint roller and ⅝"-nap sleeve. Use a 3" trim roller or a 3" paint brush for trim.

6 Paint the foundation with anti-chalking masonry primer. Start by cutting in the areas around basement windows. Then, paint the broad surfaces of the foundation with a 4" brush, working the paint into any mortar lines.

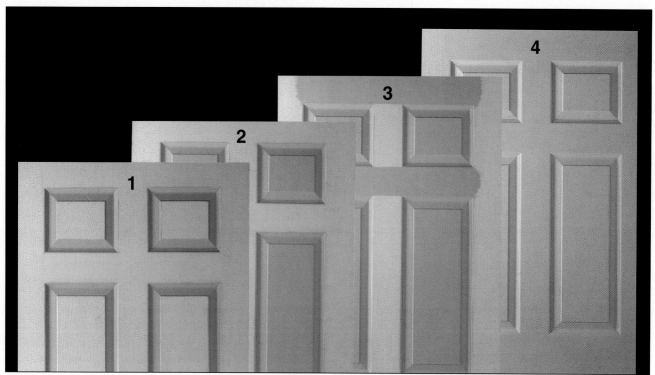

7 Paint doors and windows, using a sash brush. Follow the correct sequence: First, paint the beveled edges of raised door panels, and the insides of muntins or frames on windows; next, paint the faces of the door panels before the edges dry; next, paint rails (horizontal frame members) on doors and windows; last, paint the faces of the stiles (vertical frame members).

8 Use a trim brush or sash brush and a moderate load of paint to paint the inside edges of door and window jambs, casings, and brick molding. NOTE: The surfaces on the interior side of the door stop usually match the color of the interior trim.

9 Paint the outside edges of casings and brick molding, using a sash brush (mask off freshly painted siding after it has dried).

10 Paint the faces of door jambs, casings, and brick molding, feathering fresh paint around the painted edges.

11 Paint wooden door thresholds and porch floors. Use specially-formulated enamel floor paint for maximum durability.

Protecting & Maintaining Your Home

Maintenance and protection work hand-in-hand to keep your house safe and attractive, and to lessen the likelihood that you will need to make major repairs. Exterior house maintenance can include a wide range of activities, from cleaning siding and trim once a year to touching up minor paint problems and making small repairs. In a very real sense, creating and following a comprehensive maintenance schedule is one of the most important ways to protect your house.

Other forms of house protection go beyond maintenance to include activities like pestproofing and improving security. By securing your house against pest infestation and against intruders, you will increase your ability to relax and enjoy your home.

In the first four sections of this book, we have shown you detailed information about repairing common problems that afflict the exterior of your house. Refer to these sections when making the minor repairs that are a part of any home maintenance plan. Also refer to pages 150 to 151 for additional information on making quick repairs to concrete surfaces.

This section shows:
- Quick Fixes for Concrete & Asphalt (pages 150 to 151)
- Pestproofing Your Home (pages 152 to 153)
- Improving Home Security (pages 154 to 158)

Tips for Protecting & Maintaining Your Home

• Keep foundation plantings and tree limbs trimmed back so they are well clear of your house. They can cause damage, and they obscure entry points to your home, making it more inviting to intruders.
• Check weatherstripping around windows and doors before every heating season (pages 103 to 119).
• If you own a pressure-washer, use it to wash your siding at least once a year. Otherwise, use a garden hose and spray nozzle, scrubbing with mild detergent to remove heavy dirt buildup.

Tips for Exterior Home Maintenance

Follow a preventative maintenance schedule for the exterior of your home. The schedule should include tasks like cleaning the chimney flue (left) and cleaning out downspouts (right). Clean chimney flues with a chimney brush that fits the inside dimension of your chimney flue. Use a plumber's snake to remove clogs in downspouts. Also clean debris from gutters with an old kitchen spatula.

Quick Fixes for Asphalt

Repair materials for asphalt include: asphalt repair caulk (A), asphalt patching compound (B), asphalt sealer (C), and asphalt cleaner, which usually is a combination concrete/asphalt cleaning product (D).

You do not need years of experience working with asphalt to make effective repairs to surfaces around your house. New lines of quick-fix repair products are designed to be used by any home-owner with an asphalt problem.

Most asphalt repair products can be applied directly from the container (following manufacturer's directions), eliminating worry about mixing ratios and curing times. When surface preparation is required, it is usually only small amounts of scraping and cleaning.

Tips for Cleaning Asphalt

Clean entire area with an asphalt cleaning product to remove oil and dirt from surface. Rinse slab with hose or power washer.

Scrape cracks and holes to remove any loose material. Remove dirt and debris from cracks and holes with a shop vacuum. Flush repair area with a garden hose and spray nozzle.

How to Fix Cracks

1 Patch cracks in asphalt using a caulk gun and a tube of asphalt repair caulk. Large cracks may need several applications.

2 Spread and smooth the patch material using a putty knife. Dip scraper in cold water or mineral spirits to prevent the repair caulk from sticking to the scraper.

How to Patch Holes

1 Scrape and clean the damaged area (previous page), then use a trowel to pack the hole with loose asphalt patching material (overfill slightly). Warm the material carefully with a heat gun.

2 Tamp the patching material with a heavy flat object, such as a concrete block, so it is firmly packed in the hole and flush with the surrounding surface. Firm, smooth patches help prevent future water damage.

How to Seal Asphalt

1 Repair any cracks and holes (see photos above). Pick a day when the temperature will be above 45° Fahrenheit and dry for 24 hours after application. Pour a pool of sealer on the surface. Spread into a thin layer with a squeegee. Repeat until the entire surface is covered.

2 Allow sealer to cure well before driving or walking on it. Block drive with sawhorses or rope and ladders to prevent traffic during the drying period. Check manufacturer's instructions to determine proper drying time.

Pestproofing Your Home

Keeping pests out of your house is an ongoing battle you can win by taking some simple measures. Combating pests is mostly a matter of prompt detection and choosing the remedy best suited to the specific pests.

To detect pest problems, look for signs of entry around your house—especially holes or gaps near roof eaves, screenless or damaged vent covers, and cracks in foundations. Also look for tell-tale signs of infestation, like droppings or nesting materials. If the problem appears large in scale, or you are unsure how to address it, call an exterminator or a local agricultural extension agent.

Add a chimney cap to keep birds, bats, insects, and squirrels out of your chimney. A metal chimney cap with a cover and screening, sized to fit your flue, also sheds rainwater. Most chimney caps slip over the flue, and are held in place by fasteners or compression strips. Some chimney covers can impede air movement in the chimney or furnace—read the manufacturer's recommendations.

Tips for Identifying Infestation Problems

Look for anthills, tunnels, hives, and nests around the outside of your house. Finding their living quarters is a sure way to identify pests. Block off access points to your house near the nesting areas. For safety, use care when removing nests or hives, and avoid using chemical pesticides except as a last resort.

Examine moist areas in basements or garages for pests or signs of pest infestation, like droppings or nesting materials. Moisture attracts a host of crawling insects. If you have a minor moisture problem, try installing a dehumidifier. For major leaks, especially in foundations, call a building contractor or inspector.

Tips for Pestproofing Your House

Install protected dryer vents to help keep pests from entering your home. Because they are often warm, dryer vents are very attractive entry points, especially for small rodents. Protected dryer vents, sold at most building supply stores, are designed to be one-for-one replacements for standard flap-style vents (inset). They also help reduce energy loss.

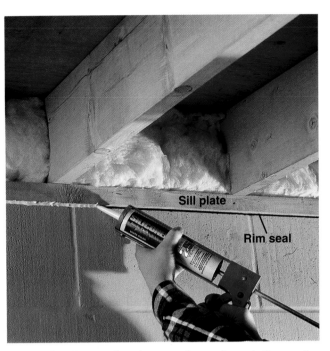

Caulk the rim seal at the top of your foundation wall (inside your basement). This is a prime entry spot for crawling insects. From outside, stuff caulking backer rope in any gaps between the siding and the foundation (page 113).

Replace damaged screening in windows and over air vent covers, using new insect screen (a 1/16" mesh). CAUTION: Do not use insect mesh to replace coarser screening on vent covers, unless you add another vent (pages 52 to 53) to compensate for lost air flow.

Look for signs of termite damage, like the characteristic tunnels they leave in wood. Termites are a very serious threat to any home. If you suspect that you have a problem, call a reputable exterminator immediately. You can purchase anti-termite chemicals, but most are difficult and dangerous to apply.

Framing members

Door jamb

Replace short hinge and lock screws with longer screws (3" or 4"), that extend through the door jamb and into framing members. This helps resist door kick-ins. Some standard hinge and lock screws are ½" to 1" long and extend only into the door jamb, making doors vulnerable to kick-ins.

Option: Install a Security Alarm System

At some time or another, most homeowners are tempted to install a security alarm system. There is some evidence that alarm systems are an effective way to deter intruders. Professionally installed systems that contact emergency operators automatically can save valuable time in dispatching emergency vehicles to your home. But alarm systems can be expensive to install and maintain, and more inexpensive models are prone to sending false alarms (which can mean substantial fines in some areas). If you are considering installing a security alarm system, first discuss your situation with a community officer from your local law enforcement agency.

Options for security alarm systems include:

Professionally installed alarm systems: Professional technicians will visit your home and work with you to decide what type of system best fits your needs. They will install and maintain the equipment. Most professionally installed systems will automatically relay the information to the appropriate emergency department if the alarm is tripped. Initial installation costs vary, but can be fairly expensive. Monthly service fees usually are charged.

Owner-installed systems: Many manufacturers sell security alarm systems designed to be installed and maintained by the homeowner. They vary from one or two simple sensors linked to a loud alarm horn, to fairly complex systems of sensors, alarms, and radio transmitters that often are wired into the electrical system in your house. Consult with a security professional, comparison shop, and do not skimp on quality.

Improving Home Security

There is a lot more to home security than simply keeping intruders out. Making a few security-minded improvements to your home has a great impact on how well you enjoy your home and surroundings: it creates peace of mind. Many security improvements also improve general safety around your house: for example, adding a motion-detector light above a door not only warns off intruders, it also improves visibility after dark for your family members.

Making your home uninviting to intruders is the primary objective of home security. Aim your home security improvements at deterrence and detection. If a potential intruder determines that he will have to gain entry by making noise or working in an area visible from the street, he will probably move on to another target.

Pay special attention to your doors—according to some estimates, more than 80% of all forced entries occur through them. Get in the habit of keeping doors and windows locked. Make sure every entry door in your home is equipped with a deadbolt lock.

For more information on home security, check with your local police department. Most will be happy to help.

Everything You Need:

Tools: screwdriver, circuit tester, electrical tape, connector caps, hammer, circular saw, nail set.

Materials: motion-detector light, 2 x 4 lumber, plywood shims, nails, screws.

Tips for Improving Security Lighting

Timer switch

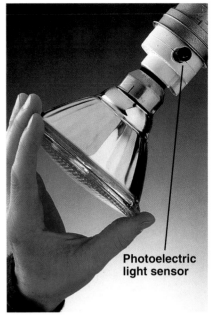

Photoelectric light sensor

Add new exterior lighting near entrances and garages. Security lights (even motion-detector lights) are available in a wide range of styles that are both functional and attractive.

Install timer switches to turn several lights on and off automatically. If you are often away from your house for extended periods of time, look for timer switches with random switching ability.

Install photo sensitive lights in your ordinary exterior light fixture. Photo sensitive lights turn on automatically at dusk, and turn off at dawn. Many are threaded so they can be screwed into a light fixture.

How to Replace an Exterior Light with a Motion-Detector Light

1 Shut off the power at your main circuit panel, and disconnect the old fixture. Carefully remove the mounting plate for your old light, then unscrew the wire nuts. Test the wire leads with a neon circuit tester. Do not proceed until you are sure the power is off.

2 Connect the wires for the new fixture, using wire nuts, and following the light manufacturer's directions. Secure the mounting plate to the electrical box. TIP: Test the motion detector to make sure it works correctly, then finish the installation by attaching the mounting plate.

3 Adjust the motion sensor for maximum coverage of entry points to your home. Select a setting so the sensor can detect motion well beyond the entry point, but not so far away that it reaches into traffic areas, like alleys (which will cause the light to turn on frequently, minimizing its impact).

How to Secure a Door Frame

1 Test the frame to find out if it needs shoring up—a loose door frame is much easier for an intruder to pry open. To test the frame, cut a 2 × 4 about 1" longer than the door width. Wedge the board between the jambs, near the lockset. If the frame flexes more than about ¼", proceed to step 2.

Gap between door jamb and framing members

2 Remove the interior jamb casing so you can inspect the shims between the jambs and the framing members. Measure the gap, then cut plywood shims from material the same thickness as the gaps. Insert the plywood between the existing shims.

Plywood shims

Original shims

3 Drive 10d casing nails through the jambs and shims, and into the framing members. Set the nail heads, and reattach the casing.

Tips for Securing Doors

Add metal sleeves to door edges around locksets and deadbolts to help prevent door kick-ins. Make sure the sleeves are the correct thickness for your door.

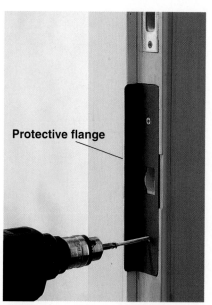

Protective flange

Add heavy-duty strike plates to reinforce your door and locks, and to help defeat kick-ins, jimmying, and prying. Some strike plates also have a flange that protects the lockset from jimmying and prying.

Install a wide-angle viewer in entry doors to allow you to see outside. Drill an eye-level hole the same diameter as the shaft of the viewer through the door. Insert the shaft so the attached eyepiece is flush against the door. Screw the exterior eyepiece onto the shaft.

Tips for Securing Windows

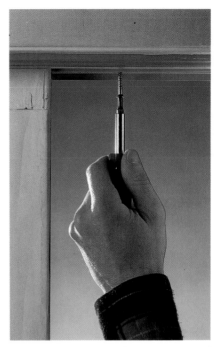

Pin sliding sashes together with ¼" x 3" eyehole bolts. With the window closed, drill a ¼"-diameter x 1¾"-deep hole, at a slight angle, through the top rail of the bottom sash and into the bottom rail of the top sash. This forces intruders to break the glass to gain entry.

Block sash tracks on sliding windows and doors by wedging a board or thick dowel between the inside (movable) frame and the door or window jamb.

Drive a screw into the top channel of side-by-side sliding windows or patio doors. This keeps intruders from lifting window sash or door panels out of their tracks to gain entry. Make sure the screw does not interfere with the normal operation of the sliding sash or panel.

Install protective bars or gates on the interior of ground-level windows to prevent entry. Swinging gates can be latched shut from the inside, so they may be opened easily in an emergency. Never install permanent obstructions in windows.

Remove crank handles from opening mechanisms on awning and casement windows. This forces intruders to climb through a frame filled with broken glass, instead of simply cranking open the window after it breaks. Create a permanent storage spot for the handle, at least an arm's length from the window.

INDEX

A

Alarm system, 154
Alignment and measuring tools, 75
Aluminum siding,
  see: Siding, metal
Asbestos shingles, 58
Asphalt (blacktop),
  cleaning and repair, 150-151
  sealing, 151
Attic, insulating, 106-110

B

Baffles (for insulation), 54, 106,
  108, 110
Base flashing, 30-31
Basement, 153
  insulating, 108-109, 111
  water in, 9, 46
Board-and-batten siding,
  see: Siding, vertical panels
Bonded roof covering, 20, 22
Bonding adhesive, 71
Brick and block,
  cleaning, 100-101
  mortar pigment, 89
  problems with, 90-91
  refacing concrete block, 96
  reinforcing, 97
  repairing walls, 92-97
  replacing damaged brick, 94-95
  tuckpointing mortar joints, 92-93
Bricklayer's hammer, 75, 89
Brick molding, replacing, 69
Brickset, 75
Brick veneer, 57
Building paper, 23
  installing, 26-27

C

Caulk, 14-15
  for weatherizing, 112-113, 115
  how to apply, 15
  types, 14, 47, 65, 107
Caulking backer rope, 15, 107
Chimney,
  adding cap, 152
  cleaning flue, 149
  flashing, 17, 23, 31
  inspecting, 6, 8-9
  installing underlayment
    around, 27
Chimney cap, 91
  repairing and replacing, 98-99
Chimney cricket, 23, 31
Circular saw to cut masonry, 75
Clay tiles for roofing, 22

Cold chisel, 75
Combination windows, 120-121
  repairing, 124-126
Concrete,
  filling cracks, 76-77
  maintaining, 86-87
  patching holes, 78-79
  problems with, 72-73
  repairing, 70-73, 76-85
  resurfacing concrete, 70, 80-81
  sealing, 86-87,
  shaped concrete, repairing, 84
  steps, repairing, 82-83
Concrete fortifier, 71, 79
Concrete patch, 71, 79
Concrete pigment, 71
Condensation on interior walls,
  9, 52, 108
Control joints,
  filling with caulk, 86
Counterflashing, 27, 31, 41
Cracks in concrete, 72-73
  repairing, 76-77
Crazing, 70, 73

D

Disposal, concrete products, 74
Doors,
  inspecting, 7-9, 104, 121
  painting, 146-147
  replacing threshold, 119
  security, 154, 156
  weatherizing, 107, 117-119
Dormers,
  installing flashing next to, 30
  installing underlayment
    next to, 27
  shingling around, 34-35
  vents in, 53
Downspouts,
  cleaning, 149
  inspecting, 7
  painting, 141, 144
  strainer for, 47
Drip edge,
  around doors and windows, 69
  installing, 26

E

Efflorescence, on masonry
  surfaces, 86, 91, 100, 131
Egg splatter, removing, 100
Energy use,
  identifying energy loss, 103-105
  monitoring, 105
  reducing, 103, 153
Exposed aggregate,
  sealing, 86-87

F

Fascia, 17
  diagram of parts, 42
  fascia problems, 19
  inspecting, 7, 9, 19
  painting, 144
  repairing, 42-43
Flashing,
  base flashing, 30-31
  bending your own, 28
  caulk for, 14
  chimney, 17, 23, 31
  drip edge, 23, 26, 69
  estimating amount needed, 20
  estimating time to install, 21
  flashing problems, 19
  inspecting, 6, 9, 19
  installing, 28-31
  nails for, 23
  removing, 24
  repairing, 38, 40
  replacing, 24, 37, 41
  saddle, 30-31
  step flashing, 30, 41
  top flashing, 31
  types, 23
  valley, 17, 23, 29, 34, 36-37, 40
Floats,
  types, 75
Foam, sprayable, 107, 113
Foundation,
  hydraulic cement to repair, 71
  inspecting, 9
  insulating, 109
  painting, 146
Framing square, 75
Frost heave, 72
Frost on windows, 104-105

G

Gable vent, 53
Garage door,
  weatherizing, 107, 119
Garage wall, insulating, 109
GFCI extension cord, 11,
Groover, 75
Gutter guards, 47
Gutter system, 17
  diagram of parts, 50
  gutter accessories, 47
  gutter problems, 19
  inspecting, 7-9, 19
  installing new system, 50-51
  painting, 141, 144
  repairing, 46-48
  replacing, 49-51

H

Heat loss, detecting, 103

Hip of roof, shingling, 35-36
Holes in concrete, repairing, 78-79
Hydraulic cement, 71, 78

I
Ice dams, 8, 18, 26
  preventing, 18, 52
Ice-guard membrane, 23, 26
  installing, 27
IC rating on electrical fixtures, 109
Infrared photo showing heat
  loss, 103, 105
Insulation and insulating, 103
  attaching, 14, 106, 111
  baffles, 54, 106, 108, 110
  for basement walls, 108,111
  inspecting, 6, 105
  installing insulation, 14, 106,
    109-111
  plastic window sheeting,
    105-107, 114-115
  products for insulating, 106-107
  recommended amounts, 104, 108
  vapor barrier, 106
Iron stains, removing, 100
Isolation joints, 72
Ivy, removing, 100

J
Jointer, 75
Joint filler, 89

L
Ladder safety, 10-13, 129
Ladder stabilizer, 13
Lead-based paint, 129
Leaks in roof system, 131
  inspecting for, 6-7, 18-19
Lighting, 6, 9
  security lighting, 155
Line level, 75

M
Magnesium float, 75
Masonry cutting blade, 75
Masonry grinding disk, 75
Masonry surfaces, 57
  cleaning, 150
  inspecting, 9, 58
  painting, 146
  removing paint, 139
  repairing, 65, 150-151
  sealing, 151
Masonry tools, 75
Masonry veneer, repairing, 85
Mason's chisel, 89
Mason's string, 75
Mason's trowel, 89
Maul, 75

Metal surfaces,
  paint for, 141, 144
  removing paint from, 139
  rust on, 131, 139
Mildew, 131
Moisture problems, 42, 59
  and pests, 152
  between windows, 105, 116
  caulking to prevent, 14
  effect on paint, 130-131
  effect on roof system, 18
  identifying source, 8, 131
Motion-detector light, 155
Mortar,
  fortified, 89, 93-94
  pigment, 89, 94
  working with, 89
Mortar hawk, 93

P
Paint brushes, 141
  tips for using, 142-143
Paint failure, 129
  causes, 8, 129-131, 140
  inspecting for, 7-9, 130-131
Painting, 129-147
  applying primer and paint,
    140-147
  brick and block, 100-101
  concrete, 71, 86
  estimating materials, 132
  preparing surface, 136-139
  removing old paint, 134-137, 139
  tools and materials, 132-133
Paint rollers, 143, 145-146
Paint stains, removing, 100
Pests,
  inspecting for, 6-7, 9, 19, 152
  protecting against, 112-113, 149,
    152-153
Plastic window sheeting, 105-107,
  114-115
Pneumatic nailer, 22
  nail coil for, 23
Pointing trowel, 89
Popouts, 70, 73
Porch,
  inspecting, 9
  painting, 147
Power cords, safety tips, 11
Power drill for masonry, 75
Power lines, working around, 11
Pressure washing, 129, 133-134,
  136,138

R
Raking tool, 89
Receptacle plate sealer, 107

Reinforcement,
  for brick or block structures, 97
Repairing,
  brick and block, 88-99
  concrete, 70-73, 76-85
  masonry veneer, 85
  shaped concrete, 84
Resurfacing concrete, 70, 80-81
Retaining walls, hydraulic cement
  to repair, 71
Ridge of roof, 17
  continuous vent for, 53
  shingling, 35-36
Roll roofing, 22
Roof and soffit vents, 9, 17
  diagram, 52
  inspecting, 42
  installing underlayment around
    roof vent, 27
  installing vents, 52-55
  types, 53
Roofing shovel, 22, 25
Roof jacks, 20, 22
  installing, 21
  when to use, 20, 33
Roof sheathing, 17, 20
  repairing sheathing, 25
Roof system,
  diagram of parts, 17
  estimating materials needed,
    20, 22-23
  estimating time for roofing
    project, 21
  inspecting, 6-9, 18-20
  installing drip edge, 26
  installing flashing, 28-31
  installing new shingles over
    old, 18, 24, 37
  installing underlayment, 26-27
  measuring slope, 20
  planning roofing project, 20-21
  removing old roof covering,
    24-25
  repairing, 17, 25
  replacing, 17, 24-25
  roofing materials, 22
  shingling, 32-37
  tools for roofing, 22
Rot, 59
  in roof system, 18-19
  using wood filler to repair,
    14-15, 46
Rust on painted surface, 131, 139
R-value,
  calculating, 104
  of insulation materials, 108

S

Safety, 10-13, 74, 96, 129, 152
and lead-based paint, 129
when painting or preparing for
paint, 139-140
when working with insulation, 109
Sand mix concrete, 71
Scaffolding, safety and use,
10, 12-13, 129
Screed board, 81
Screening, window replacing,
123-124
Sealer,
for concrete, 86-87
for exposed aggregate, 86-87
Security,
improving, 154-157
inspecting for, 6, 9
Shakes and shingles,
roof covering, 22, 40
wood siding, 58-59, 64
Shaped concrete, repairing, 84
Shingles, 17
aging new shingles to match
old, 39
buckled, 18, 38
caulk for, 14
common shingle problems, 18
estimating quantity needed, 22
inspecting, 7, 9, 18
installing new shingles over
old, 18, 24, 37
installing 3-tab shingles, 32-36
reattaching loose shingle, 38
removing old, 24-25
replacing a section, 39
types, 22, 32
Sidewalls, installing
underlayment next to, 27
Siding,
inspecting, 7, 9, 58-59
metal, 57, 66-67
repairing, 57, 60-67
shakes and shingles, wood,
58-59, 64
stucco, 65
painting, 146
vertical panels, 60
painting, 145
vinyl, 57
wood lap, 57
painting, 145
Siding sander, 135
Skylight,
flashing for, 23
installing underlayment
around, 27
Slope of roof, measuring, 20
Smoke stains, removing, 100

Soffits, 17
diagram of parts, 42
inspecting, 7, 9, 19
installing new, 42
installing soffit vents, 52-54
painting, 144
repairing, 42, 44-45
soffit problems, 19
vent types, 53
Spalling,
brick, 91
concrete, 70, 73
Splash block, 47
Spline cord, 120, 124
Stair edger, 75
Steps,
patching treads, 83
repairing, 82-83
Story pole, 75
Storm windows and doors, 112,
116-117
maintaining, 120-121
repairing, 122-126
replacing, 127
storing, 120
Swing-up elbow for gutter, 47
Switchplate sealer, 107

T

Threshold,
insert, 107,119
replacing, 119
Tiles, clay, for roofing, 22
Tools,
concrete repairs, miscellaneous,
84
masonry, 75
patching holes in concrete,
78-79
repairing brick and block walls,
92
repairing cracks in concrete, 76
repairing steps, 82
replacing chimney cap, 98
resurfacing concrete, 80-81
sealing and maintaining
concrete, 86-87
Trim,
end caps, replacing, 67
inspecting, 7, 9, 58-59
painting and preparing for
paint, 135, 144, 147
repairing, 57, 68-69
Trowel, pointing, 75

V

Valley on roof,
flashing for, 17, 23, 29, 34, 36
installing building paper

across, 26
patching damaged flashing, 40
valley flashing meeting shingles,
34, 36
Vapor barrier, 8, 106, 130-131
installing, 108, 111
V-channel weatherstripping,
107, 114-115, 118
Veneer,
masonry, repairing, 85
V-shaped mortar tool, 89
Ventilation, 42
and ice dams, 8, 18, 52
attic, 8, 17-18
diagram of roof ventilation, 52
effect of poor ventilation on
roof system, 8, 18
inspecting for, 8-9, 18
recommended amount, 52
Vent pipe, 17
flashing, 23, 29
installing underlayment
around, 27

W

Weatherizing, 103, 112-119
doors, 117-119
miscellaneous exterior
features, 113
products for weatherizing,
106-107, 112
windows, 112, 114-116
Weatherstripping, 112
inspecting, 6-9, 104-105
when to replace, 104-105
Windows and window frames,
combination windows, 120-121,
124-126
covering with plastic, 105-107,
114-115
improving security, 157
inspecting, 7-9, 104
insulating, 107
painting, 146-147
re-glazing, 121
repairing, 122-126
replacing, 127
replacing glass, 123,125
replacing screening, 123-124
weatherizing, 112, 114-116
Wood filler, 14-15, 46, 61
Wood float, 75
Wood hardener, 14
Wood surfaces,
detecting damage, 8-9, 137
repairing, 14-15, 60-64,
68-69, 137